Left: The March 1955 cover of *Dawn* featured Citizen Military Forces member Cecil Donovan. Image courtesy of NSW Aboriginal Affairs, Department of Education.

Below: Sergeant SKJ 'Len' Lenoy (far right) was an Aboriginal 3RAR serviceman killed on 24 April 1951 at the Battle of Kapyong, Korea. Image courtesy of AWM, HOBJ0116.

Three members of 3RAR with a North Korean interpreter (left). Lieutenant Reginald Saunders (second from right) was the highest profile Aboriginal soldier of the time, having also served in the Second World War. Image courtesy of AWM, P01813.866.

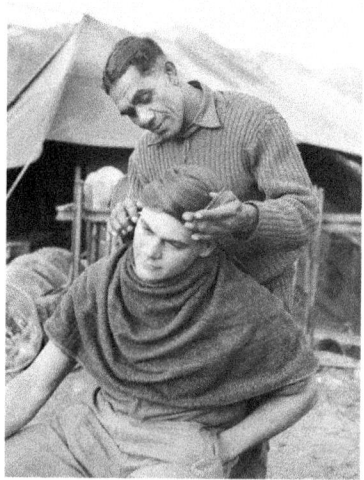

Private Richard (Dick) Hill (2RAR) of Cherbourg, Qld, doubles as a barber in Korea.
Image courtesy of AWM, HOBJ4732.

Private Steve Dodd photographed at Camp Casey, South Korea, 1953. Dodd would later lead the Adelaide Anzac Day march for many years. Image courtesy of AWM, P00969.049.

Torres Strait Islander Corporal Charles Mene (2RAR) receiving the Military Medal for bravery in Korea during Operation Blaze on 2 July 1952. Pinning the medal is the British High Commissioner to the Federation of Malay States, Sir Douglas MacGillivray. Image courtesy of AWM, HAL/57/0100/MC.

Lance Corporal Sarob Sambo, a Torres Strait Islander and ex-paratrooper, member of the 28th Commonwealth Infantry Brigade, photographed in Malaya in 1957. Image courtesy of AWM, FRE/57/0008/MC.

Lance Corporal Sue Giller (now Gordon, second from left) at the Women's Royal Australian Army Corps (WRAAC) graduating parade in 1961. For Indigenous personnel in the 1950–60s, military service was an egalitarian experience.

Gordon served in the WRAAC from 1961 to 1964. She credits the discipline instilled by the army for her success later in life. Both images on this page courtesy of Sue Gordon.

Four members of 3RAR on patrol in Borneo, 1965. The Torres Strait Islander section commander, Corporal Mial Bingarape (front row, centre), had just given directions to the forward scout. Image courtesy of Mial Bingarape and AWM, P00944.006.

Aboriginal serviceman Private Jim Molony (left) training with 7RAR for Vietnam at Shoalwater Bay, Qld, February 1967. Image courtesy of AWM, KEE/67/0020/NC.

Aboriginal soldier Bombardier John Burns (left) speaks with Gunner Bruce Morris during Operation Toan Thang, Vietnam, May 1968. Active combat cultivated strong bonds between the soldiers. Image courtesy of AWM, ERR/68/0474/VN.

Quartermaster Gunner Joseph Donovan (right), an Aboriginal sailor from Kempsey, NSW, spars on the HMAS *Parramatta*, 1970. A boxing champion, he represented Australia at the 1968 Olympics. Image courtesy of AWM, NAVYM0601/02.

Private Graeme M (Brownie) Brown, an Aboriginal member of 1RAR, on foot patrol in Baidoa, Somalia, March 1993. He served as part of the multinational Unified Task Force. Image courtesy of AWM, P01735.401.

An unidentified member of North-West Mobile Force (NORFORCE), c. 1999–2000, engaged in reconnaissance: sitting perfectly still for up to an hour to observe an area. Image courtesy of Ben Bohane.

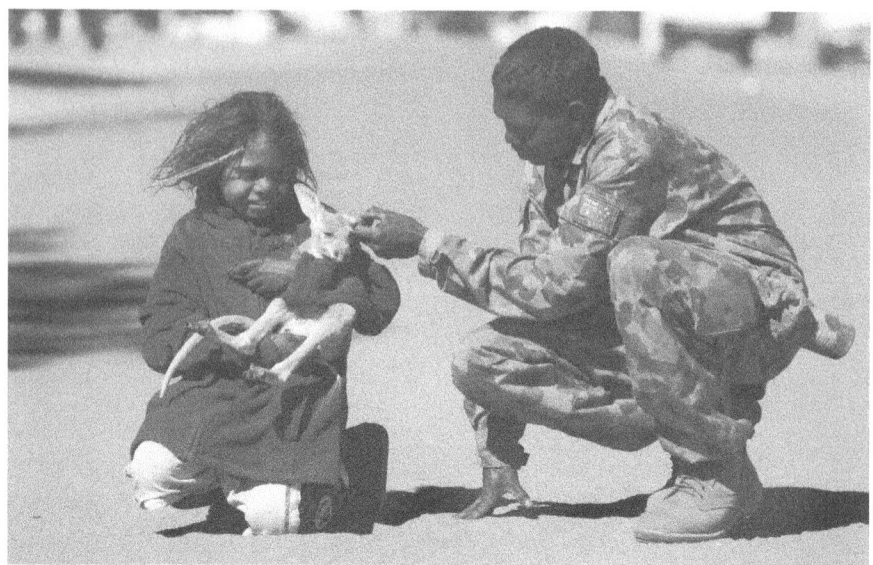

NORFORCE avoided criticism for its involvement in the controversial Northern Territory Intervention due to the goodwill it had already fostered in Aboriginal communities. Here Private Toby Cooper meets Soraya Rankin in Aputula, 2007.
Image courtesy of Chris Crerar/Newspix.

NORFORCE 'green skins': Privates Elijah Appurryarnk, Leonard Lamilami and Allen Gebadi, c. 2009. Military service can be an empowering experience for young men and women. Image courtesy of David Hancock.

Dr Noah Riseman is an Associate Professor in History at Australian Catholic University. He specialises in the history of marginalised social groups in the Australian Defence Force. His first book, *Defending Whose Country? Indigenous Soldiers in the Pacific War* (2012), was shortlisted for the 2013 Chief Minister's Northern Territory History Award.

Dr Richard Trembath has taught many university courses in a number of disciplines ranging from philosophy to military history. He is the co-author of several books, including *Witnesses to War*, a landmark chronicle of Australia's war correspondents. Much of his work involves interviews and oral history. He is currently researching potential subjects for a biography.

DEFENDING COUNTRY

ABORIGINAL AND TORRES STRAIT ISLANDER
MILITARY SERVICE SINCE 1945

NOAH RISEMAN and RICHARD TREMBATH

UQP

First published in 2016 by University of Queensland Press
PO Box 6042, St Lucia, Queensland 4067 Australia

www.uqp.com.au
uqp@uqp.uq.edu.au

© Noah Riseman and Richard Trembath 2016

This book is copyright. Except for private study, research, criticism or reviews, as permitted under the Copyright Act, no part of this book may be reproduced, stored in a retrieval system, or transmitted in any form or by any means without prior written permission. Enquiries should be made to the publisher.

Cover design by Luke Causby/Blue Cork
Cover photograph: Private Don Pickering (2RAR), in Malaya, 1956. Image courtesy of AWM, HOB/65/0673/MC (detail).
Typeset in 11.5/16 pt Adobe Garamond Pro by Post Pre-press Group, Brisbane
Printed in Australia by McPherson's Printing Group, Melbourne

Cataloguing-in-Publication entry is available from the
National Library of Australia http://catalogue.nla.gov.au/

ISBN
978 0 7022 5399 7 (pbk)
978 0 7022 5711 7 (epdf)
978 0 7022 5712 7 (epub)
978 0 7022 5713 1 (kindle)

University of Queensland Press uses papers that are natural, renewable and recyclable products made from wood grown in sustainable forests. The logging and manufacturing processes conform to the environmental regulations of the country of origin.

*To all those teachers, past and present,
who have inspired my love of history*
NR

For Anne Marie, as always
RT

CONTENTS

Preface		ix
Introduction		1
1	Defence reforms and opportunities: 1946–64	15
2	The RSL and Australian Indigenous veterans	35
3	Indigenous service and Vietnam	56
4	Skilling Indigenous women: Aboriginal and Torres Strait Islander people in the women's services	93
5	Racism, Indigenous people, and the Australian armed forces	121
6	A changing defence force and Reconciliation	142
Epilogue: Commemorating Indigenous service		171
Acknowledgements		176
List of abbreviations		179
Notes		181
Bibliography		216
Index		233

PREFACE

In January 2014 one of the showcase performances at the Sydney Festival was the Queensland Theatre Company's production of the new play *Black Diggers*. Written by Tom Wright, directed by Wesley Enoch and co-produced by the Queensland Theatre Company, the 105-minute play depicted the First World War experience of Aboriginal soldiers, drawing on key themes including long histories of colonialism, reasons to enlist, egalitarianism on the front, discrimination upon return, denial of veterans' benefits and the forgotten contributions of Aboriginal servicemen. The play successfully portrayed the diversity of experiences through clever use of the cast of nine actors across 60 scenes.

Black Diggers received rave reviews at the Sydney Festival and has contributed to a gradual awakening among non-Indigenous Australians about the role of Aboriginal and Torres Strait Islander people in defending Australia. After the play's successful run in Sydney and Brisbane, the Queensland Theatre Company received a grant from the Commonwealth arts minister to tour to Perth, Canberra, Melbourne and Adelaide in 2015. *Black Diggers* was not the first play to commemorate Indigenous service, though it was the first to focus on the First World War. Earlier productions addressing Indigenous Second World War service included *In Our Town* (1992) and *The Sunshine Club* (1999), and Aboriginal Vietnam War service was the subject of *Seems Like Yesterday* (2000). What sets *Black Diggers* apart, though, is the national tour, high-profile venues such as the Sydney Opera House, and the national press.

The positive audience and public reception of *Black Diggers* has highlighted not only the need for more histories of Aboriginal and Torres Strait Islander military service, but also the great interest among all Australians in this important topic. As Australia commemorates the centenary of the First World War, many commentators are also looking back over the last century of Australian military service, and this book tells one piece of that story. Whereas *Black Diggers* portrays the First World War experience of Aboriginal servicemen and their families, this book looks at Aboriginal and Torres Strait Islander military service since the end of the Second World War.

This project began in December 2009 when Noah conducted his first interview in Canberra with Neil Macdonald, Gulf War veteran. Very quickly it became clear that this was going to be intensive, thought-provoking and exciting research. As we conducted more interviews, we were amazed at the diversity of experiences that came across in the stories. Every ex-serviceman and woman – whether they had experienced the trauma of Vietnam, been forcibly removed from their parents as children, used the Australian Defence Force to escape domestic service or felt pride in helping rebuild East Timor – had their own story to tell. Working in the archives was also interesting, as we uncovered stories of Aboriginal men prosecuted for not registering for national service, and RSL minutes indicating support for Indigenous veterans and the White Australia Policy at the same time.

Throughout this book, one guiding principle is Aboriginal historian Gordon Briscoe's statement: 'Historians are builders of narratives in that their work is always a work in progress.'[1] Oral historian Heather Goodall further argues that 'there is now a great need to be alert to the processes of history making in order to conceive projects which allow shared work

Preface

in the early stages of these processes, not only at the end. These will be projects … which take the risk of not knowing the answers to all the questions at the outset.'² This book does not pretend to represent the complete history of Aboriginal and Torres Strait Islander post–Second World War military service. Rather, aligning with Briscoe's and Goodall's sentiments, it contributes to commemorating the history of Aboriginal and Torres Strait Islander military service. The authors hope this book will facilitate further conversations about Indigenous contributions to their country's defence, past and present.

Aboriginal and Torres Strait Islander readers are warned that this book contains images and names of persons who are deceased.

INTRODUCTION

Lance Corporal David Cook is an Aboriginal man of mixed descent born in Ebor in the New England region of New South Wales on 16 May 1945. This is the borderland of the Djungutti and Gumbaynggirr peoples, but David Cook does not self-identify with any specific Aboriginal mob. Around the time of David's tenth birthday, he and his four siblings were forcibly removed from their parents. David was placed in the notorious Kinchela Boys Home for three years before being fostered out with three of his sisters. At the age of 17 David enlisted in the army; he served two tours of duty in Vietnam before being discharged in 1968. In Vietnam, like so many other soldiers, David witnessed the horrors of war and lost close friends. Though he was a successful soldier liked by his peers, David's life spiralled out of control in the 1970s. He returned to an Australia disillusioned by the unpopular war and suffered post-traumatic stress disorder as a consequence of both his troubled upbringing and his experiences in Vietnam. Cycles of violence, imprisonment and encounters with racism threatened to turn David into another Aboriginal statistic, until he got his life back on track through reconnecting with his siblings.[1]

David Cook is one of thousands of Aboriginal and Torres Strait Islander men and women who have served in the Australian armed forces. Despite Australia's history of persecution and injustice perpetrated against Indigenous Australians, they have regularly come forward to defend their country in times of war and peace. Every Australian Indigenous serviceman or woman has a distinct story of their childhood, reasons for enlisting, time spent in military service and the opportunities and obstacles encountered post-service. These individual life stories include themes of hardship, determination, discipline and hope. Taken collectively, the histories of Aboriginal and Torres Strait Islander servicemen and women indicate that for them the military historically represented an employment opportunity and a social paradigm quite different to civilian Australia. Military discipline, sentiments of mateship and the chance to acquire new skills opened previously locked doors for them, both within the armed forces and in their post-service civilian lives. This is not to say that the military experience was always smooth or free of racism; rather, military participation represented one particular route to Indigenous empowerment. Military service had ripple effects beyond just the individuals who served; it impacted on servicemen and women's families, their communities and the non-Indigenous men and women who served alongside them.

Since the turn of the new millennium, there has been growing interest within Australia – especially within Australian Indigenous communities – to commemorate the history of Aboriginal and Torres Strait Islander military service. Such commemorations have taken the form of Reconciliation services, ceremonies at deceased veterans' graves, Australian Indigenous marches on Anzac Day, the production of documentaries, the construction of memorials, and museum exhibitions. The bulk of these commemorations has focused on the two world wars – especially the Second World War – because those conflicts have more records relating to Indigenous military service and larger numbers of veterans. What has received less attention, though, is the history of military service in the post–Second World War era. This includes service in conflicts such as Korea, Malaya, Vietnam, East Timor, Iraq and

Introduction

Afghanistan, as well as women and men who served in non-combat roles in the regular, reserve and auxiliary services. This book fills some gaps in this recent history of Aboriginal and Torres Strait Islander military service. Using both historical records and the life stories of Indigenous servicemen and women, it reconstructs the post–Second World War history of Aboriginal and Torres Strait Islander service and also examines the links between military service, civilian life and Australian Indigenous rights. Expanding the historical record beyond the two world wars allows Australians to reconceptualise the history of Aboriginal and Torres Strait Islander military service, including questioning some of the dominant narratives of Indigenous service extrapolated from the First and Second World War experiences.

Indigenous service to 1945

Beginning on the frontiers, Aboriginal and Torres Strait Islander people have long fought to defend their country. After Federation, Aboriginal people also fought to defend the Australian nation and even the British Empire in the Boer War, and the First and Second World Wars. Often they were treated as equals within the armed forces but returned home to continuing discrimination – both in individual circumstances and institutionally.

Defending their country: Frontier wars

Some Australian Indigenous service personnel consider their work as continuing a long tradition of defence of country dating back to the arrival of the First Fleet in 1788. For instance, Aboriginal ex-serviceman Jeff McCormack asserts of frontier resistance fighters: 'But you know they're the people that have got to be highlighted as Australian heroes. All you hear about is the Vietnam heroes, the Malayan heroes, the Afghani heroes and all that sort of stuff, you know. We don't hear about the real heroes – that I'd class as the real heroes – that fought with boomerangs and spears against rifles and all sorts of stuff, you know they'd be the heroes to try and keep their own country. To me they are the real heroes.'[2]

The topic of frontier conflict is contentious, particularly when determining whether or not Aboriginal resistance to colonialism constitutes 'military service'. Technically Aboriginal people defending their lands were not enlisted in a military, just as many of the white men and women in frontier conflicts were not members of police, army or militias (though some, of course, were). Moreover, there were also Aboriginal men who served in native police forces that were sent to hunt down and kill other Aboriginal people on the frontiers. Frontiers were fluid, and it is difficult to point to particular battles, let alone front lines. There was never any official declaration of war, although there are colonial documents that refer to the situation as being in a state of war; the fact that the frontier conflicts in Tasmania are collectively known as the Black War is particularly telling. Prominent Australian military historians such as Jeffrey Grey and John Connor describe the frontier conflicts as wars that form part of Australia's military history; Henry Reynolds recently dubbed the frontier wars as Australia's 'forgotten war'.[3]

The Australian War Memorial itself has grappled with the difficult question of whether or not to commemorate Indigenous resistance to colonialism as a 'war'.[4] Though there are passionate opinions across the issue, what is clear is that many Aboriginal people and military historians have argued that frontier conflicts should be recognised as wars and the sacrifices Aboriginal people made should be commemorated in the Australian War Memorial and other sites. Since 2011, Aboriginal Tent Embassy members have even marched behind the official Canberra Anzac Day parade carrying banners reading 'Lest we forget the frontier wars'.[5]

The frontier wars began shortly after the arrival of the First Fleet in 1788 and followed similar patterns – albeit manifested differently – wherever and whenever British settlement spread. Frontier war tactics included Aboriginal people preparing revenge parties, embarking on long-term surveillance of settlers, sabotaging European goods and, of course,

Introduction

spearing settlers. Europeans, for their part, shot Aboriginal people, perpetrated massacres, committed acts of sexual violence and were even known to poison flour.[6] Among the more high-profile Aboriginal resistance fighters were Pemulwuy in Sydney and Jandamarra in the Kimberley of Western Australia. Pemulwuy was a Bidjigal man responsible for several raids on settlers beginning in 1792 before ultimately being shot dead in 1802. Jandamarra was a Bunuba warrior who waged a guerrilla war against pastoralists and police in the Kimberley from 1894 to 1897. His rebellion, too, came to an end when he was gunned down. These men only graze the surface of Indigenous resistance fighters, but they have been recognised in literature and documentaries, and have become prominent symbols of Aboriginal defence against invasion.[7]

Abandoned overseas? The Boer War, 1899–1902

By the turn of the twentieth century, while frontier wars were still raging in the northern and central regions of Australia, in other parts of the continent Aboriginal people had been marginalised and forced to live on reserves and missions. Meanwhile, from 1899 to 1902, the British Empire waged war against Afrikaner Boer settlers for control of South Africa. The Australian colonies – federated as the Commonwealth of Australia from 1901 – sent about 16,000 troops to the Boer War. Among these soldiers were at least ten Aboriginal men who managed to sign up and serve as regular soldiers. A small number of other Aboriginal men were employed as trackers. The records about these trackers are sparse. They came from multiple Australian states; some were not formally enlisted in the armed forces because the British War Office opposed the enlistment of 'coloureds'; their employment as bush trackers in the Boer War was not dissimilar to work with police in Australian states at that time. Because these men were not formally enlisted, most names are unknown and there are no service records. More troubling, though, are suggestions that some of these Aboriginal men may have been left behind in South Africa. A 1907 report from the Commonwealth Agent in South Africa suggests that immigration restrictions indicative of the White Australia Policy may have barred the repatriation of these men.[8] The stories of the Aboriginal men who fought in the Boer War disappeared from the historical record, and the fate of those men and their descendants remains a mystery. Currently other historians are conducting research on Aboriginal Australians in the Boer War and the fate of the trackers, which will fill this significant gap in the historical record.

Defending empire or country? The First World War, 1914–18

Shortly after the Boer War and Federation, the Commonwealth parliament passed the *Defence Act* in 1903. In 1909, amendments to the *Defence Act* established a system of compulsory military training for Australian males but exempted from this training and wartime service 'Persons who are not substantially of European origin or descent, of which the medical authorities appointed under the regulations shall be the judges'.[9] While this released Aboriginal people from *compulsory* military service, whether or not they could still *voluntarily* enlist in the armed forces during a time of war was an ambiguous matter not addressed in the legislation.

The question of Aboriginal enlistment not surprisingly arose at the outbreak of the First World War in 1914. In the early years of the war, the Australian Imperial Force (AIF) interpreted the *Defence Act* to preclude Aboriginal enlistment. The military recruiters' handbook explicitly stated, 'Aborigines and halfcastes are not to be enlisted. This restriction is to be interpreted as applying to all coloured men.'[10] During the period 1914–16, those Aboriginal men who managed to enlist were exceptions to the rule. They circumvented regulations through a variety of means, such as pretending to be Māori, Italian or Indian, using white connections in influential positions or merely by oversight on the part of medical officers. By late 1916, with mounting Australian casualties after the Battle of Pozières, the demands for service personnel exerted pressure on the AIF and the Commonwealth government. The failure of the first conscription plebiscite in December 1916 meant that the

Introduction

AIF needed more flexible recruiting strategies if it were to maintain an independent status within the British forces. Consequently, from March 1917, a change of regulations permitted the enlistment of Aboriginal men of mixed descent, provided that one parent was white. The number of Aboriginal recruits jumped, especially in Queensland due to the encouragement of Chief Protector of Aborigines JW Bleakley. Western Australia, incidentally, continued to exclude Aboriginal recruits and consequently had the lowest proportion of Aboriginal servicemen in the AIF. By the end of the First World War, approximately 1000 Aboriginal men had served in the AIF. Of 545 Aboriginal soldiers identified by historian Timothy Winegard, 83 were killed in action, 123 were wounded and another 17 had been prisoners of war.[11]

Why 1000 Aboriginal men signed up to serve a country that had regularly discriminated against them and their kin is a difficult question to answer. Though each man had his own rationales to sign up for the war effort, some common reasons include: to seek adventure, the opportunity for better wages and hopes for equal rights during and after the war. Loyalty also appears in several Aboriginal servicemen's records as a motivating factor; letters from Aboriginal families, especially after the war, describe their men fighting 'for King and country'.

Service records, newspaper articles, photographs and family testimonies suggest that, with some exceptions, the First World War soldier experience tended to be egalitarian for Aboriginal men. There is evidence of mateship with non-Indigenous compatriots; wounded Aboriginal men were treated in the same hospitals as whites; those who died on the battlefields were buried in the same cemeteries. Scarring, shell shock, homesickness and mischief off the battlefield were all as common for Aboriginal servicemen as for non-Indigenous soldiers. Three identified Aboriginal Australians were awarded the Distinguished Conduct Medal, nine the Military Medal, three were Mentioned in Despatches and one received the Military Cross. Winegard argues that had Aboriginal men been allowed to enlist earlier in the war – when Australian combat was not primarily on the Western Front – there probably would have been even more Aboriginal servicemen with distinctions.[12]

Unfortunately for Aboriginal veterans, the return to Australia meant a return to discrimination under the law and prejudice in society. Restrictions in each state on Aboriginal people handling money made it difficult for Aboriginal men to access war gratuities. In Queensland part of Aboriginal soldiers' pay had been set aside in accounts under the administration of the Department of Native Affairs; this money would form part of unpaid wage or government entitlements collectively known as Stolen Wages. Across the country, widows or dependants of deceased Aboriginal servicemen were not allowed access to pensions, which were under control of state Native Welfare authorities. Aboriginal men were denied access to soldier settlement schemes, and in some states authorities closed Aboriginal reserves and sold the land off for soldier settlement. The only Aboriginal men known to have been granted a soldier settlement allotment – such as New South Welshman George Kennedy of the 6th Light Horse Regiment and Victorian Percy Pepper of the 21st Infantry Battalion – were successful because the authorities did not realise they were Aboriginal.

Aboriginal veterans continued to be denied rights afforded to non-Indigenous Australians, such as the right to drink, freedom of movement and even custody of their own children. Child-removal practices in every state affected the families of Aboriginal veterans, and chief protectors even threatened Aboriginal men who 'agitated' for rights with the possibility of removing their children or banishing the veterans to faraway reserves.[13] A memo from the Department of Repatriation summarised the unchanged status of Aboriginal veterans thus: 'The fact of an aboriginal having served with the A.I.F. does not remove him from the care or supervision exercisable by the Board appointed for the protection of Aborigines under the Aborigines Act [NSW, 1909]. neither [sic] does it relieve that Board of its duties towards the aboriginal.'[14]

Continuing discrimination engendered disenchantment among

Introduction

many Aboriginal veterans of the First World War, and they received only limited support at best from the non-Indigenous veterans' community. Aboriginal veterans and the families of those deceased wrote letters to newspapers, chief protectors and politicians, arguing that the sacrifices they made should afford them equal rights within Australia. They took pride in their war service and wanted it recognised by the wider Australian community. Yet still many Aboriginal men were often not allowed to march in Anzac Day parades and white Australians ignored Aboriginal families at Anzac Day commemorations.

The Returned Sailors and Soldiers Imperial League of Australia (currently the Returned and Services League or RSL)[15] varied in its treatment of Aboriginal veterans because the local branches had much autonomy. There is some evidence of individual non-Indigenous RSL members speaking out in favour of Aboriginal citizenship rights. There is also correspondence in some veterans' service records showing the RSL actively advocating on behalf of Aboriginal veterans in requests for replacement discharges, repatriation benefits or even to secure replacement medals. In 1931–32 the New South Wales RSL branch sought to compile a list of Aboriginal veterans of the AIF and sent circulars to Aboriginal protectors throughout Australia. The RSL published the lists in issues of its magazine *Reveille*. Notwithstanding these examples of support for Aboriginal veterans, there is more evidence of RSL branches not admitting Aboriginal veterans except on Anzac Day or of RSLs actively lobbying in favour of segregation ordinances.[16] Overall, the RSL's occasional interest in Aboriginal veterans' welfare reflected wider trends in Australian society. Very quickly, Aboriginal service in the First World War became relegated to a forgotten memory, retained principally in the families and communities of Aboriginal veterans.

Fighting at home and abroad: The Second World War, 1939–45

When Australia went to war against Germany in 1939, the expansion of the Second AIF, Royal Australian Navy (RAN) and Royal Australian

Air Force (RAAF) went along similar lines to the First World War. Once again, Aboriginal and Torres Strait Islander men – and this time women as well – were excluded under regulations stating 'that the admission of aliens or of British subjects of non-European origin or descent to the Australian Defence Forces is undesirable in principle, but that a departure from this principle is justified in order to provide for the special needs of any of the Services during the war'.[17] Even so, like in the First World War, a number of Aboriginal men and women managed to enlist despite the prejudicial regulations. Medical officers either overlooked the regulations or sometimes interpreted discriminatory state definitions of Aboriginality not to include so-called half-castes and quadroons. Consequently, approximately 300–400 Aboriginal people enlisted during the period 1939–41.[18]

The threat of Japanese invasion changed Australia's entire war situation, and it also impacted on Aboriginal and Torres Strait Islander people. During 1941, as the Australian government feared Japan's expansionist aspirations, the military drafted plans to form Aboriginal and Torres Strait Islander units to protect the largely undefended north coast. Two all-Indigenous forces were formed: the Torres Strait Light Infantry Battalion (TSLI) and Northern Territory Special Reconnaissance Unit (NTSRU). The TSLI was a group of approximately 440 Torres Strait Islander men who had regularly enlisted in the army. Their job was to patrol the Torres Strait and to provide mechanical and logistical support for ships passing through. This unit received significant praise from superiors and visiting officers, yet its Indigenous members received less pay than non-Indigenous men serving in the same unit. Moreover, like the experience of many First World War Aboriginal servicemen, part of their wages was quarantined by the Queensland chief protector of Aborigines and became part of the Stolen Wages. It would not be until 1982 that surviving members of the TSLI received back pay valued at over seven million dollars.[19]

The NTSRU was quite different from the TSLI. Planning for the

Introduction

force began in 1941 when Lieutenant Colonel WJR Scott approached anthropologist-turned-serviceman Dr Donald Thomson with the idea of forming a guerrilla unit of Yolngu men to patrol Arnhem Land in the Northern Territory. Thomson adopted the idea and on 15 February 1942 – four days before the bombing of Darwin – he set sail for Arnhem Land. From February 1942 to April 1943 Thomson organised and commanded a group of 51 Yolngu men, training them to use traditional bush tactics and weaponry to fight a guerrilla war against any Japanese invaders. The group operated within a traditional framework, using spears rather than guns. They embarked on patrols of Arnhem Land, constructed outposts and were prepared to launch assaults on potential Japanese invaders. They received no payment except for basic trade goods such as fish hooks, wire and tobacco. The force disbanded in April 1943 as war matters made it less necessary and other white units arose to patrol the sparsely defended north. It would not be until 1992 that surviving members of the NTSRU and deceased members' families were awarded back pay for their service.[20]

Both the NTSRU and the TSLI formed out of anticipation of Japanese aggression, which did indeed come to fruition in December 1941. Following the attack on Pearl Harbor, the desperate need for more service personnel left recruiters essentially ignoring the regulations against enlistment of persons not substantially of European descent. Consequently, by the end of the Second World War, at least 3000 Aboriginal people and 850 Torres Strait Islanders served in the Australian armed forces. With the exception of those in the specialised Indigenous units outlined above, these men and women were integrated with non-Indigenous service personnel.

Similar to the First World War experiences of their fathers and uncles, Indigenous servicewomen and men overwhelmingly reported being treated as equals – often for the first time in their lives. Military service broke down racial barriers and provided opportunities for Indigenous people to learn skills often inaccessible in civilian life. The motivations to serve in the Second World War were also similar to the First World War: better wages, an opportunity to escape the mission or reserve, adventure, defending country and loyalty to Australia. An additional motivation for some Aboriginal people was to continue service traditions begun by their fathers and uncles in the First World War. For those Aboriginal and Torres Strait Islander people living in remote regions, service in the war meant patrolling and defending their traditional lands from outside invasion.[21]

The demand for workers in remote regions also led the Australian Army to set up special labour camps to house and employ Aboriginal labourers throughout the Northern Territory. At these camps Aboriginal men and women from the surrounding areas were responsible for handling cargo, driving, construction and food preparation. In some ways conditions in these camps represented progress over their prewar situations because of improved housing, sanitation and respect afforded by non-Indigenous soldiers. Yet still their wages were unequal despite often performing the same tasks as formally enlisted soldiers, and pressure from local pastoralists ensured that Aboriginal people did not receive significant wage increases for fear of disrupting the civilian status quo. Besides the labour camps, Aboriginal people on the north coast worked with local RAAF and army patrols as trackers, to construct airfields, to guard bases and to carry out general labour tasks. Aboriginal residents worked with white missionaries as coastwatchers, and Aboriginal people were victims of Japanese bombings in places such as Milingimbi, Katherine, Darwin, Broome, Derby and Kalumburu. Most of these Aboriginal men and women never received adequate compensation for their war efforts or for their losses.[22]

Aboriginal and Torres Strait Islander veterans of the Second World War returned to a changed Australia, yet one that continued to discriminate against them. The Commonwealth and state governments recognised their valiant war service with only minor reforms. Most prominent among these reforms was an amendment to the *Commonwealth Electoral Act* in 1949 granting Indigenous veterans the vote. Western Australia

Introduction

passed legislation allowing Aboriginal veterans and others to apply for special 'certificates of citizenship' that would exempt them from restrictions imposed by the *Aborigines Act*. The cost of such certificates was the requirement that bearers sever ties with Aboriginal kin and communities.[23] What successful Second World War service did overall was 'confirm' among Commonwealth and state authorities that Aboriginal people were clearly 'ready' to assimilate into mainstream Australia. Assimilation policies would dominate Australian Indigenous affairs until the early 1970s, and as such they would also have a significant impact on the lives of Aboriginal and Torres Strait Islander servicemen and women in the post–Second World War era.

Indigenous service after 1945

Amid the assimilation policies and Aboriginal activism of the 1950s to 1970s, Aboriginal and Torres Strait Islander men and women continued to serve in the Australian armed forces. Indigenous men fought in Korea, Malaya and Vietnam; Indigenous women served in Australia in the reconstituted women's services. During the self-determination era of the 1970s to 1990s, Aboriginal and Torres Strait Islander men and women continued to serve in peacekeeping missions, the Gulf War and East Timor. These men and women's life stories both intersected with the dominant narrative of Indigenous affairs during the post–Second World War era and carved their own trajectories. As this book highlights, Aboriginal and Torres Strait Islander participation in the armed forces since 1945 has represented an opportunity for personal advancement, learning skills and often escaping the limitations imposed by assimilation policies in civilian Australia. Many Indigenous ex-servicemen and women later returned to their communities as fighters for Indigenous advancement at the grassroots. They were not activists per se; rather, they were advocates for Indigenous empowerment and sought opportunities to succeed in mainstream Australia on their own terms. This book charts the history of those individuals who served, and also how Australian Indigenous experiences in the armed forces since 1945 reflected the continuing changes in civilian Australia.

Chapter 1 begins with the end of the Second World War and the role of Aboriginal and Torres Strait Islander personnel in the British Commonwealth Occupation Force in Japan. The chapter also examines Indigenous service in the Korean War and Malayan Emergency, and the quiet changes to military policy in the 1950s regarding Indigenous service. The topic of chapter 2 is the RSL, Australia's most significant services organisation, and its evolving relationship with Aboriginal and Torres Strait Islander veterans, particularly during the period 1945–72. Chapter 3 examines the role of the at least 300 Aboriginal and Torres Strait Islander men who served during the Vietnam War, including their experiences confronting the difficulties of guerrilla war, the conditions in Nui Dat, their return to a disillusioned Australia, and their experiences of readjustment difficulties and post-traumatic stress disorder. Chapter 4 examines how and why Indigenous women participated in the women's services in 1951–85. Chapter 5 analyses the complexities of Aboriginal and Torres Strait Islander experiences and perceptions of racial discrimination in the Australian Defence Force (ADF) and its predecessors. Chapter 6 looks at the experiences of Indigenous service personnel during the self-determination and Reconciliation eras, and the ways in which the Department of Defence and ADF have responded to the needs of Aboriginal and Torres Strait Islander servicemen and women. The epilogue reflects on commemorations of Indigenous military service and the lessons that Aboriginal and Torres Strait Islander military experience can teach about Australia's past and its future directions.

1

DEFENCE REFORMS AND OPPORTUNITIES: 1946-64

The Corporal came around and he said, 'Prepare to move out. Things are getting a bit hot here.' And I said, 'I'm ready.' Never heard the word to get out, so we were left behind and I was wounded and me mate was killed.[1]

– Len Ogilvie, Korean War veteran

The aboriginal people gained further credit for themselves last week when one of their number parachuted from a plane near Newcastle. He was L/Corporal Stan Houston, full-blooded aborigine of Rockhampton, and he had just graduated as a paratrooper at the Williamtown RAAF station.[2]

– *Dawn*, April 1952

Dawn and its successor *New Dawn* were monthly magazines published by the New South Wales Aborigines Welfare Board between 1952 and 1975. The magazines reported widely on the board's activities, but they also reported news supposedly of general interest to Aboriginal Australians. One of the main objectives of *Dawn* and *New Dawn* was to promote assimilation within Aboriginal communities. Why *Dawn* and *New Dawn* are significant here is because the Australian military featured frequently throughout the magazines' publication run. Some issues featured stories about Aboriginal people serving in the armed forces, while others reported general Australian military news. The Korean conflict, for example, was a frequent subject, mentioned in 17 separate issues between 1952 and 1959. The cover image of the March 1955 issue was even a photograph of Aboriginal serviceman Cecil Donovan. The caption reads that he 'is proud to be doing his training with the C.M.F. [Citizen Military Forces] and his fellow trainees are proud to have him as a team mate'.[3]

The strong military presence in *Dawn* reflected evolving military policies in relation to Aboriginal and Torres Strait Islander enlistment, as well as the ways in which a new discourse was conflating military service and assimilation during the 1950s and 1960s. Assimilation had different meanings, both among non-Indigenous and Indigenous Australians. One feature is common to the different interpretations of assimilation: agreement that equality required an end to discrimination. This was as true for the military as it was for civilian Australia. This chapter traces the evolution of military policies and the experiences of Aboriginal and Torres Strait Islander service personnel from the end of the Second World War until just before the Vietnam War. This period witnessed important shifts from the exclusion of persons not substantially of European origin and descent during the military occupation of Japan, through to repealing such restrictions and, while not necessarily welcoming Indigenous service personnel, at least opening the door to their participation in Korea and Malaya. Meanwhile, as the military was gradually becoming more colourblind in its recruitment practices, discourse in civilian Australia promoted military service as a means to assimilate Indigenous Australians.

The traditional historical interpretation of assimilation as summarised by scholar Anna Haebich is that it represented the promise of equal citizenship rights for Aboriginal people, but in exchange 'they were required to abandon their distinctive cultural values, lifestyles, customs, languages and beliefs and conform to the national way of life'.[4] As Russell McGregor and Rani Kerin argue, there were tensions in the 1950s between policymakers, who saw assimilation as the rise of individualism and gradual decline of Aboriginal traditions (a monocultural vision of assimilation), and anthropologists and Aboriginal supporters, who advocated pluralist models of assimilation where certain features of Aboriginality would be permitted and sometimes even encouraged to endure. In the 1960s the pluralist vision was superseded by the concept of integration, whereby Aboriginal people could participate in the nation-state with equal rights while preserving their distinct cultural identities. Citizenship became the bridge linking military service with assimilation because military service has traditionally been viewed as an exercise of the duties and obligations of citizenship. Even Aboriginal activists of the 1930s to 1940s invoked participation in the first and second world wars as grounds to claim citizenship rights. Those activists considered citizenship rights to constitute political and economic equality; for policymakers in the 1950s, though, citizenship rights, military service and equality became tied up with the notion of assimilation.[5]

The British Commonwealth Occupation Force and debating exclusion

Japan surrendered to the Allied Powers on 15 August 1945, thus concluding the Second World War. The formal Instrument of Surrender was signed in Tokyo Bay on 2 September. Between those two dates the occupation of Japan by United States military personnel under the command of General Douglas MacArthur commenced. These troops remained in Japan until the San Francisco Peace Treaty, signed on 8 September 1951, came into force. Under the aegis of MacArthur, the Americans in Japan helped to implement significant changes to the Japanese political system, including establishing a democratic form of government. Not all of the occupying service personnel were Americans, though. Also present was the British Commonwealth Occupation Force (BCOF), a force drawn from the United Kingdom, India, Australia and New Zealand. The motives for the Commonwealth presence in defeated

Japan had much to do with continuing to assert a British influence in East Asia. As far as the Australians were concerned, the impetus for participation came from a sense that their role in the Pacific War had been overlooked.[6] The Australian component left for Japan in February 1946 to take up its occupation responsibilities in Hiroshima prefecture. With the departure of the British segment of BCOF to Malaya, and the withdrawal of Indian forces subsequent to that country's independence in August 1947, BCOF came to be dominated by Australians. About 16,000 Australians served as part of BCOF between 1946 and 1952, and it was Australia's major military commitment until the outbreak of the Korean conflict in 1950.[7]

The Labor government did its best to keep the Indigenous presence in BCOF to a minimum, with military selection boards again enforcing the rules about European origin and descent. As Frank Forde, the minister for the army in the Ben Chifley federal government, explained: 'In recruiting forces, particularly for the islands and Japan, a high standard of physical fitness and good educational qualifications are required. Aboriginal members of the Australian Military Forces gave splendid service during the war, but most of them cannot conform to the standard laid down for the Japan force.'[8] As with the Second World War, however, there was often a major divide between government intentions and what actually happened on the ground. If an Indigenous Australian was already a member of the 2nd AIF, then he could – and sometimes did – serve in BCOF.[9] For example, distinguished Northern Territory sportsman Steve Abala was an early volunteer for BCOF and was accepted because he was also a serving soldier.[10] If an Indigenous Australian had already been sent to Japan before the restriction came into force, then they too could stay as members of BCOF.

It was a situation ripe for confusion and criticism and an exclusion that did not make much sense. The Australian government and army might have been attempting to placate local racial sensitivities, but as academic Christine de Matos points out, there were other 'non-white occupiers'

Defence reforms and opportunities

in Japan, including black Americans, Japanese-Americans, Indians and Māoris.[11] Shortly after the Australians took up duty on Honshu, Private JS Murray, a veteran of New Guinea and Borneo, stated in the Perth *Sunday Times* that the army decision to bar Indigenous Australians from BCOF 'was inconsistent' to say the least, as he personally knew eight Aboriginal men serving in Japan.[12] There are also photographs of Aboriginal servicemen in BCOF posing merrily for the camera with their white mates.[13] One Aboriginal man who served in BCOF was Kenneth Colbung, who was a guard commander in Tokyo. He remembers the difficult situation in occupying what was essentially a nation of conquered people: 'And then I saw that what had happened to the civilian population there and how they would cower down. I could really reflect … how those people were feeling. It wasn't the civilian population, it was the military that moved in and caused all the atrocities that were around. And, of course, the civilians had to take the brunt of it.'[14]

A series of letters to the press followed Private Murray's letter, protesting at the official exclusion. For example, another Western Australian veteran wrote that he had 'worked and fought with Australian aboriginal full bloods, quarters and half castes and they do as good a job as the white Australian or any other white man'.[15] Criticism of the army was taken to another level when Australia's most famous Aboriginal soldier, Reg Saunders, wrote a balanced and thoughtful letter. No longer an officer in the army but just plain 'Mister', Saunders stated that the BCOF ban on Indigenous Australians was 'very narrow-minded and ignorant', as white 'soldiers he had met in the army were not colour conscious towards the aboriginal, and he felt sure that they would never agree with this discrimination'. His race 'did not want privileges but opportunities for advancement and fair treatment'.[16] It was unfortunate timing for Saunders that at virtually the same time as his letter appeared, an Aboriginal soldier charged in South Australia with desertion defended himself on the grounds of persistent racial insults thrown at him by his white 'comrades'.[17]

A letter from William Onus, the Victorian president of the Aborigines League, followed Saunders's. Onus placed the BCOF racial bar in the context of Aboriginal rights generally: 'Rehabilitation was not proving much help to the aboriginal. These soldiers, many with magnificent war records, were not sufficiently educated to take advantage of rehabilitation facilities. They are simply offered jobs digging or breaking stone … This is happening in all States, and our books are full of such cases.' Onus concluded by challenging the army minister, Frank Forde, 'to debate him in public on whether Aborigines were fit and proper types for the Army in Japan'.[18] After 1946 the heat, such as it was, about Indigenous exclusion from BCOF died down. Occasionally there was a reference in the press to an Aboriginal soldier serving in Japan, but generally the BCOF issue was swallowed up by wider issues of formal recognition of Indigenous military service.[19]

The army seems to have realised that it had made a mistake, for in 1948 it lifted its formal restrictions on Indigenous enlistment. *Australian Military Regulations and Orders 177* removed references to candidates needing to be 'substantially of European origin or descent', theoretically opening the door for Aboriginal people to enlist.[20] Even so, internal memos indicated that while Aboriginal people now *could* enlist, and indeed had provided exceptional service in both world wars, in principle they were still undesirable. The three primary reasons were grounded in discriminatory racial assumptions. First was a fear that given 'the ability, there would be no reason why an aborigine should not rise to NCO [non-commissioned officer] or WO [warrant officer] rank and thus be in a position to command over white troops. This may not be desirable.' The second worry was about Aboriginal soldiers' access to liquor because Aboriginal people supposedly lacked 'stability in relation to the consumption of intoxicating liquor'. Finally, there was a concern that in peacetime white soldiers would not approve of sharing barracks and mess facilities with Aboriginal men.[21] The decision, to ensure that 'only the better types were enlisted', required the senior administrative officer in each military district to personally interview Aboriginal applicants and presumably weed out those they did not want – a procedure not followed with non-Indigenous candidates.²²

The RAAF and RAN continued to adhere to restrictions against persons of non-European origin or descent because the discriminatory provisions introduced into the *Defence Act* in 1909 were still in the legislation.²³ In 1951, the Commonwealth government amended the *Defence Act*; among the changes was the repeal of section 138, which had exempted persons of non-European origin or descent from compulsory call-up in peacetime. This change was not responding to Aboriginal rights advocates; rather, the government wished to introduce national service in the same year and wanted the scheme to apply to immigrants, including those from non-European backgrounds. Though cabinet explicitly decided not to extend national service to Aboriginal Australians, it still determined in July 1950 that 'aborigines who volunteer for National Service training should be given consideration on an individual basis'.²⁴ The chiefs of General Staff (Army), Naval Staff and Air Staff all endorsed the principle that the permanent forces should retain the rules about European origin or descent, under the proviso that the respective service boards could waive the requirement.²⁵ Therefore, by 1951 the three services were at least tolerating Indigenous enlistees on a case-by-case basis, even if not encouraging them. Even in 1965, when the federal parliament amended section 61 of the *Defence Act*, they continued to exempt Aboriginal Australians from compulsory service during wartime. The references to Aboriginal Australians being exempt were finally repealed under amendments to the *Defence Act* in 1992.²⁶

Malaya and Korea

Two years after the army lifted its ban on persons of non-European origin or descent, two political crises in East Asia triggered an Australian response. One was the Malayan Emergency, where the United Kingdom was committed to counterinsurgency operations against communist guerrillas. This had commenced in 1948 but it was only in May 1950 that Australia finally acceded to British requests for military support.[27] Though Australia's involvement in Malaya lasted a decade, fighting was increasingly intermittent and small scale. Thirty-nine servicemen were killed in Malaya, 15 of these from military operations. Possibly the most distinguished Indigenous Australian who served in Malaya was Queensland Aboriginal farm worker Sergeant Cecil Anderson, who served firstly in the 2nd AIF, Korea and finally in the Emergency. There, while serving with the 2nd Royal Australian Regiment (2RAR), he was killed by a communist machine gun on 4 March 1956, the first Australian to die in Malaya at the hands of the enemy. Anderson was posthumously Mentioned in Despatches, one of the two Australians to receive this honour for service in Malaya.[28]

The second political crisis was the Korean War, which broke out on 25 June 1950 when communist North Korea invaded South Korea. Effectively, Australia deferred a major commitment to Malaya while the Korean War was in progress, as it considered its ability to deploy forces to two theatres to be limited. At the urging of the United States, the United Nations Security Council called upon members to assist in repelling the North Korean invasion. Australia was prompt in sending air and naval forces to Korea, though less prompt in committing the army. In the end Australia's decision on 26 July 1950 to commit ground troops caught the army in a state of flux. In order to supply infantry as soon as possible, a special force of volunteers was raised, chiefly from decommissioned Second World War veterans. This was christened K Force, and it was the last time in Australia's history that it used the voluntary system of recruitment to raise special units for overseas service – the last call of the bugle, as some dubbed it. Given the abovementioned policy of tolerating but not encouraging Aboriginal enlistment, the number of Australian Indigenous participants in the Korean conflict was small. At least 36 Aboriginal and Torres Strait

Defence reforms and opportunities

Islander men were among the over 17,000 Australians who served in Korea.[29]

The few testimonies from Aboriginal veterans of Korea describe their motivations to serve and the hardships they endured, particularly in the harsh climate. Like non-Indigenous servicemen, many of these men, too, had served in the Second World War. Cedric 'Ned' Egglestone, for instance, re-enlisted in the army because he believed that many of his kin were trying to 'bludge' off his Second World War deferred pay. Others, such as Leonard Ogilvie and Kenneth Colbung, who both needed permission from the Western Australian Native Welfare Department to enlist, joined for 'a better life', including fair pay. Egglestone, Colbung and Ogilvie, all members of the Stolen Generations, fitted in well with the equality and regimentation offered by the army. For men like Egglestone, who had grown up in Western Australia and served in Borneo and Papua New Guinea, the cold weather and snow were also quite a shock to the system. Egglestone was critical of how run-down the Australian Army had become since the Second World War and how reliant they were on American gear to weather the conditions.[30]

What Colbung recalls most is the toll that the war took on the civilian population. He remembers coming across a group of about 5000 displaced Korean children being cared for by the Salvation Army. Both Colbung and Ogilvie remember seeing the devastation of the terrain, towns that had been destroyed and the destitution and desperation of the people. As Colbung recollects, K Force needed to wage a hearts-and-minds strategy with the civilian population: 'We thought if we could convince them that we were decent sorts of people they would then decide that we were well worth having on their side. Because the thing is that, if you are a minority, you are always going to look for somewhere where you can seek protection and that is in with the majority in some way or another.'[31] Ogilvie was in Korea for only five weeks in 1950 before he was shot in the arm, knee and leg during a night skirmish. He was terrified that if taken prisoner he would be killed on the spot, but he survived a difficult night and was rescued by a patrol in the morning. He was evacuated to a field hospital in Japan and then sent back to Australia.[32]

The most high-profile Aboriginal soldier in K Force was Reg Saunders. While to an extent Saunders's media profile makes his story exceptional, examination of his experiences as an Aboriginal man in civilian Australia suggests that the succession of events driving him to re-enlist were not dissimilar from those of other Indigenous Australians. For various reasons Saunders had not found it easy to settle down after the Second World War. He changed jobs and his address several times. He not only protested at the exclusion of other Aboriginal people from BCOF, but he also tried to join himself and was rejected.[33] Korea saw Saunders return to the colours as an officer within the newly established 3rd Royal Australian Regiment (3RAR). Financial motives were front and centre in his decision to re-enlist; Saunders recalls: 'Where else can I get £21 a week, all hospital expenses, three meals a day and an allowance for my wife?'[34] He served on the Korean peninsula from November 1950 to early 1952, being promoted to the rank of acting captain. He participated in some of the hardest fighting the Australians saw in that conflict, from the Chinese entry into the war in late 1950 to the Battle of Kapyong in April 1951. Journalist Cameron Forbes portrays Saunders in Korea as a hard-bitten warrior anxious for the United Nations forces to stop retreating from the Chinese and to 'stand and fight', but Saunders was more than that stock-standard image might suggest.[35] He was also photogenic, articulate and good with a quick retort. Not all soldiers could come up with Saunders's widely quoted response to the line that Korea was 'no country for white men': 'And it's not much ruddy good for black men either.'[36]

Saunders's achievements in the Second World War had been widely publicised and his encounter with war correspondent Harry Gordon in Korea later brought him renewed public attention in Australia. The Korean War was, for the most part, poorly reported by the Australian

Defence reforms and opportunities

media, but coverage did note the different aspects of Saunders's life – frontline hero and supposed symbol of his race versus domestic squalor back home.[37] After Korea, Saunders remained in the army and was responsible for training national servicemen. He resigned from the army in October 1954, citing the low quality of national servicemen as the reason. He commented, 'There were too many officers' parties at weekend camps. The men at times were allowed to do much as they pleased.'[38]

Another well-known Aboriginal soldier from the Korean War was Cecil (Cec) Fisher from Queensland, who served as a member of 2RAR and who recalled with pleasure the cheers the Brisbane crowd awarded his unit upon their return. As with other Indigenous veterans, that rousing welcome may have been a rare example of acceptance back home. Marches and parades in this period occasionally featured returning Indigenous servicemen. For example, Korean veteran Stephen Dodd of Colebrook, South Australia, led the Anzac march in Adelaide for years after the war.[39] Press articles on soldiers departing for Korea noted the presence of Indigenous Australians, as when the *West Australian* newspaper pointed to two 'full bloods' in the ranks of the 1st Royal Australian Regiment (1RAR) in Sydney. In the same period the Rockhampton *Morning Bulletin* was proud of local Lance Corporal Stanley Houston, who had recently graduated as an army paratrooper. Torres Strait Islander Charles Mene received the Military Medal for courage and devotion to duty while serving.[40] Newsreels highlighted the Indigenous contribution more frequently, perhaps partly in response to international criticism of Australia's treatment of Aboriginal people.[41]

Once in Korea, the Aboriginal presence was noted more often than in previous conflicts, such as when an unnamed Aboriginal soldier was filmed sighting a mortar in the Imjin River area in 1951.[42] The United Nations was formally committed to racial equality and Korea was, after all, a United Nations war. Perhaps, too, a traditional stereotype of the 'passive' Aboriginal Australian, as compared to a New Zealand Māori or a Torres Strait Islander, was being tweaked a little. Prior to the Korean War, popular opinion might have held that the Māori were 'natural' warriors and the Torres Strait Islanders were more warlike than Aboriginal people. This, in 1947, was the opinion of the Queensland minister for health and home affairs: 'Mr Jones said the Torres Strait islanders were a particularly virile and energetic race, and their standard of intelligence and industry was much superior to the Australian aborigine. To some degree it could be compared with the Maori.'[43] The elevation of Aboriginal Australians to a similar level would, as outlined below, align with the assimilation discourse about uplifting them.

The postwar legacies for Aboriginal Korean War veterans were in many ways similar to those of their non-Indigenous comrades. The notion of Korea as the Forgotten War permeates testimonies. To an extent this aligns with historian Alistair Thomson's observations about veterans constructing their memories to fit their experiences within dominant narratives, though the veterans differ in their interpretations of why Korea was 'forgotten'.[44] Egglestone states: 'I do think that it's a forgotten war. I sort of think we've been overshadowed … because it was so close to the Second World War and there wasn't conscription.'[45] Ogilvie believes that it was overlooked by the public mainly because 'the government had forgotten about it', with servicemen returning piecemeal and never marching in parades upon their return. (In fact, returning Korean servicemen often did enjoy such parades, but the contrary belief was widespread.)[46] Aboriginal veterans remained close friends with their army mates, uniting with them regularly and on Anzac Day, and many joined the Korean Veterans Association of Australia. Aboriginal Korean War veterans are proud not only of their service protecting South Korea, but also of being members of the first force to fly under the United Nations banners. They also suffer post-traumatic stress disorder from the horrors they witnessed. Ken Colbung in particular singled out the smell of burning, rotting flesh as one memory he could not shake even 36 years after the war. He reflects: 'Wars should never be. I think we should look more for peace. We should aim for it.'[47]

Defence reforms and opportunities

Korea seems to have shaken the Defence establishment a little. This was not just due to the greater attention given to Aboriginal soldiers spearheaded by Reg Saunders, but was also perhaps due to the postwar remodelling of a professional Australian Army. Several Aboriginal veterans of Korea, including Colbung, Egglestone and Ogilvie, continued to serve in the army into the late 1950s and 1960s (though by then they were too old to serve in Vietnam). Within this new structure the contributions of professional career soldiers may have been more easily spotted irrespective of the colour of their skin. And, as we shall see in the next chapter, there was also growing recognition of the part played by Indigenous Australians in the Second World War.

Military service and assimilation

For a variety of reasons beyond the Korean War, the military virtues of the 'Aboriginal race' were enhanced during the 1950s. For example, in October 1952, a Western Australian critic of slurs directed at Aboriginal people argued that we 'import thousands of new Australians to help us to develop and defend this continent but right here in Australia we have the makings of the finest defence forces in the world'. Only 'the necessary training' was needed plus, of course, 'the recognition in high places that the aboriginal is a man – not some sort of nuisance'.[48] This article appeared around the same time as the *Medical Journal of Australia*'s editor stated that there was no scientific basis to any form of white superiority over Aboriginal people and such a claim was a 'monstrous fiction'.[49] In the wake of the Second World War, science was disposing of some of its racial baggage. In 1951 *Mufti*, the journal of the Victorian branch of the RSL, proposed an all-Aboriginal battalion for the Australian Army. The magazine argued: 'Captain Saunders has provided proof in abundance, if proof were ever needed, that with training the aborigines can become as good if not better in many respects as the white.'[50]

Reg Saunders often appeared in the media and government publications during and after the Second World War. Much of the reporting focused on Saunders as a 'model' Aboriginal person who had successfully assimilated in Australian society. Wheeling out 'model' Aboriginal people, particularly 'celebrities', was dual-purpose propaganda. It encouraged white Australians to accept assimilated Aboriginal people as 'like them', while concurrently suggesting to Aboriginal people that they, too, could make it in mainstream Australia.[51] Reports in 1944–45 frequently mentioned Saunders as the first Aboriginal officer in the Australian Army. Coverage after the war ranged from a photo of Saunders's daughter on Santa Claus's lap, to Saunders starring in a local pantomime revue, to Saunders's wife, Dorothy, and daughters greeting him at Spencer Street Station when he returned from Korea. Such imagery aligned with government efforts to 'sell' assimilation to the white Australian public. One article from the Melbourne *Herald* encompasses the media's attitude towards Reg Saunders: 'It has been frequently demonstrated that an Aboriginal of normal intelligence … can lift himself to the standard of his white brethren. The case of Lieut. Saunders emphasises this truth.'[52] As Haebich summarises, stories such as these sent the message 'that they had been able to succeed in spite of this impediment [being Aboriginal]'.[53]

Most media coverage of Saunders the war hero and model of assimilation did not mention the difficulties he confronted as a civilian Aboriginal man. Between the Second World War and Korean War, Saunders worked in low-wage jobs such as a tram conductor, foundry worker and tally clerk. After the Korean War he again returned to low-wage positions. His daughter Glenda recalls, 'Dad had done extremely well … yet at the end of it, there was nothing for him. Some of the guys have said to me, "I can't believe that he wasn't offered the types of jobs other people were offered." I can only think the reason was the colour of his skin.'[54] Saunders had amicable relations with his colleagues but had to confront racial discrimination from the public. He recalled several incidents when tram passengers racially abused him, though he always stood his ground and often kicked those passengers off. He also confronted racial vilification on the streets of Melbourne and Sydney, and on the football field. He was often refused alcohol in pubs.[55]

Notwithstanding the discrimination he confronted, throughout the 1940s to 1950s, Saunders embraced assimilation for its promise of equality. He tried to live and work with white Australians and no longer resided in Aboriginal communities. When his marriage with Dorothy fell apart in 1953, he subsequently partnered with and eventually married a white woman. A line in Saunders's Aborigines Welfare Board file commented in 1956 that 'Reg's present partner I am told is a white woman possibly a nurse so he is at least being assimilated'.[56] Saunders commented in his 1962 biography: 'Ultimately, I suppose, there'll be assimilation, but it will take hundreds of years.' He used his son Chris as an example: 'He could be totally assimilated. He's a good-looking boy, not too dark, very popular, better than average at sport. And he's very bright at school. You never know ... Chris might one day get to university. And he'll certainly marry a white girl.'[57] That even Saunders argued an assimilationist approach to Aboriginal affairs demonstrates the strength of the ideology within 1950s and early 1960s Australia. As Kerin asserts, many historians and Aboriginal people are hesitant to admit 'that many Aborigines supported assimilation' because of the negative connotations associated with the term today.[58]

Assimilationists asserted that the army was the catalyst for Saunders's 'successful' assimilation and therefore was a possible path for other Aboriginal people. Saunders's military prowess was cited as one proof of Aboriginal capabilities, as were the art of Albert Namatjira and the concert success of singer Harold Blair.[59] Yet playing Indigenous people against one another in terms of their putative martial virtues did not cease. For example, *The Cairns Post* stated in April 1951 that the 'history of the [Torres Strait] islanders [was] replete with song and story depicting their head-hunting activities, their warlike attributes, unequalled seamanship and a pride of race that is not paralleled in the Australian aboriginal'.[60] Despite racial stereotyping and a sense of surprise in some articles that Indigenous Australians were actually capable of functioning as soldiers, it is clear that the armed forces in the 1950s were seen as one way of assimilating Aboriginals and Torres Strait Islanders into mainstream society.

In the late 1950s and 1960s, the links between the armed forces, citizenship and assimilation became more explicit. Publications such as *Dawn* and *New Dawn* frequently promoted the armed forces as a site of opportunity for Aboriginal men and women to perform obligations associated with citizenship. Taken collectively, the *Dawn* and *New Dawn* articles read almost like a series of recruitment advertisements. For example, an article from May 1964 was entitled 'Aborigines discover advantages in army life'. The opening sentence summarises the article's message: 'Serving side by side with many thousands of other Australians in the Regular Army today are a number of young Aborigines who have discovered advantages in this career.' The article details the different aspects of training, life in the army, skills development, education opportunities and wages. There are images of Aboriginal servicemen happily working with and learning from white servicemen. It concludes with a contact address for Aboriginal people interested in signing up.[61] Formal recruitment advertisements appeared in later issues of *Dawn*, particularly during the Vietnam War. An advertisement in August 1967 even promoted careers in the women's services.[62] The presence of these advertisements in *Dawn* – a magazine designed to promote assimilation – reveals that the New South Wales Aborigines Welfare Board clearly saw the armed forces as a vehicle to achieve its goals. Stories would continue to profile Aboriginal service in Vietnam in issues from 1965 to 1970.

A series of Commonwealth Department of Territories information pamphlets beginning in 1957 with *Our Aborigines* promoted to white Australians the 'successful' assimilation of Aboriginal people.

Defence reforms and opportunities

These pamphlets were rife with primitivistic stereotypes about 'traditional' Aboriginal societies, as well as information about the 'assimilated' Aboriginal people who were functioning as active citizens in mainstream Australian society. Among these pamphlets was one in 1961 entitled *One People*. The final section of the booklet was headed 'Some Successful Aborigines', profiling 'assimilated' Aboriginal people 'who – sometimes largely by their own efforts, sometimes with the generous help of other Australians – have established for themselves an honoured place in our community'.[63] The profiled Aboriginal people included sportsmen, entertainers, pastors and Aboriginal servicemen – Reg Saunders, Second World War veteran Timothy Hughes and Phillip Prosser. Of Prosser, the pamphlet stated:

> The original Australians are still worthily represented in their country's armed forces – by such men as Driver Phillip Prosser. Driver Prosser got his taste for soldiering in the Cadet Corps of the Perth High School. Subsequently he left his apprenticeship as a carpenter and joiner to enlist in the army. In 1957, after completing a Driving and Maintenance Course at Sydney's North Head, he became the Commanding Officer's driver.[64]

This description of Prosser, both as an individual and in conjunction with the popular image of Saunders, was another government attempt to link the armed forces to the project of assimilation. The brochure summarised: 'in war, aborigines, or men of aboriginal descent, have *won* the respect and affection of their fellows'.[65] Such propaganda is similar to discourse about uplifting the primitive before granting citizenship rights, and it had some impact on non-Indigenous readers. Noongar Elder Hazel Brown recalls encountering proponents of Aboriginal service in Vietnam in Gnowangerup, Western Australia. One argued: '"Look Hazel you know the trouble with your people is, your people are lazy. Most of them [Aboriginal people] won't work."

He said, "Army'll be good experience."'⁶⁶ Brown rejected such assertions of idleness, but her testimony reveals the strength of the discourse about 'lazy' Aboriginal people and the army representing a 'positive' site of assimilation.

Many of those Indigenous men and women who served in the 1960s and 1970s interpreted assimilation differently from the monocultural approach. By this period many advocates of assimilation did not believe that Aboriginal people should have to sever their cultural ties to become equal citizens. As Kerin argues, there were some who considered assimilation an opportunity to bring Aboriginal culture into mainstream Australian life. She describes such interpretations of assimilation as 'an assimilation which celebrated rather than suppressed Aboriginality'.⁶⁷ Phil Prosser's testimony aligns with this pluralist vision of assimilation. He describes how he did learn leadership skills in the army, but not at the cost of his own culture. He remarks: 'To me it was a way of getting away from this welfare mentality that you could see what was happening in the terms of the old Native welfare days. The way they treated Aboriginal people or Aboriginal people were treated. And so to me it was a way out.'⁶⁸ Prosser used the opportunities provided in the army to set himself up for later in life: 'Well, it gave me the chance that I'd been looking for. A polite way to do things and to prepare me for later stages of my life. It furthered my, I was able to further my education.'⁶⁹

Lingering inequality

It is hard to generalise about Indigenous Australians' experience of the services in the immediate postwar period. The subsequent return to civilian life was not always smooth – as it was not for many non-Indigenous Australians too. In some cases, though, the transition for Indigenous veterans was made harder by the fair go (or fairer go) they had received when in uniform; for them readjustment to civilian life meant returning to discrimination. Cecil Fisher may have enjoyed

Defence reforms and opportunities

his parade in Brisbane but he did not relish the entrenched racism at Cherbourg in Queensland and elsewhere. Many years after his time with 2RAR, Fisher wrote to the Australian War Memorial that he had 'good relations with my fellow soldiers … [we] wore one another's shirts etc borrowed money from one another and had no personality or race problems'.[70] Back home was different. Fisher penned a number of poems that reflect upon his experience of the contrast between army acceptance and domestic indifference or outright hostility. Probably the best known of these is 'Black Anzac', but here we shall quote from another verse where he describes how his grandmother, widow of a First World War veteran, was feted on Anzac Day, but 26 April saw things return to normal:

> Granny was treated like a Queen Anzac Day
> See the shiny medals flashing from far away
> Next day they crossed the street racism was back
> Didn't treat her equal just because she was black.[71]

The drink laws in the multiple jurisdictions of Australia were an obvious irritant and there is no need to multiply examples here.[72] One instance that attracted some attention will suffice – the treatment of Lance Corporal Des Parfitt, formerly of 3RAR, with 12 months' service in Korea. In late 1952 Parfitt was wearing his cluster of service medals when he attempted with some other Aboriginal people to order tea and sandwiches in the West Australian country town of Williams. The woman in charge refused them service and apparently said that 'even a native who is a Korea soldier' and a citizen would be knocked back.[73] The rather confused response from the assistant commissioner of the Native Welfare Department was that 'the law as it stands' made it obligatory 'for a hotel to refuse liquor to a native' even though in Parfitt's case it was an 'absurd' application of the regulations. Yet this was a café not a hotel.[74] Parfitt seemed destined to be humiliated by public acts of discrimination, as the next year he and his new wife were refused entry to the rooms in Perth they had booked for their honeymoon.[75]

The treatment of Australian Indigenous veterans did not pass unnoticed by all elements of Australian society. Church groups, some political groups and concerned individuals protested. 'Good enough to fight, not good enough for a drink' represented one level of this criticism. At another level the message was 'good enough to fight, good enough to be a citizen'. The next chapter will show how this apparently simple proposition was championed by one of Australia's more conservative organisations – the RSL.

2

THE RSL AND AUSTRALIAN INDIGENOUS VETERANS

> Any man who has donned the uniform of this country for service is entitled to full citizenship rights, and that applies also to the aborigines.[1]
>
> – HL Willis, delegate from Narrogin at Western Australian State Congress of the RSL, 1952

In April 1946 the secretary of the Victorian branch of the RSL wrote to the federal executive of the organisation, raising the matter of the 'high service rendered by Australian Aborigines' in the defence forces that contrasted with 'their subsequent treatment as civilians'. He drew attention to 'the high regard the general public has for their services in war time'. The letter asked the RSL's federal executive to request the Commonwealth government to ease 'the regulations restricting the social life of Aborigine ex-servicemen'.[2] This initiative of the RSL's Victorian branch marked a period of approximately ten years in which Australia's premier veterans' body took a strong interest in 'rewarding' the services of Indigenous Australians during the Second World War by improving their rights as citizens, lifting the bars on their social lives and smoothing their passage into military careers. Easing regulations restricting social life – in other words allowing Aboriginal veterans to purchase alcohol legally and drink with their white mates – might not seem a radical proposal, but it is evidence of a sincere, if limited, desire to acknowledge the participation of Indigenous Australians in the great wars of the twentieth century. The RSL's initiatives, some more successful than others, indicate the degree to which Indigenous service personnel could integrate into mainstream Australian society and also the degree to which this was not possible in this period.

The RSL, while not the only veterans' organisation in Australia, was undoubtedly the most significant for much, if not most, of its history. Though some scholars have regarded its influence as 'one of the great myths of twentieth-century Australia', and others have bemoaned some of its more reactionary outbursts, the RSL was a prominent pressure group on a range of national issues and often succeeded in gaining benefits for its members.[3] In the period immediately after the Second World War, its relationship with the federal government was close and its ability to attract public attention pronounced. Its newfound interest in the rights of Indigenous people also had its limitations. Firstly, with some rare exceptions, which are noted below, the RSL restricted its attention to those who had served in the forces; the organisation ignored the mass of Indigenous Australians, even though the RSL was prone throughout its history to extend its activities to 'issues well outside' its 'stated charter'.[4] Secondly, there was a gender divide: the RSL was a single-sex organisation until 1965 and therefore, not surprisingly, spoke only of servicemen in this period.[5] Indigenous women who had served in the auxiliary forces during the Second World War were not mentioned. Thirdly, the RSL's attention was firmly fixed on Aboriginal Australians, not Torres Strait Islanders.

The war's proximity to Australia after 1941 aroused the attention of sections of the RSL to the contribution of Australia's Indigenous servicemen and women, both in the past and in the present. The official policies to rebut potential Indigenous recruits during the war struck some members of the RSL as both unjust and idiotic given the threat posed by the Japanese. A prime example of this new attitude was that of the Boulia sub-branch of the league in central-west Queensland, who stated in 1942 that: 'We consider it a gross injustice that such men should be refused the right to take their place in the AIF on account of their colour ... Many served in the last war ... With the war at our doors this is no time to allow petty prejudices to interfere with the defence of Australia.'6

After the war the league threw itself behind such moves for recognition of Indigenous service personnel. The federal executive of the RSL endorsed the initiative from the Victorian branch outlined above and passed it on to the Commonwealth government. It did not meet with an immediate response nor was it greeted enthusiastically.7 Several reminders and acknowledgements passed to and fro before the secretary of the Prime Minister's Department stated in August 1946 that Mr Chifley intended 'as soon as practicable to implement a progressive policy for the amelioration' of Aboriginal conditions. A rider was attached to this hopeful announcement that was to be repeated many times over the next decade: the authority of the Commonwealth government for Aboriginal affairs was limited to the Northern Territory, the Australian Capital Territory and the Jervis Bay Territory, which included Wreck Bay Aboriginal Station. As apparently there were no Aboriginal ex-servicemen in the latter two areas, there was no need for change there. Within the Northern Territory, officials drew an inappropriate and misleading racial distinction that seemed, temporarily anyway, to get the Commonwealth off the hook. The secretary of the Prime Minister's Department had been advised that a 'number of [full blood] aborigines' had worked for the army during the war but not as enlisted personnel. So-called half-castes had enlisted but they supposedly already enjoyed 'full citizen rights in the Northern Territory'.8

To its credit the RSL did not let this rebuff dampen its newfound enthusiasm for Indigenous veterans' rights. At the organisation's thirty-first annual congress held in Melbourne later in 1946, resolution number 433 read that 'the Commonwealth Government be requested to grant the franchise to Aboriginal ex-servicemen'.9 Thus from the original generalised desire to improve Aboriginal veterans' 'treatment', a specific demand for extension of the franchise at the Commonwealth and state levels had developed. Between 1946 and 1956 the RSL advanced this proposal many times. In this decade it also petitioned the government for two other reforms. Firstly, the RSL sought the removal of the drink regulations that prevented Aboriginal veterans in many parts of Australia from freely buying alcohol or legally entering hotels. As a significant portion of the RSL's attraction was its social activities organised at the local or sub-branch level, this prohibition was an obvious target. Secondly, it wished to encourage the recruitment of Indigenous Australians into the various components of the defence forces. These threads were intertwined, but it will be less confusing here to treat each issue, as much as possible, in turn.

Voting rights

The first sustained effort by the RSL to ensure extension of voting rights to Aboriginal veterans was largely successful. As before, it was the Victorian branch that took the lead in resuscitating interest in the matter when in March 1947 it urged action 'to obtain the granting to Aboriginal Servicemen of all citizens' rights including the Commonwealth Franchise'. Over the next ten years the state executive repeatedly gave the same reason for granting the vote to Aboriginal veterans: 'In the opinion of the Executive, the fact that an Aborigine has served his country in the Armed Forces should be sufficient to warrant his enjoying all the privileges of an Australian citizen.'[10] In other words, service in the forces was proof that one had qualified as an Australian.

It is less clear how widespread the support for this position was among the rank and file, the ordinary returned servicemen in the suburbs and country towns. A sprinkling of letters in archives and newspapers shows that Indigenous service in the Second World War had given a number of non-Indigenous veterans a more positive view of their Aboriginal comrades. Boulia was not unique. For example, in March 1947, William F Wannan from the Caulfield Central sub-branch of the Victorian RSL wrote to *The Argus* that a recent meeting there had unanimously agreed that the franchise be extended to Aboriginal ex-servicemen:

> It is to be hoped that other sub-branches of our league, as well as every progressive organisation throughout the country, will take up this cause. We cannot regard ourselves as an enlightened or democratic community while a section of our citizens, which played so proud and worthy a part in our war effort at home and abroad, is denied those rights which are an essential part of democracy.[11]

A later gesture of support from Gippsland in Victoria indicated that such sentiments were not restricted to metropolitan centres. In February 1949 a Morwell newspaper reported that no less than 11 sub-branches in that area had been calling for some time for the extension of the vote to those Aboriginal veterans who did not yet possess it.[12] What is noticeable in this period is that the most enthusiastic supporters for reform within the RSL came from the southern states.

In August 1947 Chifley informed the federal executive of the RSL that a wartime expedient, whereby serving or discharged Aboriginal service personnel had received the federal franchise under the *Commonwealth Electoral (War-time) Act*, might be made permanent.[13] Throughout 1947 and 1948 the RSL maintained the pressure, on several occasions widening the debate and calling for 'better educational and social facilities' for Aboriginal ex-servicemen or 'full political and economic rights'.[14] Though these wider rights were rarely specified, the pressure regarding the vote was successful, and the last months of the Labor government saw the passing of the *Commonwealth Electoral Act 1949*, which automatically enfranchised Aboriginal veterans.[15] This was for Commonwealth voting only, of course, as the situation within state jurisdictions remained patchy and confused. By September 1948 Aboriginal Australians were already entitled to vote in four states, but not in Queensland, and only under certain circumstances in Western Australia. Despite these problems the amendment to the electoral laws was a real, if qualified, achievement, and historian Richard Broome rightly attributes its passage to the pressure exerted by the RSL.[16]

At the end of 1949 the Chifley Labor government was ousted at the polls. In 1951 Paul Hasluck became minister for territories under the Menzies Liberal–Country Party government, a post he held until 1963, with responsibility for the Northern Territory, including its Indigenous inhabitants. Even before Hasluck took this position, his influence within the government over Australian Indigenous matters was pronounced. Unusually for a politician, perhaps uniquely, Hasluck entered office having published on the subjects of Indigenous history and policy.[17] Hasluck's characteristic mixture of assimilationist rhetoric, paternalism and emphasis on Aboriginal people's gradual development may be seen in an early message (January 1950) from the Menzies government about its intentions in the Indigenous sphere. After the usual disclaimer that the Commonwealth's power was constitutionally limited in this area, the government informed the RSL that it intended to 'endeavour to raise the status of aboriginals to enable them to take their place as members of the community with full citizen rights'. This was a lofty ideal but one that would not come overnight, apparently, as this 'goal, of course, can only be attained progressively over a period of years, as many of the aboriginals still range from primitive to backward'.[18]

Aboriginal veterans' entitlement to the vote continued to occupy the attention of the RSL after 1949 chiefly because of the differences in Aboriginal rights across Australia. Once Hasluck became responsible for the Commonwealth's Aboriginal policies, he argued that 'enjoyment of citizenship rights should be withheld only where a person needed special care and assistance'.[19] The newspaper reporting this lofty statement was suitably cynical, having heard much of this rhetoric previously. *The Argus* – in its dying years a more radical organ than ever before in its history – asked the minister:

No Strings, Mr Hasluck? – We should like to be certain that the Commonwealth Government intends to give the Australian Aborigine full citizenship as a right ... Often in the past we have heard other promises of a better future for our aborigines. And the aborigines have been the only ones to remember those promises ... Can we be certain a fine piece of Australian history has just been written?[20]

In the early 1950s what was actually meant by 'full citizenship' or 'full citizenship rights' was vague. The RSL generally meant the extension of the franchise to all states that were yet to give Indigenous veterans the vote; sometimes it referred as well to removing restrictions on movement, entertainment and the need to get permission for a range of activities from some government authority. For example, in September 1951, the federal executive, using the racial distinctions of the period, asked the prime minister to ensure 'full citizen rights' for 'all Australian returned servicemen'. In clarifying this item the general secretary noted that he was referring 'of course, to [both] aborigine and half-caste members of the Forces'.[21] It was also notable that pressure within from the RSL was now coming from the northern and western areas of Australia, not just the south-eastern states. Thus, in 1951, after the federal executive and the general congress of the RSL had renewed the call for the granting of full citizenship rights, the Alice Springs sub-branch applied pressure on the Northern Territory's only member in the House of Representatives to raise the matter with the Commonwealth government. They lamented that the matter had 'evidently become lost in the pigeon-holes at Canberra'.[22]

In the following year a debate among the sub-branches in northern Queensland illustrated the combination of issues that could be placed under the heading of 'citizenship rights'. This was the annual meeting of the RSL sub-branches in 'the Far North'. A motion was put to the meeting, and lost by a 'big majority', to the effect that the state government should examine all Aboriginal reserves to see if there was land that could be excised for soldier settlement, a scheme from which virtually no Indigenous Australian ever benefited. The opposition to the attempted land grab was vigorous, though it was sustained by well-worn myths that 'the aborigines were a dying race', so it was important to be kind to the terminally ill. Speakers from Edge Hill did proclaim that it 'was one of the League's fundamental principles to preserve the rights of the aborigines'.[23] This was probably news to Indigenous Australians as well as most members of the RSL. More typical of the RSL's attitude to northern Australia was the resolution from the 1928 annual congress of the league that, as the area was dangerously empty:

> [This] Congress insistently press for the initiation of a nation wide policy designed to open up the sparsely settled areas of our great continent, and urge the immediate pushing on and completion of the North to South railway, the extension of the Border Railway Agreement, the construction of cross-country developmental lines, water supply and new Sea Ports; that this is the only practical solution of populating Australia with prosperous contented people, sufficiently powerful to make our nation secure to the white race.[24]

The sentiments expressed by the Edge Hill branch in 1952 indicated changed attitudes. Yet, at the same time as the RSL pressed for an extension of Indigenous rights, it also proposed the separation of part of northern Australia as a Cold War security measure. In March 1950 the state secretary of the Victorian branch argued that ceding Cape York to the United States as a 'second Alaska' would bind the Americans more closely to the defence of Australia. The interests of local Indigenous Australians, whether Aboriginal or Torres Strait Islander, were not mentioned.[25]

The RSL's enthusiasm in the extension of the franchise to Aboriginal veterans ceased towards the end of the 1950s. Perhaps it felt that those who could be granted the right to vote had, for the most part, registered to do so or were not particularly interested one way or the other. Also, in 1962, amendments to the *Commonwealth Electoral Act* granted all Indigenous Australians the right to vote at Commonwealth elections, though they were neither compelled to do so nor to register in the first place. In 1962 and 1965 Western Australia and Queensland respectively became the final states to enfranchise Aboriginal and Torres Strait Islander people. Though Aboriginal and Torres Strait Islander Australians continued to fight for citizenship rights, the franchise battle was over.

The right to purchase and consume alcohol

In the years immediately after the Second World War, Australian newspapers featured a number of court cases in which Aboriginal veterans ran afoul of their state laws and were hauled up before courts for purchasing alcohol. In those cases where Aboriginal returned soldiers were fined for breaking the no-grog rules, it was not uncommon for magistrates to refer to the anomaly of punishing a veteran for something that had been legal when he was in the forces. As a result the RSL proposed cautious amendments to state protection legislation so that all members of a local branch, for example, might share drinks together. As opposed to extension of the franchise, this was not an issue adopted nationally and pushed forcefully with the Commonwealth government. These moves occurred at local and state levels, and reflected a newfound sensitivity to a shared wartime experience with Indigenous Australians.

The timidity with which the RSL approached the issue of drinking rights for Aboriginal Australians was demonstrated in 1951 when Clive Evatt, the colonial secretary in the McGirr Labor government in New South Wales, provisionally relaxed the restrictions on Aboriginal people buying alcohol and drinking in public places. *The Sydney Morning Herald* reported that Evatt had done this 'following representations from the Returned Servicemen's League' because it was 'absurd to speak of emancipation when aborigines who served in the fighting forces with some distinction, some gaining commissions and decorations … are being treated as social outcasts'.[26] Giving the vote to Aboriginal veterans might have enjoyed strong support within the community; 'drinking rights' did not, it seemed. A week after the appearance of the article cited above, the editor of *The Sydney Morning Herald* condemned the proposal and its 'dusky beneficiaries'.[27] The RSL was also at pains to distinguish itself from such a liberal extension of rights. Early in 1951 *The Bulletin* argued that the RSL was responsible for allowing homicidally inclined Aboriginal people to drink. In the trial of a 'half-caste' for murder in New South Wales at the time, counsel argued that both the victim and the accused were drunk, and this was because the colonial secretary, at the RSL's urging, had lifted the embargo on the sale of alcohol to 'colored people of native birth'. Next day the panicked RSL went into damage control, 'saying that all it had done was request that aboriginals who had served in the fighting forces, and had a badge to prove it, should be exempt from the ban'.[28] Self-control, acquired in the services, was apparently the key to why Indigenous veterans could drink responsibly. As the RSL in New South Wales explained it, Aboriginal veterans 'had the discipline to serve with the forces, so they should be able to drink with equal discipline'.[29]

Reg Saunders and the Coronation Contingent

The RSL displayed considerably more enthusiasm at national, state and local levels over the Coronation Contingent issue of 1953. Here, the position it eventually adopted resonated with a large section of the wider public. As outlined in the previous chapter, many people from a range of social, political and religious backgrounds viewed Reg Saunders as a hero. His exclusion from the Coronation Contingent therefore sparked widespread criticism of the federal government's position.

King George VI died in February 1952 and the coronation of his successor, Queen Elizabeth II, took place on 2 June 1953. The development of television and the expansion of a more public role for the monarchy in the twentieth century meant that media coverage of the event was extensive. The Empire had been rebranded as the Commonwealth and the new monarch was head of state of newly independent countries such as Ceylon and Pakistan. There were some grumblings about the cost, but the first television coronation, with its 'trumpetings and hurrahs', 'was a superb spectacle' in spite of the heavy rain that fell on the day.[30] Each Commonwealth country participated in the coronation and associated celebrations and ceremonies; a number provided military personnel for the big day and other pageantry. The route from Buckingham Palace to Westminster Abbey and the longer trip back to the palace was lined with soldiers, sailors, airmen and airwomen from the Commonwealth. Australia's Coronation Contingent was sizeable – 250 in all – and their duties consisted of forming the guard at Buckingham Palace and being part of the Spithead Naval Review, as well as participating in the procession itself.[31]

In February 1953, when the composition of the Australian contingent was made known, the RSL, Aboriginal organisations and members of the public vigorously objected to the absence of an Indigenous representative in the party. For example, on 8 February 1953, the Sydney *Sunday Herald* reported that key 'members of the aboriginal community … thought an aboriginal should go to the Coronation'. Josiah Francis, the army minister, replied flatly that 'it was not proposed to send an aboriginal among the Army contingent to the Coronation' though Aboriginal servicemen 'had been considered among other Army personnel'.[32]

Newspapers then revealed on 12 February that the executive of the Victorian RSL would discuss the possibility of Reg Saunders's inclusion in the contingent.[33] The Victorian branch's case for Saunders was really a collection of separate arguments covering a wide range of issues. Firstly, there should be at least one Indigenous representative in the force and this should be Reg Saunders. 'This Branch,' stated the Victorians, 'has a high regard for Captain Saunders and believes he is a suitable nominee for the Contingent.' Secondly, the executive 'was mindful … that it is important to Australia that overseas countries should be given an assurance that the "natives" are represented'. New Zealand would, of course, have Māori servicemen in London, and if Australia did not attempt something similar this would attract 'questioning and unfavourable comment overseas'. Given that Australia had 'often been charged overseas, falsely of course, with ill-treating its Aborigines … this opportunity should be taken by the Government of off-setting anti-Australian propaganda'. Any proposal that put 'Australia in a better light overseas in regard to the treatment of her coloured population should be encouraged, especially when it can be arranged at a comparatively low cost'.[34]

Similar proposals came from 'prominent members of the aboriginal community'.[35] The wider public generally supported the inclusion of Saunders too. The title of an article in the Perth *Sunday Times* encapsulated an argument that would be repeated over the ensuing months: it read 'Good Enough to Fight – Not Good Enough for Coronation'.[36] Despite the refusal of the army minister to reconsider the original selection of the party, the intervention of an influential organisation such as the RSL boosted hopes for an eventual change of mind. *The West Australian* thus printed a picture of Saunders underneath the optimistic heading 'May Join Contingent'. The mere possibility of Saunders going to London sparked a wave of interest within western Victoria in Reg's life and family, where readers were reminded that he was the son of Chris Saunders of Portland, a Great War veteran.[37]

The federal executive of the RSL decided on 24 February 1953 that, rather than nominating an individual Aboriginal veteran, a 'party of aboriginal servicemen' should attend.[38] Optimism was sustained in some quarters. According to the Adelaide *Advertiser*, the minister for defence, Philip McBride, would 'consider a request' for Saunders to attend.[39] All this optimism was misplaced, though. McBride was characteristically resolute in March 1953 in saying that the three services had already selected the coronation party and there would be no changes to this original decision.[40]

That was the end of the Coronation Contingent as an issue. However, a number of alternatives were put forward by which Saunders could go to London. For instance, ND Wilson, president of the Victorian branch of the RSL, argued that Saunders could go as 'a fine honorary aide for the Prime Minister'.[41] A letter writer to the Adelaide *Advertiser* supported the RSL's action and included the following paragraph, which probably went further than the RSL wanted: 'Why not? These men who served in both wars should be eligible for the contingent. I feel sure that Australia should be represent [sic] by true-born Australians and not by immigrants from other countries.'[42] McBride and the government remained unmoved and the aide idea vanished.

Other suggestions included some recognition of Saunders's service during the much anticipated royal visit in 1954 or, more generally, a tangible reward for Indigenous war service that would benefit a wider community. Thus, it was suggested that Saunders be one of the 'attendants' of the Queen during her progress around Australia.[43] A West Australian woman 'indignant at the Federal Government's omission of a representative of aboriginal servicemen from the Coronation contingent' called for the establishment of enlarged or totally new quarters in Perth 'so that aborigines coming into the city for special medical treatment may be housed in decent surroundings'.[44] None of this happened, and public disapproval of the federal government's decision was reflected in a newspaper picture of Saunders looking on wistfully as he watched the army contingent being reviewed in Royal Park, Melbourne, in March 1953.[45]

Public disapproval did not die down, though, even after it was clear that the government would not budge on the matter. The RSL had obviously decided that there was little it could do. It bowed out, but columnists, editors, church representatives and the concerned public continued to protest for several months longer, the issue finally expiring around the middle of 1953. The RSL might not have liked the way the argument was going, either. For many the government's attitude was typical of the wider racism in Australia, which, despite what the RSL maintained, was not a mistaken perception on the part of other countries. As the Reverend Crookes Hull, secretary of the Methodist Overseas Mission, argued in May 1953, the 'exclusion of aboriginal representatives from the Coronation contingent was a grim reminder of the official attitude to these people'.[46] The changing social and demographic structure of postwar Australia was wonderfully reflected in the comments of 'a New Australian of only four years' standing' who spoke about that 'Old Australian' Reg Saunders: 'The refusal to include an aborigine reminds me most sickeningly of racial discrimination in Germany, of which I among millions, was a victim … You Australians regard yourself as a modern people – in this instance you are 500 years behind the times.'[47] Few RSL office holders shared such sentiments. It was fine to celebrate small groups such as Indigenous veterans or distinguished individuals such as Saunders, the artist Albert Namatjira or the singer Harold Blair and other 'successful' Aboriginal people as described in the previous chapter. Criticism of fundamental government policy and entrenched racial attitudes was another matter.

Waning interest in Indigenous advocacy

The RSL was on safer ground as far as it was concerned when it encouraged the federal government and the three services to enlist more Indigenous personnel. In September 1955 the RSL called for increased participation in the armed forces of not only 'Australian aborigines' but also 'coloured people of British extraction'. The federal executive of the league was especially anxious to learn 'whether any limitations' were 'imposed against the enlistment of such persons into the Royal Australian Navy'.[48] The singling out of the navy here is interesting as it may indicate a feeling that the navy was more discriminatory than the other services.

In response to the RSL's inquiry, the navy insisted that Aboriginal people were indeed currently serving in that force, and the army provided a similar answer. The minister for air reiterated the old regulation: 'an applicant for enlistment' in the RAAF 'must be a natural born or naturalized British subject of substantially European descent, but that, in special circumstances, enlistment may be approved of an applicant who is a natural born or naturalised British subject but who is not substantially of European descent'.[49] The RSL seems to have suspected that the services were being defensive about existing opportunities for, or barriers to, Indigenous enlistment, for they continued to nag away at the issue. In March 1956 Defence Minister Philip McBride emphasised once again that the services had the 'discretionary authority' to waive the European descent clause. He did not say how often this discretionary authority was actually used.[50] At least one state branch of the RSL thought that the answer was probably 'not often', because in August 1956 Queensland asked the federal executive to ensure that 'all aboriginals and/or half castes joining the forces be given opportunities equal to those of members of European descent'. The leadership of the veterans' body seemed to have lost interest in the matter, for they took no action on the request.[51]

In fact, by this time, approximately a decade after it had first intervened on behalf of Aboriginal veterans, the RSL was losing interest generally in Indigenous matters. With some rare exceptions its world view did not take in broader issues of Indigenous rights, and it maintained throughout this period, and for some time after, a ferocious belief in the White Australia Policy. Here there was no bending. For example, in December 1954, the Melbourne *Argus* cited an article in the Victorian RSL's *Mufti* in which it was urged 'TO LET ASIATICS INTO AUSTRALIA'. By doing this, it was argued, 'Australia could make friends with half the world, and friends in these days of international tension [were] often hard to find'.[52] The explosion within the RSL, and community surprise, was considerable. Within three days the alleged author of the article, ND Wilson, the Victorian president, had to write an abject letter to his national president denying authorship of the controversial but unsigned piece.[53] The following statement of national policy from the RSL in 1958 indicates that Indigenous veterans were really seen as exceptions in a society constructed on racial grounds:

> The stand of the RSL on this question [i.e. the White Australia Policy] has remained constant since 1916. It is based not on racial discrimination but on a desire to ensure that this country, for whom so many have worked and died in its short history, and who have by sacrifice succeeded in building up a great nation shall not have its settled, traditional, and proved social pattern jeopardized by misguided sentimentalists and appeasers, however altruistic their motives may be ... [It is] a basic principle of the Australian way of life.[54]

By the early 1960s the attention of the RSL was oriented firmly towards international affairs, with a renewed interest in an external threat from communism as well as the presence of actual or alleged communists within Australia itself. Indigenous affairs now were not part of the league's remit. In 1962 a Select Committee on Voting Rights for Aborigines sought comment from significant organisations as part of the process leading to the amendments to the *Commonwealth Electoral Act* that finally federally enfranchised all Aboriginal people. The RSL declined to participate on the grounds 'that this matter is hardly one which comes within the range of activity encompassed by the League'. The national secretary seemed to have a poor grasp of corporate history or chronology generally, for he then added that 'many years ago we were most concerned to ensure that aboriginal ex-servicemen were given the vote; that right now exists'.[55] At the end of that same year there was a last burst of activity on behalf of Aboriginal service personnel, though it seemed to contradict what the RSL had said seven months before. A resolution from that year's national congress was sent to the prime minister. It shows a belittling of Indigenous people, and indeed Indigenous veterans, which was not present in RSL statements a decade before:

The RSL and Australian Indigenous veterans

THAT the Commonwealth and/or State Governments be urged to provide legislation enabling a returned ex-serviceman of Aboriginal stock to be granted full citizen's rights without the necessity of having to apply for a certificate ... It is quite clear that the Aboriginal problem is not nearly as simple as many people would have us believe, particularly having regard for the fact that many of them are ill-equipped to cope with conditions of modern day society. However, our application is made on the basis of a very small number who have served their country to an outstanding degree. Our simple belief is that as they were advanced enough to share the dangers of active service they are, by the same token, sufficiently advanced to cope with the privileges and responsibilities of full citizenship.[56]

During the 1960s and 1970s the nature of Indigenous politics, identity and activity changed far beyond what the RSL might have envisaged in the late 1940s. Broadly speaking, RSL leaders and rank and file were unsympathetic to such issues as land rights, the Aboriginal Tent Embassy in 1972 and the Reconciliation movement of the 1990s. In this new world the league grew apart from mainstream Indigenous campaigns, their more reactionary leaders being critical of moves they saw as threatening the integrity of the nation. By 1989 one historian of the Indigenous contribution to the Second World War could write that 'the League now seems to have forgotten its obligation to Aboriginal ex-servicemen'.[57]

Such statements need to be qualified. Even a hardened right-wing culture warrior like Bruce Ruxton, long-time head of the league's Victorian branch, could assert that he was not prejudiced because he had known and liked Aboriginal diggers in his time in the forces.[58] Yet some of his outbursts were toxic and showed the RSL's struggle for relevance in an era when many saw it 'as a Dad's Army of hawkish old diggers'.[59] Ruxton's intemperate language, which had the distinct advantages of sooling on his constituency and attracting the media, was at its worst in collisions in 1982 with Charles Perkins, senior public servant and Aboriginal activist, and Al Grassby, then federal commissioner for community relations. In the former case Ruxton used his column in a reactionary magazine to abuse Perkins, referring to 'the stupid and provoking mind of an overpaid public servant who paports [sic] to be black'.[60] In the latter case a debate between Grassby and Ruxton quickly became an exchange of unpleasantries. For the Victorian RSL president Aboriginal people apparently did not share in the Anzac legend:

RUXTON: There's 104,000 Australians who died for this country and the Australian flag …

GRASSBY: Do you know how many Aboriginal people died for the flag?

RUXTON: Don't you bring the Abos into it.

GRASSBY: What do you mean Abos? I'm talking about the Aboriginal people. What's wrong with Aboriginal Australians after 40,000 years?

RUXTON: You mean all the no-hopers and mugs that are doing all the stirring at present?

GRASSBY: Are you saying that all the leaders of the Aboriginal people are no-hopers? Come on, Bruce. Be fair.[61]

Two years later Ruxton, fresh from being elected Victorian state president of the RSL for the fifth time, blasted the concept of land rights and once more divided Aboriginal Australians into real and not-so-real categories. He called for both levels of government to 'ban part-Aborigines from making claims to land rights' as 'the RSL did not regard Australians with just a drop of Aboriginal blood in their veins as being Aborigines'.[62]

The RSL and Australian Indigenous veterans

In 1988 the RSL was in danger of sounding out of touch about immigration issues and Indigenous activism. This occurred in the context of a change in the federal leadership of the league as Sir William Keys, who had strongly opposed the RSL's attempt to restrict Asian immigration to Australia, was replaced as president by outspoken conservative Alf Garland. Internally the RSL was coming to terms with an ageing membership almost 40 years after the end of the Second World War, and externally it faced the challenge of younger Vietnam veterans who had formed their own separate organisations. The RSL had a choice between adapting or holding the line.

In a rambling interview in *Australian Playboy* in April 1988, Bruce Ruxton once again said that Australian soldiers had not left these shores so 'you could give Australia away to the Aborigines'. Yet he also asserted that there was 'no difference between an Aboriginal soldier and a white soldier and I was in a Queensland battalion during the war and they had plenty of Aboriginal soldiers … we've got some good friends who are Aboriginals in Queensland'.[63] Ruxton's biographer picked up these statements but they must be compared with his support for Garland's call in September 1988 for the government to 'consider blood tests to check the racial mix of Aborigines receiving government payments'.[64] At least, that is how the media reported the RSL federal president. In fact, he may well have been misquoted but he certainly called for tests of a person's Aboriginality.[65] Predictably the reaction from the Indigenous community was furious, and not all members of the RSL were happy with this combination of racism and unscientific gibberish. That most famous of Aboriginal soldiers, Reg Saunders, was reported as saying he would have joined the subsequent protest march to federal parliament except for his war wounds, which was a nice touch. Charles Perkins said that his father who had 'served in New Guinea … must be turning in his grave' and later debated Ruxton on Channel 9.[66] Their unedifying exchange concluded with Perkins telling the RSL state president, 'Ah, go and get stuffed.'[67]

More significant were the reactions of Aboriginal veterans, who in a number of cases also happened to be RSL members just like Reg Saunders. One of these, Hewitt Whyman, had served in Vietnam. He told *The Sydney Morning Herald* that it was 'funny' but he did not 'remember needing to quote' his 'caste when ... called to service this country in war'. The letter 'called on all Aboriginal RSL members to resign' because its leaders 'had apparently forgotten that a lot of Aborigines had fought for Australia'.[68] The intransigence of several prominent RSL leaders in this period and their intemperate language dismayed many Indigenous Australians at a time when senior members of the armed services were attempting to establish units in northern Australia with significant Indigenous participation and which re-affirmed links with units from the Second World War (as discussed in chapter 6). It was perhaps not surprising then that, despite the ubiquitous media presence of Bruce Ruxton at this time, *The Australian* newspaper in 1991 argued that 'the story of the RSL in the past 20 years has been one of decline', whereas in 'the 1960s and 1970s, the RSL was one of the most powerful pressure groups in the country, rivalling the farmers and churches in the ability to wield influence with decision-makers'. Once the 'organisation could boast instant access to prime ministers, premiers and defence chiefs', but that had now been lost.[69]

As self-proclaimed guardian of the Anzac legend and intermediary between veterans and the government, the RSL has played a major role in asserting that the voice of former service personnel should be heard and that this group should occupy a prominent place in the Australian community. Therefore, their advocacy – limited, cautious and curtailed – of the rights of Indigenous veterans after the Second World War was important in linking some Aboriginal and Torres Strait Islander Australians to what Jeffrey Grey has called one of 'the great defining influences in our history': war and service abroad.[70] The relationship deteriorated in the 1980s but perhaps is now more amicable than it has been for some time. The wider official acknowledgement of Indigenous

The RSL and Australian Indigenous veterans

participation in Australia's external wars has seen the modern leadership of the RSL, distant from the right-wing warriors of the past, honour the military contribution of Aboriginal and Torres Strait Islander servicemen and women. Thus in July 2000 the national president of the RSL spoke at the ceremony on Mount Ainslie in Canberra, coinciding with NAIDOC (National Aboriginal and Islander Day Observance Committee) Week, which celebrated the achievement of Australia's Indigenous soldiers. He referred to Indigenous servicemen carrying the flag at Anzac ceremonies, a mark both of incorporation into the national legend and the revitalisation of that legend in the twenty-first century. And of course Mount Ainslie rises above the Australian War Memorial, one of the key sites for the commemoration of Australia's military history.[71]

3

INDIGENOUS SERVICE AND VIETNAM

He had been brought up in an era when Aboriginal people were still stereotyped as no-hopers by many in the white community and this was one of the few times in his short life that he felt like he was an equal. The trust, bonding and acceptance he had experienced in Vietnam warmed him then, and would remain with him for a very long time.[1]

– Kenny Laughton

I didn't really understand what Anzac Day was about until I had been to Vietnam in fact. I used to think Anzac Day was a day for playing footy after one o'clock and cricket after one o'clock and all those sorts of things. I didn't understand what that one was about, I didn't understand what the RSL meant … after I had been to Vietnam you understand what the bond is all about because the bond is something that saves your life and sets you up for life forever and it is done by somebody, or with someone else's assistance, who you may never see again, because that is exactly what happened when we came back from Vietnam.[2]

– Glenn James

Indigenous service and Vietnam

> Don't get me wrong. I was no angel. But because everything just sort of went haywire from the organised life I had in the army to the disorganised life that I had out in civilian street.³
>
> – David Cook

The 1960s in Australia are often remembered as times of upheaval, social change, youth rebellion and activism. The Vietnam War and its impact on civil society have traditionally been central to studies of the 1960s, and in recent years the significance of the fight for Aboriginal civil rights has also emerged as a key social movement in that decade's narrative. If race and war were two themes permeating the 1960s, then one area overlooked by historians is their intersection: Aboriginal and Torres Strait Islander service in Vietnam. As in previous conflicts, Australian Indigenous servicemen were integrated with other troops and served alongside them. For non-Indigenous personnel, this was often the first time that they interacted with Aboriginal people. Non-Indigenous veterans have described their service with Aboriginal servicemen favourably and have argued that Aboriginal people were treated as equals. Retired non-Indigenous officer Colonel OM Carroll writes, 'I would make the point strongly that the men I am referring to were first and foremost Australian soldiers. There is no discrimination in the Australian Army on account of a man's background, his race, his colour or his creed.'⁴ Carroll's statement has echoes among the testimonies of Aboriginal veterans, but only Indigenous people themselves can verify his observations about their lives in the armed forces, their motivations to serve, their experiences in Vietnam and the impact of military service on their lives.

As a brief background to Australia's Vietnam War: in August 1962 the Commonwealth despatched 30 military advisors known as the Australian Army Training Team Vietnam (AATTV) to South Vietnam. Australia's commitment expanded in 1965 alongside the United States, sending 1RAR and 3 Field Troop, Royal Australian Engineers, to accompany the US 173rd Airborne Brigade in the Bien Hoa province. At least three Aboriginal men and one Torres Strait Islander were part of this deployment. From March 1966 the Australian forces worked independently from the Americans, based at Nui Dat in the Phuoc Tuy province of South Vietnam. It was near Nui Dat that Australia's most famous engagement in the Vietnam War – the Battle of Long Tan – took place on 18 August 1966. The majority of Australian troops continued to be stationed at Nui Dat for the duration of the Vietnam War. The Australian presence in Vietnam peaked between 1967 and 1970, and that too would be when the majority of Australian Indigenous soldiers were there. By late 1970, as the United States began staging a gradual withdrawal of its own forces, so too did Australia begin to reduce its commitment. The bulk of ground troops were out by the end of 1971, leaving only a small contingent of advisors and embassy guards until mid-1973. Through the course of Australia's entire military commitment from 1962 to 1973, almost 60,000 men served in Vietnam; there were 521 deaths and over 3000 wounded.[5] The Australian War Memorial has identified at least 260 Aboriginal and Torres Strait Islander men who served in Vietnam, including at least eight killed in action. Though this number is admittedly incomplete, it represents an under-studied demographic. All of the identified Indigenous service personnel are men; only 43 Australian women in the Royal Australian Army Nursing Corps served in Vietnam, and none have been identified as Aboriginal or Torres Strait Islander.[6]

There can never be a uniform Indigenous Vietnam experience, just as there is no homogeneous non-Indigenous veterans' history. Yet a stark number of parallel themes permeates many Aboriginal and Torres Strait Islander Vietnam veterans' testimonies, regardless of when they served or their particular unit or corps. Among the more pronounced subjects are: motivations to join the military, sentiments of equality, experiencing the hardships and trauma of war, witnessing American racism, an ambivalent return to Australia, and professional links to Aboriginal affairs later in life. Many of their experiences are not dissimilar to non-Indigenous Vietnam veterans – particularly their memories of Vietnam, their alienated homecomings and the lingering impacts of post-traumatic stress disorder. This convergence of narratives again reflects historian Alistair Thomson's observations about how public memory and national narratives may shape veterans' oral histories of war.[7] Such warnings do not mean we should disregard the common portions of veterans' testimonies. Rather, we should be aware of the impact of popular memory and take it into account when analysing oral histories of war. In the context of Indigenous service in Vietnam, though, the hitherto lack of public discourse suggests that there is less scope for public memory to shape Aboriginal and Torres Strait Islander veterans' testimonies. Unlike non-Indigenous veterans, Aboriginal and Torres Strait Islander Vietnam veterans had to confront life as Indigenous men after the war. Diverging from the dominant Vietnam veterans' narrative, the skills they acquired in the armed forces in conjunction with their newfound self-confidence made Aboriginal and Torres Strait Islander Vietnam veterans apt community leaders in various capacities.

Veterans' backgrounds and motivations to serve

Like most Vietnam veterans, the majority of Indigenous men who served in Vietnam were born either during or immediately after the Second World War. This was a time when assimilation policies dominated Indigenous affairs in all states and child removal was widespread. Some Vietnam veterans were themselves members of the Stolen Generations. Those men faced childhood hardships including institutionalisation in boys' homes, physical and mental abuse, and emotionless foster relationships. Even many men who were lucky enough not to have been removed have memories of hiding from the Welfare Department as children, fearing removal.[8] Many members of the Stolen Generations who signed up for the armed forces required permission from chief protectors or other state-appointed guardians, which was sometimes a demeaning experience for the enlistees. Once in the armed forces, though, Aboriginal servicemen from the Stolen Generations often responded well to military life because their regimented upbringings suited them to the discipline, communal living environment and rigid social structures. Phillip Prosser, for instance, recalls: 'I was able to accept a lot of discipline because the discipline that was meted out to me in the army was nothing compared to what I had to have when I was a young kid growing up in the home.'[9] The armed forces were a common destination for an unknown number of survivors of out-of-home 'care' in Australia – both Indigenous and non-Indigenous – because they provided stability, discipline, steady income and shelter.[10]

Over 100 service records of Aboriginal and Torres Strait Islander Vietnam veterans were canvassed, and the most common education level listed on enrolment forms is 'Reasonable Primary', usually meaning completing up to year seven. This was not uncommon among non-Indigenous Vietnam servicemen as well. The majority of service records list Indigenous servicemen's previous occupations as 'labourer'. Some of the more common industries listed include: railroads, forestry, farm labour, meatworks and construction. The vast majority of Indigenous servicemen in Vietnam were single and between ages 17 and 20 when they enlisted, but at least half of them married during their time in the armed forces. Some Indigenous servicemen had Anglo-Australian friends in their pre-service lives, while others recall that Southern European migrants tended to be more accepting of Aboriginal people. All recalled experiencing some racism in their youth, such as taunts at school, police harassment and segregation in public places. But the veterans do not dwell on specific incidents of racism. Former soldier Dick Bligh summarises the attitude of several Aboriginal veterans towards childhood racism: 'It never bothered me, and it doesn't bother me now. It was something that happened back in that era, and as far as I'm concerned it can stay back in that era.'[11]

How and why Aboriginal men enlisted in the armed forces varied, which suggests that, like non-Indigenous men, everyone had his own personal reasons to join. Even so, a few common threads are discernible

Indigenous service and Vietnam

among veterans' testimonies. For instance, Ron Wenitong entered the army because it was one of the few opportunities for an Aboriginal man living in Gladstone, Queensland. He states: 'There was nothing else. All the young kids, my two cousins were both in the army, one was in the SAS [Special Air Service Regiment], I don't know what the other was in, and it was just a way out. You know, there was a job; you got fed; you got a roof over your head basically.'[12] Frank Mallard was working in rural Yuna, Western Australia, and similarly saw the army as a chance to earn a better wage: 'I'd been working on the farms and I was getting £5 a week and my keep, and believe it or not, the military was offering £22 a fortnight and travel. They didn't, at that stage, they didn't say to you that where your travel was going to be but you get to travel overseas and I thought that was a good idea, so I joined up in '62.'[13] Phil Prosser, also from Western Australia, says: 'I made up my mind that I was going to use the army, or the services, to benefit me at the better part of my life. 'Cos to me it was a way [of] getting away from this welfare mentality that you could see what was happening in the terms of the old Native Welfare days.'[14] Geoff Shaw responded to an advertisement in the *Australasian Post*; Dick Bligh claims that he accidentally signed up for the army when responding to a similar announcement in the *Post*. He then filled out the application forms with a friend's assistance, and when he was summoned to training he went. George Bostock also joined on a whim; he was at the employment office in Sydney, and the army recruitment office happened to be next door. He thought it would be a good job opportunity, which would keep him out of trouble.[15] Bob Blair does not even remember why he signed up for the army. He says: 'I just signed up and that was it.'[16]

Several Aboriginal veterans acknowledge family connections to the army, and a few indicated that it was their main motivation to join.[17] Family reactions to the men's enlistment varied, with male relatives generally more supportive than the females. Frank Mallard recalls: 'Well, my mum was not all that happy to sign the paperwork. I took it home to her and I said I really want to join the army. And she was saying you know it's a dangerous job and that you can get killed there.'[18] Mallard's mother's reaction is quite striking because his family has a long history of military service. On the other extreme, though, was Jeffrey Duroux, whose parents encouraged him to enlist. Jeff's sister Dianne Gage remarks: 'So, being young I think Dad had a word to him and Mum, get yourself together, do something with your life, join the army. And of course people thought the army would be good discipline, motivated, keep you under control. So maybe they thought he needed those things, so he did that.'[19] For all of the Aboriginal and Torres Strait Islander men who served in Vietnam, what was clear was that they were continuing a tradition of Indigenous service to Australia, and despite some misgivings, they received the support of family and community to serve their country.

National service and Aboriginal people

Out of the Aboriginal and Torres Strait Islander veterans identified by the Australian War Memorial, 61 – nearly 24 per cent – were national servicemen. This compares with total figures of 19,000 national servicemen out of 60,000 who served in Vietnam, or nearly 32 per cent. The reason for the significantly lower percentage of Aboriginal and Torres Strait Islander national servicemen is that technically, under the law, they were to be exempted from national service. That almost one out of every four Aboriginal and Torres Strait Islander soldiers in Vietnam was a national serviceman suggests those exemptions were not so clear. Indeed, inconsistent application and interpretation of the *National Service Regulations* created a fraught situation for Aboriginal and Torres Strait Islander men.

Under the *Defence Act 1903* and amendments in 1909, Aboriginal people were explicitly exempt from call-up and from compulsory training. In 1951 the Menzies Liberal–Country Party government introduced a new national service scheme, citing communist disturbances in

Indigenous service and Vietnam

Southeast Asia and Korea. Section 18 of the *National Service Act 1951* followed the *Defence Act* precedent and exempted Aboriginal people from registering for national service.[20] In the 1950s there was little discussion in the media or government about their exclusion because Aboriginal affairs were not high on the federal government's or the public's agenda. Even so, during this first period of national service, there were inconsistencies in the implementation of the racial exclusion clause. For instance, when now-renowned Torres Strait Islander Eddie Koiki Mabo received a letter summoning him for national service, he refused to enlist. He went to his local member of parliament, who found out that Indigenous Australians were exempt, and the matter went away. But Mabo recalled another Torres Strait Islander who did not protest and wound up serving.[21] Such examples would become more prominent, and also more complicated, during the Vietnam War.

The Menzies government passed an amended *National Service Act* in November 1964, reinstating what had been a defunct scheme since 1959. The government cited the need for national service because of the deterioration of the situation in Southeast Asia, including Indonesia's policies in Malaysia and the continuing conflicts in Borneo and Vietnam. Among the people required to register for national service were almost all males aged 20, including resident foreign nationals. Aboriginal people, though, were the only civilian British subjects legally not required to register. The updated section 18 of the *National Service Act* again excluded 'aboriginal natives of Australia, as defined by the regulations, other than a class of aboriginal natives as so defined that is specified in the regulations'.[22] Whereas in 1951 such clauses did not attract attention, as early as January 1965 the Commonwealth had to justify its position excluding Aboriginal people from conscription. Aboriginal affairs now garnered public interest because of domestic and global interest in minority civil rights. HA Bland, secretary of the Department of Labour and National Service (DLNS), defended the government in May 1965: 'there is no foundation for the suggestion that the Government intends any discrimination against Aborigines by reason of their not being required to register … it would be impracticable for many primitive or tribalised Aborigines to register and hence be liable for national service and to require this of them would create special hardship'.[23] Administrative difficulty and impracticability were recurring defences against repealing the references to Aboriginal people from the *National Service Act*.[24] Moreover, the government regularly pointed out that Aboriginal people were only excluded from *compulsory* national service; they could still volunteer for national service, and an unknown number of Aboriginal people did.

Calls for Aboriginal inclusion in compulsory national service came from various sectors of society, including politicians, concerned citizens, local councils, political party branches and Indigenous organisations. The first politician to raise the matter in federal parliament was ALP senator Joe Fitzgerald, citing valiant Australian Indigenous and Papua New Guinean service in the Second World War as proof of their effectiveness.[25] Individuals wrote letters to newspapers and politicians, claiming that the exemptions discriminated against Aboriginal people. One letter from a school child even stated, '[A]re Aborigines conscripted for National Service[?] If not, why not? We feel that if we are striving for their welfare, they should be given equal treatment wherever it is possible.'[26] Other letters advocated national service for 'lazy' Aboriginal people on the grounds that it would '[p]rovide a new sense of responsibility and national spirit'.[27] Local councils and other individuals similarly argued that discipline would benefit Aboriginal people in their wider communities.[28] Even the Federal Council for the Advancement of Aborigines and Torres Strait Islanders (FCAATSI) resolved in 1965 '[t]hat the Federal Council call upon the Commonwealth Government to remove discriminatory clauses against Aborigines in the National Service Act'.[29] In 1967 the Western Australian state Liberal conference endorsed a motion to repeal the references to Aboriginal people from the *National Service Act*. From 1965 through 1971, the Commonwealth–State

Indigenous service and Vietnam

Aboriginal Welfare Conferences regularly called for Aboriginal inclusion in national service on equal terms.[30]

Aboriginal people, too, expressed opposition to the discriminatory provisions in the *National Service Act*. Some Aboriginal people voluntarily signed up for national service as a form of protest. Yorta Yorta veteran Graham Atkinson testifies: 'I thought, in terms of being equal, that was sort of discriminative. I was aware that technically, I didn't have to enrol [in national service]. But I thought, that time as a young bloke, who had a lot of friends who were conscripted too … '[31] Others signed up for the armed forces because their non-Indigenous mates were being conscripted. David Williams remembers: 'My mates were with the national service. We were 18 getting called up and so I said, well, if I'm going to go, I know now that I didn't have to, because I was Aboriginal, but my mates are going … So I stayed in there for 29 and a half years.'[32] Western Australian veteran John Schnaars describes how originally the DLNS refused his application: 'Yep. Got a letter back saying that they didn't want me; no explanation. So I wrote them another letter then saying, well this is gonna look good in the media. I'm volunteering for national service and you're knockin' me back and you're forcing others to go in that don't want to go in. So it was about two to three weeks later got another letter saying: go for your medical.'[33] As previously mentioned, there were also Aboriginal men who were called up and served because nobody told them that they were exempt from national service.[34]

Such inconsistencies were common because, in response to public calls for Aboriginal inclusion in national service, the DLNS argued that the provisions of the *National Service Act* applied only to certain 'nomadic' classes of Aboriginal people. Those who lived more settled lifestyles could still be obligated to register for national service if they did not fit the definition of Aboriginal laid out in the *National Service Regulations*. Regulation 18 defined an Aboriginal person as:

(a) a full-blooded aboriginal native of Australia;

(b) a person who is a half-caste aboriginal native of Australia or has an admixture of aboriginal blood greater than a half-caste; or

(c) a person who has an admixture of aboriginal blood and lives as an aboriginal native or amongst aborigines.[35]

The complex definition of Aboriginality was meant to appear non-prejudicial while still discriminating. For instance, the original 1951 *National Service Act* only excluded 'aboriginal natives of Australia as defined by the regulations', whereas the 1964 Act added the phrase 'other than a class of aboriginal natives as so defined that is specified in the regulations'.[36] HA Bland wrote that '[o]ne reason for this amendment was to counter any charges of discrimination against aborigines'.[37] Historian Pam Maclean argues that the real purpose of such a complex definition of Aboriginality in the *National Service Regulations* was so that Aboriginal people 'should only be called up if their fellow conscripts considered them to be "acceptable", in other words fully assimilated'.[38]

The flaw with the government's position was that providing a stipulated definition of Aboriginality did not circumvent discrimination or promote assimilation; rather, not counting all Aboriginal people merely compounded the discrimination. Bureaucrats and politicians recognised this in their internal memos. Regular correspondence between the DLNS and the Council for Aboriginal Affairs (formed after the 1967 referendum granted the Commonwealth government power to legislate in Indigenous affairs) deliberated the prospect of removing references to Aboriginal people from the *National Service Act* and administratively excluding 'tribalised' Aboriginal people. Arguments for such change focused on public opinion, international obligations and the Coalition government's pronounced agenda to repeal discrimination from all federal legislation. The DLNS dismissed the Council for Aboriginal

Affairs' suggestions on two grounds: firstly, it would be too much of an administrative burden, and secondly, it would merely introduce discrimination into the administrative process.[39] By 1970 the DLNS accepted the inclusion of Aboriginal people in compulsory national service as part of its agenda, but stated 'there is no intention of opening up general discussion of the Act by introducing amendments relating only to Aborigines'.[40]

As the internal debates waged over whether or not to amend the *National Service Act*, there were also concerns across the different states about the applicability of the definition of Aboriginality. As early as 1965 the Victorian superintendent of Aborigines welfare flagged:

> there is a variety of interpretations in this State as to whether or not a part-Aboriginal who lives in a house with other part-Aborigines is liable for registration or not … What is the test to be applied as to whether a part-Aboriginal is living 'as an Aboriginal native' or 'amongst Aborigines'. Is the Department influenced by the State definition of 'Aborigines' … [?][41]

The fact that each state had a different definition of Aboriginal people complicated matters further, as an individual could be deemed Aboriginal in some states but not others. The South Australian Department of Aboriginal Affairs reported in 1969: 'there is no legitimate way in which the caste can be proved with any degree of certainty. As a result, an Aboriginal, who in fact should register for National Service in accordance with the National Service Act, may fail so to register and there appears to be no method whereby he can be required to do so.'[42] Victorian and New South Welsh officials expressed similar difficulties determining which Aboriginal people would fit under the *National Service Regulations* definition. Queensland, on the other hand, had a larger Aboriginal population and a stronger regime of segregation, making the definition of Aboriginality more 'workable'. The Northern

Territory and Western Australia similarly presumed that there would be few Aboriginal people liable for national service due to both the predominantly 'tribalised' population, but also the poor literacy skills of Aboriginal people of mixed descent.[43]

Auditing the situation in 1966, the DLNS received reports from state welfare departments approximating the number of Aboriginal people who may be eligible for national service under existing regulations.[44] The diverging state responses did not raise concerns among the DLNS staff; instead, the audit reinforced the DLNS's false assumptions that individuals could easily fit into the categories of 'Aboriginal' or 'non-Aboriginal' under the *National Service Regulations*. Various parties external to the DLNS raised the alarm about potential complications. BG Dexter, the director of the Office of Aboriginal Affairs, wrote in 1968: 'No definition or judicial discretion has been made on the actual meaning of the phrases "lives as an Aboriginal" or "lives amongst Aboriginals".'[45] The South Australian Department of Aboriginal Affairs wrote in 1969: 'It would appear from discussions with Aboriginal Affairs officers, National Service authorities and the Aboriginals themselves, there is no clear understanding of the subject.'[46]

The confusion over the definition impacted on the lives of Aboriginal men. Victorian Aboriginal veteran Glenn James recalls: 'I was twenty [in 1968] when I got a notice to say I was called up for National Service. Then I got a notice to say I didn't need to go because I was Aboriginal. Then I got a third notice to say I had to go after all. I tell you, that put a damp outlook on the whole thing right from the start. I was going, then I wasn't going and they'd raised this question of Aboriginality right at the start.'[47]

In 1968 a Western Australian man named Stephen Henry presented himself at registration, identifying as a 'half-caste', but was told that he still had to register. Henry consulted a lawyer and produced a family tree showing that he was slightly more than 'half-caste' under Western Australian law. When the state Department of Native Welfare supported

Henry's claim, the DLNS ruled that he was not liable for call-up.[48] In 1970 Queenslander and Rugby League World Cup contender Eric Simms was nearly prosecuted for failing to register because he thought himself exempt as a 'part-Aboriginal' man. A press release from the DLNS declared: 'I am satisfied after careful enquiry by my officers that Mr Simms, at the time he was obliged to register for National Service, was under the impression that he was not a person affected by the National Service Act.'[49] Simms was ultimately allowed to register without penalty and was treated the same as all other Australians registered for national service. As this chapter will later outline, by the early 1970s, the Commonwealth government began to prosecute Aboriginal people who failed to register for national service, fuelling the debates over national service.

Training

Whether they entered the armed forces voluntarily or as national servicemen, many Aboriginal and Torres Strait Islander servicemen in Vietnam also served in places such as Borneo and Malaya. Those in the army – the most prominent service in Vietnam – underwent basic training at Kapooka before being sent to further corps training. Glenn James recalls of Kapooka: 'Oh it looked enormous; it was just something ... Imagine a twenty year old these days going to a complex where there are something like 6000 people there, including the recruits, and all the training personnel, staff and bases ... different units set up there and trucks going back and forwards with big guns on and 'cos they would be going out to the range and people marching everywhere ...'[50]

At Kapooka Aboriginal and Torres Strait Islander soldiers often stood out, which could have both positive and negative ramifications. Bob Blair comments: 'So I stood out in the crowd because I was the only blackfella in the platoon. So I think that people got to know me but, at the end of the day, also, if I stuffed up, they'd also get to know me very, very quickly too.'⁵¹

Given the lower education levels of the vast majority of Aboriginal and Torres Strait Islander recruits, it is not surprising that approximately 60 per cent of Australian Indigenous soldiers identified by the Australian War Memorial entered the Royal Australian Infantry Corps. The next most common corps was the Royal Australian Engineers, with 12 per cent. A small number of Indigenous servicemen joined more specialised corps such as the Royal Australian Corps of Signals or the Royal Corps of Australian Electrical and Mechanical Engineers. While the infantry was of course the largest army corps, that so many Aboriginal soldiers wound up there or in other front-line positions demonstrates that Aboriginal soldiers who enlisted through the period 1965–70 were likely to see active duty in the Vietnam War.

Most Indigenous Vietnam veterans describe army life positively: most responded well to the discipline and regimentation; their previous work as labourers had made them physically fit; they participated in sport and they easily made friends with other soldiers. Military sport is quite prominent in the testimonies of Indigenous veterans. Many service records list football (meaning either rugby league, union or Australian Rules football), cricket or swimming under 'hobbies' on the enlistment papers. Football and boxing continued to be popular extracurricular activities and ways of bonding with other servicemen. David Cook remembers playing rugby league in Sydney, Borneo and Papua New Guinea. At one stage he even played against the touring British National Rugby League team. He recalls: '[I]t was a pretty close game because they couldn't handle the heat, coming from England. It was a friendly but it was pretty hard. It was a hard game. So I played against the British Lions. That's one thing a lot of people can't say.'⁵²

Boxing stories also echo across veterans' testimonies. At times, though, Indigenous soldiers' interest in sports led to stereotyping. Glenn James remembers:

Well, I can remember an issue in the army when at Puckapunyal they were asking for boxers to represent our company that I was part of, and of course in the army boxing is a high-profile sport and always has been. And the sergeant was standing up on this little dais asking us were there any volunteers and I was standing in the line and he said … no one volunteered. And he poked his head around the corner and he looked at me and he said, 'What about you, James?' I said, 'No, Sergeant, I don't want to fight.' He said, 'Well, do you know what?' I said, 'I don't know, Serg.' He said, 'You are the only abo in Australia I know doesn't like a fight.' And he said, 'You are fighting' and I said, 'No, I am not.' He said, 'You are on charge,' and I said, 'Well, I am fighting, Serg' because I didn't want to be on charge … so I jumped in the ring and had a fight. I won; I won two fights.[53]

This incident leads to the question of racism and stereotypes in the armed forces, which is dealt with in more detail in chapter 5.

Service in Vietnam

The notion of all soldiers needing each other's support rang true in Vietnam, where Indigenous and non-Indigenous servicemen alike experienced the horrors of war. Most of the veterans did not feel comfortable discussing their combat experiences and the atrocities they witnessed, though they did dwell on incidents when friends died. They were more prone to discuss memories of friends, life in the base at Nui Dat or the trouble they got into in the town of Vung Tau. The interpersonal relationships with other soldiers form a significant component of veterans' histories, and these patterns permeate the veterans' testimonies regardless of corps or when they were in Vietnam. One famous friendship was between Aboriginal soldier Billy Coolburra and non-Indigenous serviceman Snow Wilson, both from 3 Field Troop, 1st Field Squadron

(1965–66). They were so close that they were nicknamed twins even though their appearances were strikingly different. At one stage Snow Wilson met the visiting prime minister, Harold Holt. Holt asked where his twin brother was and did not realise that his 'twin' was actually an Aboriginal man.[54] Every testimony recalls the striking of close friendships among Aboriginal, Torres Strait Islander and non-Indigenous servicemen, highlighting the equal nature of life among the 'grunts' in Vietnam. Bob Blair encapsulates the spirit in his statement: 'But I think the mateship was the thing that got you.'[55]

The sorts of memories veterans are willing to share depend on their tasks in Vietnam. Bob Blair (2RAR, May 1967 – June 1968) remembers commanding an infantry platoon: 'I was a platoon sergeant in the infantry. We had an infantry platoon. You know, just normal patrolling, ambushing, looking after fire support bases, anything to do with going out there … I might end up with a 15-man patrol being out there for five days, 15 of us. So things were pretty hairy, bit scary, but you sort of believed in each other and that was it, yeah. So it wasn't too bad.'[56] Hewitt Whyman (Royal Regiment of Australian Artillery, 1st Field Regiment, December 1969 – February 1970) expresses frustration that when patrolling villages like Hoa Long: 'it was hard to realise that they were probably cheering you one day then fighting you that night'.[57] Glenn James (Royal Australian Engineers, 17th Construction Squadron, May 1969 – April 1970) similarly comments: 'sometimes those people were friends by day and enemies by night, and that was quite evident to us in some cases because the guy who managed the market place in some cases was our friend during the day and he would get caught and be in the prison compound when you come back into camp'.[58]

Patrols were, of course, dangerous business that may end in deaths, and particular incidents took a severe toll on veterans' psyches. Dick Bligh (8RAR, November 1969 – November 1970) recollects:

Indigenous service and Vietnam

We were in an area where there were a lot of landmines and we lost two blokes through a mine incident, and it was a pretty low point at that particular time. Then the next day we sort of harboured up as a company and the next day we moved off as platoon groups and our platoon had a mine incident. And the section I was in, there was only two of us left in the section and all the rest of them had to be evacuated out, because they were involved in the incident. So yeah, I think that was the lowest point in my life, losing all those blokes. None were killed – they were all wounded – but we lost them all and we were out in the jungle and there was two of us left in the section. That night, it just felt so lonely, not having these blokes around because they were there all the time. You didn't know what was going to happen during the night or what was going to happen the next day. Because our platoon lost about six blokes or something I think it was, and that is a big loss for the platoon, because we only usually had around 22 or 23 blokes in the platoon at one particular time.[59]

The theme of ambush permeates several veterans' testimonies. Geoff Shaw (2RAR, May–November 1967 and 9RAR, November–December 1969) remembers one double-ambush: 'In the meantime, while we had this VC [Viet Cong] on the stretcher and waiting for the winch to come down to take the VC away, another group of VC came along and took us by surprise and opened up on us. And that's where my scout got it; he was badly wounded. We had to throw the VC out of the stretcher to make sure we could winch Kevin out and get him to the hospital … I lost three of my men and I could've been killed at the same time. But having people shot next to you and killed creates that strong relationship with other soldiers around you.'[60]

Men in non-infantry corps performed other duties. One of the many tasks Royal Australian Engineers member Frank Mallard (3 Field Troop, 1st Field Squadron, September–November 1965 and

January–September 1966) had to do was to check Viet Cong tunnels: 'You go down and have a look and see what it's all about and of course the engineers then were the first to sort of go down tunnels in Vietnam, searching for the Viet Cong and whatever else. You probably don't know that but we found a lot of equipment and stuff underground which has been recognised and photographed, and we did quite a good job really.'[61]

Although the majority of Australian servicemen in Vietnam were army, the navy too played a key role patrolling the seas and as transport. David Williams is an Aboriginal naval Vietnam veteran. He recollects:

> You escort it [HMAS *Sydney*] up there and you'd anchor in the harbour and then you do dives every four hours. It's called an Operation Awkward, where one-third of your defence is closed up at action stations while the other two-thirds get on with the daily chores … One night, we had a bit of a ruckus. The current got up over three knots and we got in a bit of strife and they found me floating out in the South China Sea at about quarter to one in the morning. I don't know how they found a blackfella in the middle of the night, but they did … I couldn't swim against the current and I was the surface swimmer and the boys underneath me got into strife. It's called a half necklace, when you just search the ship's bottom for bombs and mines or whatever they're going to put on it.[62]

Amid the high-stress environment, life at the Nui Dat army base was a bit more relaxed. John Schnaars (Royal Australian Armoured Corps, Detachment, 1st Forward Delivery Troop, February–June 1968) describes the mess hall thus: 'there was a huge [mess] hall where everybody had their meals … and you had tables and then the passage up the middle where you'd go up the front and get your tucker, and they had all these tables lined up and stools. And I don't know how much; it must have held a couple of hundred at least.'[63] Frank Mallard commented on the living conditions: 'Well, it was always muddy and wet, and living in the tents under the rubber plantations. Well, one particular incident I can remember, it was terribly hot there in the summertime and we had our tents surrounded by sandbags, so we were sleeping on stretchers below the sandbags in case of shells coming into the place. And we had the tents rolled up so you get a breeze coming through.'[64]

Despite the physical difficulties at Nui Dat, there was a psychological comfort about the base. Mallard summarises: 'But I enjoyed my time there, if you can say enjoyed wartime. But you either enjoyed it or you suffered too much from it all.'[65] George Bostock (4RAR, May 1968 – May 1969) specifically remembers Nui Dat as a place of relief, contrasting sharply with the battlefields: 'Where we would be out in the operations and that, it was shell scrapes and bloody sleep on a hard ground or bloody waiting up all night in the rain in an ambush or patrolling and all that shit. But when you come back to Nui Dat, you had a mattress. You had a bloody stretcher to sleep on. You would go up to the boozer and have a beer. You could leave lights on late at night and scream and talk and carry on like pork chops, and it was a luxury. And then we'd go to concerts and things and in the movies and then just sort of relax and, the next time a couple a week or so later, we're out on operations again.'[66]

Dick Bligh similarly testifies: 'Nui Dat was great. You felt safe there, the environment was good, it had wire all around Nui Dat and you felt pretty safe there and you could have a beer and relax and enjoy yourself, but you were still on alert virtually all the time … There was a couple of times when, I think Col Joye came over there and Little Pattie, and we were able to go and see their show … We did get to Vung Tau, down at the Peter Badcoe Club a couple of times that I remember.'[67]

Vung Tau was the principal rest and recreation location for servicemen, and Australian troops – Aboriginal, Torres Strait Islander and non-Indigenous – ended up causing lots of mischief, including boozing, fighting and sexual relations with Vietnamese women. As Frank Mallard summarises:

There was always incidents of one kind or another in Vung Tau. When we used to go in, we used to get the opportunity to go in there and have a beer in the bars and so on and you'd be coming back and you'd go down to the local pickup point where you had to wait for your trucks to take you back. All the locals would set up their little stalls and that there and we were always saying we go down there and have a meat soup or a hepatitis roll before we'd go back to base camp. And of course you had all the problems with guys being drunk and coming out of the bars and causing problems and the local police being trigger happy, [you] were very very lucky that you didn't get shot. A couple of guys had been shot by the white mice as they called them.[68]

Some of the stories that veterans shared about Vung Tau were off the record, such as stories about sexual relations. Like non-Indigenous veterans' memoirs, the Indigenous testimonies paint a picture of many Australians behaving atrociously in Vung Tau, including excessive drinking, fighting with other servicemen, Americans or locals, sexual relations and the spread of venereal disease. Service records are filled with reports of men going absent without leave (AWOL), and several include descriptions of misconduct charges such as staying out past curfew, threatening superior officers, losing their identity cards, or even in one instance creating 'a disturbance at the GRAND HOTEL, causing damage to two glass windows and a shaving stand'.[69]

Tales on the record often involved drinking. Dick Bligh recollects: 'The Peter Badcoe Club was great and it was a great rest and recuperation area and everybody that went there enjoyed themselves. It was just a rest area and you just went there and most people just drank themselves silly, into oblivion sometimes and would just stay there the two or three days.'[70] Many of the drinking stories ended in brawls or other trouble. For instance, Darryl Wallace (2nd Air Service Squadron and 3RAR, February–November 1968) got into a fight with a boy on a motorbike and wound up in jail.⁷¹ Overall, though, memories of Vung Tau tended to put a smile on the face of Aboriginal veterans more so than any other aspect of their testimonies.

Relations with the Americans

From 1966 when the Australian forces moved to Nui Dat, contact with the Americans in Vietnam was limited. Most Indigenous servicemen were happy not to work with the Americans for several reasons, most prominently because they considered the Americans to be wholly undisciplined, ineffective and dangerous soldiers. Frank Mallard, who served early in the conflict alongside the 173rd Airborne Unit, comments: 'No, we didn't particularly like going on patrols with the Americans because they were not professional as we saw it. They talked too much, they chatter when they're out there in the bush, they're listening to Radio Vietnam on their little radios with the thing stuck in their ear when you're supposed to be on patrol and you're not paying attention. We can remember a couple of incidents where we got into fire fights because people were not being more attentive to what they were doing, or what they should have been doing.'⁷²

George Bostock similarly states: 'I'm glad I never had to work with them [Americans], because they were loud out in the bush and their methods that they had was unbelievable. Where we would have scouts and we would go into a harbour position at night and no noise and everything like that, and we would stand to for a certain hour until dark, the Yanks would all sit in the pits, their front-line pits, and they'd open up. Their theory was if anybody was out there, they'd be hit by all this per-per-per-per. They would hippie shoot. I thought, "Hang on, what's going on?" "Oh, that's the, the Americans doing a clearing patrol."'⁷³

Notably, many Aboriginal veterans observed racial tensions within the American army. Even though the United States military had been officially desegregated since 1948, several Aboriginal testimonies describe black–white tensions and segregation within the American ranks. These observations are especially pronounced among the members of 3 Field Troop, Royal Australian Engineers, who served alongside the United States 173rd Airborne in 1965 before the construction of Nui Dat. David Cook observed: 'There, in the 173rd Airborne, they had black lines and white lines. The whitefellas lived here, the blackfellas lived here. The blackfellas ate in this mess and the whitefellas ate in this mess. And here we are in our outfit, we had three Aboriginals: one Thursday Islander, me, and Billy Coolburra, who came from Arnhem Land. Even the Australians were shocked at the racism that it was because they've never seen it so blatant. And it became apparent that they – the 173rd – I believe comes from the South of the USA, and they were shocking racists.'[74]

Frank Mallard, who also served in 3 Field Troop, similarly describes American racism: 'But they did treat their Hispanics and their Negroes with contempt. They were always calling them by name and whatever; there was always some sort of a fight going on within their ranks and we found it difficult to understand that because we – as I said – we were professional soldiers who got on with the job and it didn't matter what your colour or creed was. You looked after one another 'cos that was what you were trained to do. We couldn't understand how the Americans sort of had a dislike for one another and they were all in the military.'[75]

Ron Wenitong (7RAR, April 1967 – April 1968) describes segregation practised in several areas of the American Army:

> I got malaria and they flew me out to the 36 Evacuation Hospital, which was an American hospital in Vung Tau. And the one thing I noticed I was the only black man in the hospital. So I said – because there were a lot of Negroes and this is the thing that really stuck in my mind – 'Where are all the Negroes servicemen who are injured, wounded, sick?' And they didn't bring [them] to that hospital, which I found, I mean it was really – I don't know what happened there.

But I did notice when we did do operations with the Americans' 11th Armoured Cavalry Regiment, the tank crews, the ones I saw and the personnel, Armoured Personnel Carrier crews, they were either all black or all white.[76]

Americans even segregated their morgues, which was a salient observation for Indigenous servicemen.[77]

The historical literature about black Americans in the Vietnam War supports these anecdotal testimonies. Historian James Westheider has described situations where bigoted officers used their positions of authority to impose excessive discipline or obstruct promotions. Westheider describes Confederate flags flying in Vietnam and graffiti on latrine walls and in enlisted men's clubs with sayings such as 'I'd rather kill a nigger instead of a gook'. Accounts of verbal racial abuse were common, with terms such as 'spear chucker', 'boy', 'spook' and 'nigger' regularly reported among black Vietnam veterans, though incidents of physical racial violence were rare in combat units. From the period after approximately 1968, the rise of Black Power in the United States as a response to racism also infiltrated the armed forces. Racial tensions in Vietnam even erupted in race riots between white and black Americans. It was not until new programs designed to stamp out racism in the armed forces emerged in the early 1970s that the racial tensions eased in the American military.[78]

Despite witnessing racism against black Americans, the Aboriginal servicemen did not experience it themselves at the hands of Americans. One reason is the limited contact most Australians had with American servicemen in Vietnam. But even those Indigenous men who served early in the war with the American 173rd Airborne were not targets of American racism. David Cook states: 'They didn't treat me different ... probably because I was from another country, and that was okay I suppose. 'Cos they probably knew then that I couldn't take anything that belonged to them.'[79] Graham Atkinson (Royal Corps of Australian

Electrical and Mechanical Engineers, B Squadron Section, 1st Armoured Regiment, Light Aid Detachment, December 1969 – August 1970) says that Americans did not understand what a Koorie person was, and suggests this was why they did not discriminate against Aboriginal people. Frank Mallard speculates that American ignorance of Australian race relations led to their non-prejudicial attitudes. Billy Coolburra sometimes found himself acting as a mediator between white and black American soldiers. He remarks: 'I told him [American soldier] I was a full blood Aboriginal and I said we should be making friends because we never knew when we would have to depend on each other. The next night we all got together and sang songs together and started talking about our homes.'[80]

Several Aboriginal testimonies indicate that both Indigenous and non-Indigenous Australian servicemen felt more comfortable with black rather than white American soldiers. Darryl Wallace relays a story in which he chose to play ping-pong with a black American who used to spend his rest and recuperation time with the Australian SAS. When they were in the same mess as the Americans, he and the other Australians used to sit in the black wing. White Americans questioned him and other Australian soldiers, and he responded: 'I know I'm in the right mess, mate! … Because I'm a blackfella.'[81] George Bostock recalls a similar anecdote when drinking with some Americans in Vung Tau. He writes: 'One of our blokes had noticed a black American sitting by himself and went over and asked him to join us. He was reluctant at first, but after some coaxing decided to join us. When the other Americans at the table saw him coming over they all stood up and left. You would have had to be living on the moon not to know anything about the racial problems that existed between black and white Americans, but that was the first time I had seen it close up.'[82]

Bostock also writes about another occasion when there was a brawl in Vung Tau involving Australians, New Zealanders and Americans in response to a racist remark white Americans made against black

Americans. He writes: 'The black American said they couldn't believe what had happened. They never thought they would see the day when whiteboys [sic] would fight for them over racial remarks.'[83] Hewitt Whyman similarly commented on how black Americans were confused by the fact that Australians tended to socialise more with them than the white Americans.[84] Though most Aboriginal testimonies sympathise with the discrimination suffered by black Americans, Graham Atkinson expressed disdain for both black and white Americans. He considered all Americans to be arrogant, but what bothered him most was that 'they used to look down on the Vietnamese, I mean the blacks, and even more so than whites, and even the Australians. Jesus, so ethnocentric.'[85]

These testimonies all highlight the racial complexities at play in Vietnam and serve as a vivid juxtaposition between the Americans and Australians. For Aboriginal and Torres Strait Islander servicemen, who were generally treated as equals in the army, witnessing American racism both heightened their awareness of racial discrimination while concurrently reinforcing their sentiments of equality in the Australian military. Yet the problematic racialisation of the enemy could cause unease among Aboriginal servicemen. Aboriginal veteran Geoff Shaw states:

> We shouldn't have been there in the first instance because basically it was a civil war amongst people from Vietnam. I shouldn't have been there because they were Indigenous people such as myself – who belongs to the Aboriginal race. They were as poor as us, but they owned the land where us Aboriginal people owned the land but it was taken off us. Some of the things that I've seen over there makes me think that they're just as poor as us as far as building. Where we had to build humpies, I seen buildings over there made out of sheets of Colt 45 and Schlitz beer cans and all those American beers that were drunk over in Vietnam.[86]

Aboriginal people, national service and the anti-war movement

The politics of race continued to play out in Australia during the Vietnam War, and the national service question finally came to a head in 1971. An Aboriginal man from Western Australia named Mervyn Eades was charged for failing to register under the *National Service Act*. Eades argued in court that under section 18 of the Act, he was exempt from registering because he was Aboriginal. The question at trial became whether or not Eades could prove that he actually fitted the definition of an 'aboriginal native' prescribed in the *National Service Act* and its accompanying regulations. Under Western Australian law, Eades was classified as 'three-eighths caste' and thus an Aboriginal person under the *Native Welfare Act 1963*. But 'three-eighths' did not constitute 'Aboriginal' under the *National Service Regulations* because it was less than 'half-caste'. When charged with failing to register for national service, Eades thus had to prove that he fitted the definition of Aboriginal under regulation 18(c) as 'a person who has an admixture of aboriginal blood and lives as an aboriginal native or amongst aborigines'.[87]

The magistrate, HJ Ryan, determined on 13 December 1971 that Eades was indeed Aboriginal under Western Australian law but not under the *National Service Act*. Ryan declared: 'It is clear from the foregoing inconsistencies between the State and Commonwealth legislations that a person having an admixture of aboriginal blood of halfe [sic] caste or less than half caste could be an aboriginal native in Western Australia and yet under the National Service Regulations not be an aboriginal native. It seems to me possible also for such a person to be found to be an aboriginal native under the National Service Regulations and yet not be an aboriginal native under the Western Australian Act.'[88] That Eades held a regular job, dressed well, owned a car and spoke English implied to the magistrate that Eades did not live as an Aboriginal man because he had successfully 'assimilated'. He was convicted and fined 20 dollars for failing to register for national service.[89]

The press reported Eades's conviction and focused primarily on the absurdity of Eades being classified as Aboriginal under Western Australian law but not the *National Service Act*.[90] A scathing editorial in *The Australian* declared:

> The State of Western Australia is satisfied that Mr Eades is an Aboriginal. The Commonwealth is not. Its reason is that he cannot be so long as he is well dressed, speaks English, lives in a house like a Housing Commission one and drives a car. His wife is even less black to look at than he is, so he cannot be said to be living with Aboriginals. Therefore, he must be white.[91]

Media coverage seemed to interpret the fundamental problem to be the inconsistent and unfair definitions of Aboriginal people, without commenting on the interrelated fact that being Aboriginal was an excludable factor from national service.

Newspaper coverage of the Eades verdict was significant enough to worry the Commonwealth government. JE Cooper of the Office of Aboriginal Affairs wrote: 'we are now in a position where the courts are saying when an Aboriginal is an Aboriginal … It would be preferable to make <u>all</u> Aborigines exempt compared to the present situation where many young Aborigines don't know whether they should register or not.'[92] The press also inadvertently recognised a critical issue often lost in public memory about Aboriginal civil rights: the ineffectiveness of the 1967 referendum. *The Australian* accurately reported: 'After the 1967 referendum, most of us assumed that the Commonwealth had the power to make special laws to help Aboriginals … But, judging by the result of the Eades case, this power will only be applied in certain circumstances … Australians overwhelmingly demanded an end to this kind of bias through their vote in the 1967 referendum.'[93] As the Eades case highlighted, granting the federal government concurrent powers to pass legislation in relation to Aboriginal people did not standardise the state regimes or definitions of Aboriginal people.

From 1968 the Commonwealth minister responsible for Aboriginal Affairs – William Wentworth – was already in the process of adopting a more favourable definition of Aboriginality based on cultural connections rather than blood quanta. By August 1972 the Commonwealth definition for the purposes of any special assistance programs read: 'An Aboriginal is a person of Aboriginal descent who claims to be an Aboriginal and is accepted as such by the community with which he is associated.' Yet the DLNS refused to accept Wentworth's definition and would not amend the *National Service Regulations*. The DLNS argued that their department was not defining who was and was not Aboriginal, but merely: 'Their sole purpose is to specify categories of Aborigines who, for the reasons mentioned above, are exempt from national service obligations and, by definition, to specify those who are not exempt.'[94] This semantic attempt to avoid the question of 'definitions' through an emphasis on 'categories' represented another DLNS bid to avoid confronting the matter of discrimination in the *National Service Act*.

In late 1971 the government amended the *National Service Act* to reduce national service from two years to 18 months, hoping to ameliorate public opposition to conscription.[95] The amended tenure of national service was meant to foster the appearance of *reducing* conscription in Australia. To amend the *National Service Act* at the same time to include Aboriginal people would appear to be *widening* national service. The DLNS worried that adding Aboriginal people into the national service scheme would merely contribute to the anti-war movement. PH Cook, secretary of the DLNS, wrote in 1972:

> (c) with the then identification of national service with Vietnam it would doubtless be said that the Government had now reached the stage where it was even calling up Aborigines to fight in Vietnam;

(d) there was, indeed, the real risk that while Australian troops remained in Vietnam successful attempts would be made to join and exploit what have been separate protest causes, namely Vietnam and Aboriginal rights;[96]

The Council for Aboriginal Affairs concluded: 'On the whole, Labour and National Service's reply does not indicate that they are anxious to amend the Act at all, despite the fact that they were so "upset" by the Mervyn Eades case.'[97] Removing the racial provisions would have ended another form of legal discrimination, but in the process Aboriginal people including Eades would then have had to sign up for national service anyway.

After the Eades case and the government's obstinate refusal to amend the *National Service Act* or its regulations, another case in Western Australia resulted in the conviction of Stanley Ward for failing to register for national service. The magistrate in Ward's case used similar assimilationist criteria applied in the Eades case and determined: 'The defendant lives in what is apparently a normal address, he is well dressed. There has been no suggestion he lives in a camp, and he apparently lived in a house in Derby. The defence hasn't established to my satisfaction that he comes under Regulation 18c.'[98] Ward's verdict in June 1972 received even more publicity than the Eades case. It sparked letters criticising the narrow, assimilationist view of Aboriginality, with statements such as: 'Presumably if Stan had painted his face and done a rain dance in the court he would have been all right. But he didn't. He behaved like a man proud of his race. For his pains, he was stripped of his dignity – and $40.'[99]

The government's desire to avoid the conflation of anti-Vietnam and Aboriginal rights protests became untenable when convictions such as Eades's and Ward's brought public attention to the intertwined issues. An editorial published in *The Australian* argued: 'If ever there were fertile ground for the seeds of its own destruction it is in the administrative, legal and social swamp that has developed around Aboriginals and national service.'[100] Realising the government's worst fears, anti-draft activists also publicised the problematic status of Aboriginal people in relation to national service. Prominent draft resister Robert Muntz wrote a satirical letter in *The Australian*, arguing 'it was high time that whites were given equal rights with Aboriginals in this matter, by abolishing the offensive and racially based law requiring whites to register for national service'.[101] Muntz's piece spooked the DLNS. The issue of discrimination in national service had come full circle; Eades's, Ward's and others' failed attempts to use the racial provisions of the *National Service Act* to avoid national service had revealed the discriminatory nature of the Act for all Australians.

Interestingly, though, there is little evidence that Indigenous activists became significantly involved in the anti-war movement. This is an important contrast to the United States, where both Native Americans and black Americans – including veterans – played significant roles in the anti–Vietnam War protests. Indeed, the Vietnam War was a significant issue on the Black Power and Black Panther Party agendas in the United States, yet there is no reference to Vietnam in the literature about Black Power in Australia. There are only two historical references to Aboriginal people and the anti-war movement. The first comes from anti-war activist Denis Freney's recollections of a march in Sydney in 1970. Even that reference was more about Aboriginal rights than the Vietnam War. Black Power activist Paul Coe demanded the right to speak and made an impassioned speech: 'You are our oppressors. You worry about Vietnam, about the Black struggle in the USA or South Africa. But what about us, here? You raped our women, you stole our land, you massacred our ancestors, you destroyed our culture and now – when we refused to die out as you expected – you want to kill us with your hypocrisy.'[102] The only other mention of Aboriginal people and the anti-war movement is within the wider context of Aboriginal union organiser Kevin Cook's participation in anti-war marches with the Builders Labourers' Federation.[103] Aboriginal activists of the 1960s–70s were more concerned with domestic issues such as land rights and access to health, housing, legal services and education. The prosecutions of Eades and Ward raised the stakes and threatened a convergence of Black Power and the anti-war movements. Such fears never came to fruition; the election of the Whitlam Labor government in December 1972 defused both the Black Power and anti-conscription movements. Stanley Ward appealed his conviction and in December 1972 a court stayed his appeal indefinitely.[104] Whitlam's government subsequently repealed the *National Service Act* in 1973, and the discriminatory provisions ended with the demise of national service.

Life after Vietnam

If the Vietnam combat experience for Aboriginal people mirrored that of their non-Indigenous comrades, veterans' postwar lives represented both a convergence and divergence of experiences. The commonalities are most clearly post-traumatic stress disorder, social dislocation and confronting the legacies of an unpopular war. Several interviewees commented that they had to return to Australia at night and leave their transport in civilian clothes so that they would not be harassed by anti-war protesters. Vietnam veterans also received an ambivalent welcome from their local communities and rejection from the RSL. Graham Atkinson states: 'When I got back I found that no one wanted to talk about Vietnam. If you went into the pub people would say, "Oh you're back," and that'd be it. No one wanted to know about it.'[105] Several veterans have spoken of psychological problems and the inadequacy of the Department of Veterans' Affairs (and its precursor the Department of Repatriation) to address their problems. Alcoholism and marriage breakdown – common also among non-Indigenous veterans – permeate several veterans' stories.[106]

Unlike non-Indigenous veterans, though, Aboriginal and Torres Strait Islander people also had to confront racial discrimination. Geoff

Shaw describes how he was turned away from entering the Alice Springs Memorial Club even though he was a veteran.[107] Phil Prosser recalls an incident in Western Australia: 'And we went down into town to have a few drinks. And we walked in, sat down in the lounge area of the Hotel Manly, as it was known in those days. And the steward came up to take orders. Of course he went around the table, and when he came to me, he turned to me and the guy said, "I'm sorry; I can't serve this gentleman because he's Aboriginal." And of course they became pretty upset, the guys. They said, "But he's in the army. You've got to serve him." He said, "I'm sorry but we can't." So he refused to serve me.'[108]

David Cook experienced some extreme examples of racial discrimination in the form of police harassment, contributing to years spent in and out of prison. Cook was both a Stolen Generations survivor and a Vietnam veteran, and much of his life trajectory reflects the findings of both the Royal Commission into Aboriginal Deaths in Custody and the *Bringing Them Home* Stolen Generations inquiry.[109]

Another area where Aboriginal veterans went on diverging paths from non-Indigenous veterans was in their pursuit of Aboriginal causes. This was by no means a universal path, and many interviewees indicated that they had no interest in Indigenous affairs upon their return to Australia. Even so, several Aboriginal veterans did find employment in Indigenous affairs and have attributed their army experience as preparing them for such career paths. George Bostock and Hewitt Whyman both became involved in the land rights movements of the 1970s. Whyman then became a field officer for the New South Wales Aboriginal Legal Service. After a stint as a prison officer, Darryl Wallace worked for various Indigenous organisations: Aboriginal housing in Queensland, Aboriginal and Islander Dance Theatre in Sydney, and Aboriginal medical services in Sydney. Graham Atkinson took advantage of ABSTUDY to complete a social work and arts degree. Subsequently, he worked in the Victorian Department of Aboriginal Affairs as a social worker, then as a program director for the Victorian Aboriginal Child Care Agency, and

Indigenous service and Vietnam

then as regional director of the Aboriginal Development Commission for Victoria and Tasmania. After many years Atkinson left the public service and started his own consultancy. Atkinson says: 'I'd like to highlight my involvement in Aboriginal affairs because I think it all started through my experience in the Army. It was Vietnam which forced me to become more aware of the social and political issues facing Aboriginal people.'[110] Geoff Shaw explained in 1988 how military service prepared him for work in Indigenous community advancement:

> One of the things that my years in the army have assisted me [with] was giving me the ability to negotiate with white people, especially the bureaucracy. In fact, I came back and at that time we were living in car bodies and lean-tos. And I thought, look – I'm going to have to do something, not only for my people, I'm going to have to try and better myself. I've got some skills that I can offer to my people, so I decided to join the Aboriginal movement. I've been working for my people now for the last 14 years [at Tangentyere Council]. That was the beginning of me being spokesperson on other Aboriginal organisations such as ones that relate to health and welfare, land acquisition, and dealing with mining companies and so on. We've fought hard, we've built so many houses so far, and we've still got a long way to go to build more houses for Aboriginal people, especially on Aboriginal town leases.[111]

While the abovementioned veterans pursued causes for Aboriginal advancement, other veterans pursued alternative career paths. Max Gardner had difficulty finding work, but ultimately found employment in a milk factory in Shepparton. Ron Wenitong worked in construction all over Queensland for 35 years. John Schnaars also worked in construction in Perth until a residual knee injury forced him onto a disability pension. He then became a stay-at-home dad, raising his four children. Other veterans such as Lionel Duroux, George Bostock and Frank

Mallard remained in the army until the 1980s, which was also common among approximately one-third of the service records examined. Mallard subsequently joined the Army Reserve and in 1993 responded to a call for retired army engineers to join United Nations peacekeeping forces in Croatia and Bosnia. Dick Bligh stayed in the army until 1975, then joined the Army Reserve while working for the defence department. Bob Blair remained in the army until 1982 and then drove a taxi for three years. One of the more high-profile veterans was Glenn James, who became a Victorian Football League (VFL) umpire and in 1984 the first Aboriginal person to umpire an AFL–VFL Grand Final.[112]

Yet even for these abovementioned veterans initially not interested in Indigenous affairs, later in life several have become respected Aboriginal Elders involved in their communities in various capacities. George Bostock has become a playwright, with his first play *It Seems Like Yesterday* performed by the Kooemba Jdarra Indigenous Theatre Company in 2001. He was a consultant and actor in the acclaimed 2014 production *Black Diggers*, about the Aboriginal First World War experience. He also sat as an Elder on the Murri Courts in Queensland. Dick Bligh worked for Aboriginal Hostels from 1987 to 1996 and then as an Aboriginal community development officer in the Pilbara for five years. In 2003 John Schnaars founded the organisation Honouring Indigenous War Graves to commemorate Indigenous service.[113]

Bob Blair has done remarkable work for the Indigenous business community since he gave up taxi-driving in 1985. First he worked for the Central Queensland Aboriginal Corporation for Training and Resources, providing training to several Aboriginal organisations in Central Queensland. In 1987 Blair was approached to put in an application for the position of CEO of the Dreamtime Cultural Centre in Rockhampton. Since opening in 1988, the centre has been a major tourist attraction that has employed Indigenous and non-Indigenous staff, worked with Indigenous contracting services such as catering and has expanded to include a conference centre and hotel. Blair has also been the deputy chairperson of Indigenous Business Australia and has worked with the ADF to assist in Indigenous recruitment. Bob Blair says that he runs the centre with military precision and attributes his own management skills to his army training. Blair effectively encapsulates the links between military service and the postwar success stories of many Aboriginal Vietnam veterans: 'there's no doubt in my mind, whatsoever, without my army background, this place wouldn't be where it is today'.[114]

Vietnam, Indigenous Australians and memory

The histories presented in this chapter are only a snapshot of the experiences of the hundreds of Aboriginal and Torres Strait Islander men who served in Vietnam. Their experiences both complement and confront the wider histories of Australia's role in Vietnam. Despite the efforts of military and social historians, much of the popular memory of Australia's Vietnam War continues to be clouded by myth based on the United States experience. Among the casualties of such misunderstandings of Australia's Vietnam War are the forgotten histories of Aboriginal and Torres Strait Islander servicemen. Furthermore, the historiographical trends among Australian Indigenous histories of the twentieth century tend to focus on the impact of colonialism and assimilation, with Aboriginal and Torres Strait Islander people inevitably forced to accommodate and/or resist discriminatory and devastating policies and practices such as child removal. Histories of Indigenous Australian participation in the armed forces during the First and Second World Wars offer tales of reconciliation and Indigenous people joining the armed forces hoping for equal citizenship rights through military service. Yet Aboriginal and Torres Strait Islander military service in Vietnam does not sit well with this narrative. It was an unpopular war that did not entail a mass mobilisation of Australian citizenry. Veterans of Vietnam did not receive fanfare or significant benefits upon their return to Australia. Fights for Aboriginal civil rights, Black Power and land rights were occurring at the same time as Vietnam, with little indication that there were links between Vietnam service and these social movements. For such reasons, the histories of Indigenous veterans of Vietnam have been subsumed among the histories of all Vietnam veterans and forgotten by the majority of Australians.

Individually and collectively the experiences in this chapter demonstrate the hardships, accomplishments and legacies of military service and the Vietnam War for Aboriginal and Torres Strait Islander veterans. Many of the issues confronting Aboriginal Vietnam veterans are indeed indistinguishable from non-Indigenous veterans, such as the horrors of war, the impact of post-traumatic stress disorder and the difficult readjustment to Australian life. But it is clear also that being Aboriginal meant diverging pathways both before and after Vietnam. While some themes permeate many of the interviews – difficult childhoods during the assimilation era, racial equality in the armed forces, witnessing American racism – each veteran has his own personal reflections and experiences. Despite some hardships along the way, even today all of the Vietnam veterans interviewed remember their time in the army fondly because of the friendships they made, the skills they learned and the opportunities the military provided. As Frank Mallard summarises: 'Oh, I love the armed forces; if I could be back in the military uniform tomorrow I would be but my age is against me.'[115]

4

SKILLING INDIGENOUS WOMEN: ABORIGINAL AND TORRES STRAIT ISLANDER PEOPLE IN THE WOMEN'S SERVICES

> Even though there wasn't a war when I joined, I joined in case there was a war. I was prepared to fight for my land regardless of whether the Queen did it or whether it was for Aboriginals; it was still our land.[1]
>
> – Jacqueline Shaw

At a 2001 conference celebrating 100 years of the Australian Army, ex-servicewoman Judy Costello declared: 'Outside of the military, their [women's] options broaden rapidly and many have become very senior very quickly using in their new profession the mix of skills they gained in the military. It is good for Australian industry and the public sectors – and a loss for the military.'[2] Costello was discussing glass ceilings in the present-day army and how many dissatisfied servicewomen simply leave the ADF and take their skills elsewhere. Though she was describing the situation around 2001, Costello's statement is applicable to the history of the Australian military. Women who served in the separate women's services during the Second World War and in postwar peacetime acquired skills they were able to apply in their post-service lives. As feminist author Dale Spender writes: 'seeds were planted at this time in the minds of [service]women, seeds that perhaps would lie dormant for a few years, but which would bloom within the next generation'.³

If military service sowed the seeds of women's liberation among many servicewomen, for Aboriginal and Torres Strait Islander women, work in the military represented an opportunity to challenge both gender and racial discrimination. During the assimilation era of the mid-twentieth century, Aboriginal and Torres Strait Islander women had even fewer education or employment opportunities than non-Indigenous women. This was an era when state and territory governments used policies such as child removal and urban relocation to attack Aboriginal culture and to compel Aboriginal people into predominantly low-paid, unskilled employment. Government and institution policies and practices geared Aboriginal girls' education primarily, though not exclusively, towards becoming domestic servants.⁴ The Second World War and the creation of women's services in the armed forces provided Indigenous women with an alternative path. Testimonies suggest that racism was rare in the military of the 1940s to 1970s, and thus Aboriginal and Torres Strait Islander women were treated on the same level as other servicewomen. Through military employment, Indigenous servicewomen were learning skills otherwise not accessible to them, and such training imbued leadership abilities that would position Aboriginal and Torres Strait Islander ex-servicewomen as active fighters for Indigenous rights and as community leaders later in life.

This chapter examines how Indigenous women's participation in the armed forces during the 1950s–70s provided one possible escape from the few options open to Aboriginal and Torres Strait Islander women in civilian life, and contributed to future leadership roles at the community, state and national levels. It is difficult to estimate the number of Aboriginal and Torres Strait Islander servicewomen. One piece of evidence that suggests small numbers is Jan 'Kabarli' James's compilation of Western Australian Aboriginal service personnel from the First World War to the present day. Of the 631 Aboriginal ex-service personnel named in her book *Forever Warriors*, only 21 are women.[5] This admittedly incomplete list includes four women who served in the Australian Women's Land Army during the Second World War, which technically was not part of the armed forces.[6] This of course does not diminish the significance of those women's work, as well as the work of Australian Indigenous women who served in civilian capacities in factories and labour camps, and in support services such as the Australian Comforts Fund.

Though Indigenous ex-servicewomen may be small in numbers, the importance of their work in the armed forces has been significant both for the individual servicewomen and for Australian society because of the leadership roles Aboriginal and Torres Strait Islander ex-servicewomen filled in their post-service lives. Contemporary Aboriginal women have reflected on conceptions of Indigenous women's leadership. Samantha Joseph of the New South Wales Aboriginal Justice Advisory Council says: 'Indigenous women are therefore fundamental in advocating for change. As women we must … empower our young ones to speak out about the issues they are facing.'[7] Historian and former co-chair of Reconciliation Australia Jackie Huggins argues that Aboriginal women leaders 'have the interests of our community at heart'. They remain grounded in their local communities and families and '[t]ake an interest in everybody, no matter how significant or insignificant they are, or think they are'.[8] Finally, Huggins considers Aboriginal women's leadership to entail an ability to communicate with a variety of audiences and to mentor the next generation. Education – whether through formal channels, life experiences, cultural upbringing or through work – has been central to imbuing these leadership qualities among Aboriginal and Torres Strait Islander women.

Links between work in the military, escape from assimilation and Indigenous women's leadership are discernible through understanding the lives of Indigenous ex-servicewomen, so four case studies form the crux of this chapter. The women include a mix of high-profile figures and women who have been strong advocates at grassroots community levels.

Each woman participated in a different service – the Royal Australian Army Nursing Corps (RAANC), Women's Royal Australian Army Corps (WRAAC), Women's Royal Australian Air Force (WRAAF) and Women's Royal Australian Naval Service (WRANS). These women's stories complement much of the wider histories of the women's services, but they differ through their experiences as Aboriginal and Torres Strait Islander women. Themes permeating the Indigenous women's testimonies include their limited prospects before enlisting, joining the armed forces to improve their social positions and learning new skills. After their times of service, these Aboriginal and Torres Strait Islander women used new education opportunities and the discipline instilled in the military to break free from the constraints of assimilation and to fight for the betterment of Indigenous Australians. Reflecting Huggins's and Joseph's conceptions of Indigenous women's leadership, they remained grounded in their communities and families while working to empower youth, to improve Indigenous lives and to respect the dignity of all Australians.

Background on women's services

Australia did not have women's services during the First World War or at the outbreak of the Second World War. Women could serve as nurses, but this was skilled employment that was inaccessible for the majority of Indigenous women until after the Second World War. In 1941 the cabinet and various services of the military finally approved the enlistment of women in support tasks to free up male labour for combat. The new auxiliaries formed were the Women's Auxiliary Australian Air Force (WAAAF), the WRANS and the Australian Women's Army Service (AWAS). Women represented 4.9 per cent of army, 12.5 per cent of air force, 10 per cent of navy personnel and 6.6 per cent of overall enlistments. When the Second World War ended, all three services gradually demobilised by 1948.[9]

With the disbandment of the women's services, only nurses remained enlisted in the armed forces in the all-female nursing corps. Then, in July 1950, with fears that there would eventually be another total war and women would again be needed in support roles, cabinet approved the reintroduction of women's services. The WRAAF and a reconstituted WRANS formed in late 1950, followed by the WRAAC in February 1951. All three forces had similar roles as their Second World War predecessors: employing women primarily in clerical and other non-combat capacities to free up male labour. As in the Second World War, pay was set at between two-thirds and three-quarters the male rate, although equal pay for officers was introduced in 1978. Though there were distinctions in policies and practices across the services, the impact of work in the armed forces on women's opportunities – including Indigenous women – was universal.[10]

When women were first commissioned, cabinet and military commanders envisioned that they would take jobs such as typists, drivers, telephonists, wireless operators, orderlies and cooks. Besides being work that did not challenge gender norms, the military favoured women for non-combat tasks because they could be acquired as cheap labour. Depending on their occupations, servicewomen learned a variety of physical, clerical, intellectual and communication skills. For instance, women in all three services worked in the respective Signal Corps. Tasks included enciphering and deciphering messages, operating several pieces of wireless equipment and working around the clock with access to top-secret information. Their work was so top secret that many ex-servicewomen still will not give specific details about it. Women in all three services who worked as drivers not only had to know how to operate a variety of heavy motor vehicles, but they also had to learn different driving methods, maintenance and roadside repairs. These and all other jobs not only taught women their particular tasks, but also imbued abilities in budgeting, management, mathematics, communication and delegation of work. For the majority of Aboriginal and Torres

Strait Islander women growing up under assimilation policies, these were life skills often not provided in their limited pre-service education or unskilled employment.

By the 1970s the purpose of the women's services was less about releasing male labour, and there was a gradual recognition of the military as a possible career path for women. WRAAF disbanded in 1977, and from 1978 cabinet approved the full integration of women into the mainstream army and navy. This process was completed in 1984 and 1985 with the disbandment of WRAAC and WRANS respectively. Women's employment opportunities in the military have expanded greatly since the 1980s. For instance, the first woman commenced study at the Royal Military College, Duntroon, in 1978; combat-related jobs opened up from 1990 and the first female RAAF pilot graduated in 1991. From September 2011 the Commonwealth cabinet approved the gradual integration of women into combat roles over the next five years.[11] Though certainly gender discrimination still exists, the employment opportunities for women in the ADF have improved significantly beyond the realm of solely 'women's work' since the integration of women into the mainstream forces.

For the period of the separate women's services, notwithstanding discrimination in pay and available jobs, servicewomen were equal regardless of race. Aboriginal and Torres Strait Islander women fitted well into this paradigm, though notably there were no identified Indigenous women among the senior women officers. Like their non-Indigenous colleagues, work in the military was an opportunity to acquire skills that could serve them beyond a wife/mother career. Unique to Indigenous women, military service also provided new prospects beyond the customary employment in domestic service. The following four case studies demonstrate the myriad ways that Indigenous ex-servicewomen used their armed forces experiences to escape the limitations imposed in civilian life.

Nurse and health-care worker: 'Louise'

Queensland had some of the strictest legislation regulating Aboriginal people's lives. Such legislation persisted after the Second World War and only gradually began to be dismantled from the mid-1960s through the 1980s. Different legislation controlled Torres Strait Islanders under the Office of the Director of Native Affairs (renamed the Department of Aboriginal and Islander Affairs in 1966), but it afforded Torres Strait Islanders more autonomy than Aboriginal residents. Torres Strait Islanders living outside of the Torres Strait had even more freedom, and essentially the further south one lived, the less likely one was to come under government control. Therefore, Torres Strait Islanders like 'Louise', who moved to Brisbane as a child during the Second World War, had more education and employment opportunities than Aboriginal women. Indeed, Louise's prospects were not dissimilar to those of working-class white or immigrant women during the postwar period. Louise trained as one of Australia's first Indigenous nurses and was the first-known Torres Strait Islander in the RAANC, serving in 1953–57.

Louise was born in 1936 in the Murray Island region of the Torres Strait. In her early years she resided on Murray Island with her extended family in what she describes as a relatively carefree environment. They fished, tended gardens, visited family on other islands and occasionally took a big boat to Thursday Island. When the Second World War came, Louise's family was uprooted like almost all Torres Strait Islander families. Sometime in 1941 or 1942, Louise's family was evacuated on her father's pearling lugger. Whereas most Torres Strait Islander evacuees wound up in Cairns, Townsville or at Aboriginal missions such as Barambah (Cherbourg),[12] Louise's family caught the train to Brisbane, where they settled permanently in the suburb of Breakfast Creek. They were the only Torres Strait Islander family there; Louise does not even recall any other Torres Strait Islander families in all of Brisbane during her childhood except when kin came to visit. The adjustment was not easy; Louise and her three brothers did not speak English, so they had to attend elocution classes at the local primary school. She does not recall any specific incidents of racism as a child, which she speculates is because there were no other Torres Strait Islander, Aboriginal or South Sea Islander families in her area. Essentially, as Louise summarises: 'we often talk about having grown up in this white area and all the kids were, you know, there was no racism towards us. So, we were all from working-class families. And we had a great childhood.'[13]

Even though Louise does not recall individual incidents of racism, she still faced institutional barriers as a black woman from a working-class background. After the war Louise's father resumed work as a seasonal labourer on luggers in the Torres Strait, which did not produce a stable income for the family. Therefore, when Louise was 13, she left school in year seven in order to work. For two years she made party hats and baskets at a small business, then for two years she worked in a laundry. Louise found both of these unskilled jobs to be tedious and isolating, but she was determined to improve her situation. She paid for night classes in a typing course and at age 17 applied both to the taxation office and to the Brisbane General Hospital (now Royal Brisbane and Women's Hospital) to do a nursing course. Louise received job offers from both and decided to go with the nursing program because it offered a living-in option and her family home was getting crowded.[14]

Louise's entry into nursing in 1952 was at a time when Aboriginal and Torres Strait Islander women were only beginning to join the profession. Like Louise, these women saw nursing as an alternative option to domestic work and were breaking new ground. In fact, one other Torres Strait Islander nurse named Ellie Gaffney, who entered the profession at the same time, identifies as 'the first Torres Strait Islander to become a qualified nursing sister'.[15] In the 1950s some regions excluded Indigenous people from hospital-based training and in most locations they could train only as nursing aides. Though most pioneering Indigenous nurses remember their work with fondness, several recall discriminatory policies in the hospitals such as segregating patients based on race and sometimes medical treatment such as sterilisation being forced upon Aboriginal patients.[16] Fortunately Louise does not recall any such discrimination, but instead remembers the hard work associated with her profession. She comments: 'Like it was hard then, like doing the meals and most of the junior nurses used to do all of the cleaning, so that first year was awful. Many times I'd think, "Oh, what did I come nursing for?" Have a bit of a cry in the linen room. But I just loved the rapport with the patients, and meeting other people.'[17] The challenges Louise describes as a nursing aide indicate that while some doors were opening for Torres Strait Islander and Aboriginal women, their position within the profession still remained primarily at the entry level.

Louise worked at the Brisbane General Hospital for two years before she decided to join the Australian Army. When asked why she joined up, she replied: 'Well, I think it was because I wasn't sure what I wanted to do. Whether I wanted to, because all my friends, the ones I'd started nursing with, had probably moved on. They would have finished second year, so they would have been in their third year. I often regret it, but then I think, well, I wouldn't have met my husband if I hadn't have gone nursing. So I thought, "Oh, it's an adventure, you know, you're young."'[18] Louise's sentiments about an adventure and looking for something different mirror those of many non-Indigenous women who joined the RAANC. Historian Jan Bassett argues that most female recruits saw the army as an opportunity to receive training denied them in civilian life.[19]

Louise was 19 when she joined in 1953. She was sent to Queenscliff in Victoria where she underwent RAANC basic training alongside WRAAC recruits. They learned elementary drills, marching and army history. Although Louise was not a fan of marching, she adapted well to the strict hours of army life because they were not dissimilar to the hours she had previously kept in the hospital. She then went through further medical corps training in Healesville, Victoria, before being posted back to Brisbane. Only nurses aged 21 and over could serve overseas. Louise therefore never saw overseas service because, by the time she was 21, all 142 nurses who served in Japan under BCOF and during the Korean War had returned.[20]

Louise lived with the other nurses at Yeronga Camp in Brisbane and her role was to look after soldiers who were ill. Many of the patients Louise treated were national servicemen; Yeronga Camp did not tend to major injuries, but rather problems such as flu, minor operations, football injuries and some psychological issues. It was in the Yeronga Camp Hospital that Louise met her husband. He was a soldier returned from Korea who was suffering from what turned out to be hepatitis. He was prescribed bed rest, and Louise was one of the nurses who tended to him. Remembering the beginning of their relationship, she says: 'And gee, I think I felt sorry for him more than anything when I first saw him sitting up in that hospital bed … And so, anyway, going out, I was on my day off and we met going up to catch the bus – because no one had cars, I never knew anyone with cars, except the priest that used to come and visit us. So we just went, he asked me where I was going and I said, oh, I was going home. He said, "Oh, would you like to go to the movies?" So that started that off.'[21]

Louise married in 1957; before she married, she had to leave the army under regulations forbidding married women from serving. Her story is similar to that of many non-Indigenous women who served: falling in love with servicemen, getting married and leaving the forces.[22] Louise says that she probably would not have stayed in the army longer even if the regulations permitted it: 'I think at 21 I was ready to settle down and have children, you know, start a home and get on with our lives.'[23]

Louise's husband did two more years in the army and she continued to work in civilian life while also having children. She was able to use her nursing training to work at an aged-care facility in Sydney before moving to Perth in 1960. Louise worked as a nurse assistant in a maternity hospital and then on night duty twice a week at an aged-care facility for over 30 years. She managed to balance her nursing responsibilities with raising five children. She remained a nurse's aide this entire period because she did not have the time to pursue the further education necessary to become a registered nurse. She does not regret her life choice to concentrate on raising a family; Louise states: 'But I could have gone and finished my training. But it meant that I had to leave my kids, so, and I just didn't think that I could do it.'[24]

After her children were grown up, Louise found that she had more free time and was ready to enhance her work skills. In 1995 she enrolled in a course at the Marr Mooditj Aboriginal Health College in Perth. She learned clinical practice, first aid, drug and alcohol abuse information, and Aboriginal history and culture. She also helped to facilitate a trachoma survey and ultimately received a diploma qualifying her as an Aboriginal health-care worker.

Louise became more involved in the Western Australian Aboriginal community, working as a relief officer for the Aboriginal Medical Service and then in a permanent role in the Home and Community Care service. She continued to work in several of the Aboriginal Medical Service sites across Perth, even in a managerial role at one stage, before finally retiring in 2004. Louise reports that what she valued most in the various healthcare roles was always working with the patients. A few years later she moved to Canberra, where a chance meeting at the Aboriginal Health Service led her to leave retirement. She started working one day a week as a training assistant, then as a mentor for a drug and alcohol education class, then as a project manager and then part-time on the desk at the Aboriginal Health Service.[25]

Louise's time in the army was a small part of her life, but her observations about army life and the role of Indigenous women in that life are significant. First, she does not recall encountering any other Torres Strait Islander or Aboriginal women during her time in the army from basic training with the RAANC and WRAAC through to her discharge in 1957. In fact, she recalls that, until enrolling at Marr Mooditj, she had only ever met about three other Indigenous nurses in her entire career. She does not suggest feeling isolated as a lone black woman in the armed forces, but rather that she was treated as an equal with the white members. Louise insists that she was never the target of racism or sexism in the armed forces, whether from other nurses, superior officers, soldiers or patients. It was even a white male patient with whom she fell in love and married. In contrast, testimonies from the few other Indigenous nurses in civilian Australia during the same time period suggest that segregation and racial discrimination were regular occurrences. Patients sometimes even made disparaging remarks when being treated by black nurses.[26] Yet, in terms of the army, Louise comments: 'I never ever had any racism that affected me. It might have been overt, but just didn't affect me.' Louise's suggestion that there may have been racism opens other questions. Indeed, later in her testimony, when discussing civilian life in Perth, she comments: 'I can honestly say it [racism] never affected me. But if I was with someone I would get really upset over it. But I wouldn't make an issue, you know. You could go somewhere else.' These sentiments suggest that Louise had a strong character and was determined not to be derailed in her life choices, whether as a nurse, army member, mother or health-care worker. In reflecting on the army as a career option for other Torres Strait Islander or Aboriginal people, Louise summarises: 'I think it's a great life, you know, they get the discipline, they get their health service, three meals a day.'[27]

Public advocate: Sue Gordon

Arguably one of the most high-profile of all Aboriginal and Torres Strait Islander ex-servicewomen is Sue Gordon. A Yamatji woman born in 1943 near Meekatharra, Western Australia, Gordon was forcibly removed from her family at the age of four and sent to Sister Kate's Home in Perth. Gordon was raised believing she was an orphan with no family, even though she actually had cousins also living at Sister Kate's. Gordon does not speak ill of her time at the home. She knows she should not have been removed, and she remembers discrimination when outside the institution and acknowledges some cases of abuse at the home. But she herself was not abused and prefers to focus on the close-knit relationships formed among the Sister Kate's children, who continue to consider each other as family.[28]

Like at other institutions at the time, the education at Sister Kate's was geared towards training boys in manual labour and girls as domestic servants. At the age of ten Gordon was already being sent out to work as a domestic during the school holidays. Several historians and Aboriginal women have written about the experience as domestics, and cases varied from being treated as an extension of the family to outright physical, sexual and mental abuse.[29] Gordon was not abused, but she hated domestic work. She was fortunate, though, that she happened to be at Sister Kate's during a short period when high-achieving students could go on to further study. She was one of only seven who were selected to attend high school, where she learned to type. From there, Gordon won a scholarship to business college and then got a job working as a secretary for an automotive company.

Gordon was now 17, and because she was working she was no longer allowed to live at Sister Kate's and was forced to fend for herself. She was walking through North Perth (now Northbridge) one day and happened to pass the army barracks there, at a time when the army was recruiting. She says: 'I went in and it sounded all exciting. They were going to pay me and send me to Sydney. Where's Sydney, you know?'[30] Gordon needed the support of Sister Kate's, and at first the manager would not back her. But Gordon was stubborn and managed to get Sister Kate's to provide the documentation she required to join the army. So, at age 18 in 1961, Sue Gordon enlisted in the WRAAC. As she states: 'I swapped one institution for another, but it was the only way I could get away [from Sister Kate's and domestic service].'[31]

Gordon went through basic training in Sydney before being sent to work in Signal Corps in Melbourne. Her experience with discipline and regimentation at Sister Kate's helped her adapt well to army life, which mirrors the experiences of other Stolen Generations survivors who served in the armed forces.[32] When asked about her work in Signal Corps, Gordon responds: 'If I tell you, I'll have to kill you.'[33] Though she will not reveal the details of her work, she does indicate some of the skills obtained: 'Now, you've seen old movies, where these tapes relay machines there and they spit this tape out. Well, we, as part of our training, we had to learn to read the holes in those tapes. That's the Murray Code. You would – you could read these tapes without any typing on them.'[34]

Gordon states that being in the army was an egalitarian experience with non-Indigenous women: 'I didn't encounter any racism in the army, we all just had our job to do and we did it, and "sexism" hadn't been invented then. As women we just accepted our lowly place.'[35] Gordon was involved in some important events during her three-year stint in the army. She did communications work at the Empire Games in Perth in 1962 as a teleprinter typist, typing up the Reuters and Australian Associated Press reports. She also was on duty during the Cuban Missile Crisis of 1962, receiving incoming messages of the highest priority. At the end of her three years the army wanted Gordon to re-sign, but she decided that she did not want a military career because she wanted to travel and pursue other opportunities.[36]

Through the contacts Gordon made in the army, she was able to continue skilled employment after her time of service. She did a short stint training as a ledger machinist with a WRAAC friend while working in the office at a Queensland hotel. In 1967 she got a job with NASA at the tracking station in Carnarvon. All of her colleagues were ex-army, navy or air force, so she fitted in well with the routine and regimentation of the work. Gordon then briefly did administrative work in Perth before moving to the Pilbara in 1969. It was there that she began a long career in Indigenous affairs in several capacities. She first worked with organisations representing the Iergamadu people, then for the welfare department and then for the Commonwealth Employment Service in Port Hedland. It was while working with traditional Aboriginal people that Gordon received significant community support and went in search of her own Aboriginal family. She did reconnect with her family in the 1970s and they continue to be a significant part of her life. Meanwhile, she continued her involvement with Aboriginal communities, even taking part in some of the peaceful land rights demonstrations against oil drilling at Noonkanbah in 1980. She remembers: 'I actually sat on the side of the road in Hedland with all the old people from the 12 Mile Reserve to watch the convoy go past and we were protesting in silence on the side of the road ... so I was involved in Aboriginal affairs on the ground, not in the protests interstate.'[37]

By the early 1980s Gordon's leadership abilities had propelled her into national roles in Aboriginal affairs, but still grounded in Western Australian Aboriginal communities. She worked with the Aboriginal Employment Committee, managed the Aboriginal Development Commission in Port Hedland, and after years of working with traditional people she was appointed as the commissioner of Aboriginal Affairs – the first Aboriginal person to head a Western Australian government department. In that role Gordon continued to emphasise integrity and the needs of Aboriginal people. She states: 'I always believed in being honest with people. I never made promises, even when I was in charge of anything, I never made promises. So I was getting more involved in national issues. But, and then, when I was asked to be a magistrate, to take that on, without a formal qualification, I did that.' As Gordon alludes, in 1988 she became the first Aboriginal magistrate of the new Western Australian Children's Court. For the next eight years while working as a magistrate, she also completed a law degree part-time at the University of Western Australia. Again Gordon attributes her discipline – instilled both at Sister Kate's and in the army – as the key to her success. She states: 'But I battled at uni, like a lot of mature-aged students, but we had the discipline. The young ones don't have the discipline.'[38]

Gordon served as a magistrate until reaching mandatory retirement age in 2008. She has also sat on national bodies including the National Committee on Violence, chaired the Western Australia Inquiry into Response by Government Agencies to Complaints of Family Violence and Child Abuse in Aboriginal Communities, and headed the Howard government's short-lived National Indigenous Council (2004–08). Her most high-profile national position was as the chair of the Northern Territory Emergency Response Taskforce (colloquially known as the Intervention) for the first 12 months. Though the Northern Territory Intervention has been controversial, Gordon was quite determined to make it work to stamp out child abuse in remote communities. She accepted the appointment, saying to her critics: 'When I got asked to do the Northern Territory, I was treated like a pariah there by some people, and I said, "Well, hang on. This is about child abuse. This is about bettering Aboriginal people's conditions who've been neglected by governments of all persuasions for decades. So what do you want people to do? Let the kids continue to be abused? Do you want change in communities or do you want people to stay?"'[39]

Gordon has come a long way since both her time at Sister Kate's and her tenure in the WRAAC. She maintains ties with the WRAAC as a member of their organisation and marches with other WRAAC ex-servicewomen every Anzac Day. She is also a member of the Honouring Indigenous War Graves organisation. Gordon credits the leadership skills she has used in the last four decades to the sense of discipline instilled in her early life. She remarks: 'I think it was the discipline from the army. That I realised that if something was going to happen, I had to make it happen.'[40] The army was not the only reason for Gordon's success and her leadership contributions to local, state and national Aboriginal community development. But work in the army catalysed the development of an independent woman who has consistently contributed to Aboriginal empowerment and fought for the rights of Aboriginal Australians.

Grassroots education leadership: Mabel Quakawoot

Mabel Quakawoot, born in 1937, is both Aboriginal and South Sea Islander. Three of her four grandparents were indentured labourers from present-day Vanuatu, brought to north Queensland to work in the sugar cane fields.[41] Her other grandmother is Baialai, from present-day Curtis Island near Gladstone, Queensland. Quakawoot grew up in a large family outside Rockhampton with strong connections to both cultures and kin. Because of their South Sea Islander heritage, her family was exempt from much of the restrictive legislation against Aboriginal people in Queensland. Nonetheless, she did experience racism as a child and recalls segregation against all black Australians – Aboriginal, Torres Strait Islander and South Sea Islander.[42]

Quakawoot was an avid learner and finished school after grade ten. Even so, finding skilled work was difficult because of discrimination. Consequently, she had little choice but to work as a domestic servant. She recalls: 'Well, I did housekeeping, housework, because no, they didn't believe that dark people could be in an office. They didn't think that you could understand reading and writing and be in an office, which I wished I had gone and challenged them, but that would be cheeky of me in those days.'[43] Quakawoot worked as a domestic servant for four years, and during that time she saw little other opportunity for personal advancement. What set her on a different path, though, was the good fortune of working for a kind family whose father happened to be an ex–Second World War fighter pilot. According to Quakawoot: 'He was the one who gave me the incentive, and he said, "You have enough brains to join the air force." [I] thought it was quite funny. But it was really great because they believed in me, even though I didn't believe in what I was doing. And I put in an application to join and I had to have an aptitude test, and I passed my aptitude test, and so I was in the air force.'[44]

Quakawoot's story of how she joined the WRAAF parallels those of the other Aboriginal women in several ways. Like Gordon, this was an escape from domestic service, and she had not even thought about signing up until a chance encounter with the services. Like all other women in this chapter, she felt she had few other opportunities to advance herself, so joining the WRAAF for work made sense.

Quakawoot did not know anything about the WRAAF or what she was getting herself into when she signed up in 1957. She scored well on her aptitude test and was sent to work in the signals mustering as a telegraphist. She completed her training at Point Cook and Ballarat in Victoria before doing most of her service in Canberra. Like Gordon, Quakawoot would not discuss her work in the WRAAF because of the top secrecy of signals. She worked as a telegraphist until she became engaged in 1960. Being engaged lowered her security clearance and Quakawoot was transferred to become a telephonist. Quakawoot was sociable and recalls no racism whatsoever in the WRAAF; neither does she recall any individual examples of gender discrimination, though she does note the unequal pay. In 1962 Quakawoot married a man of Solomon Islander descent and, under WRAAF regulations, was discharged and moved to Mackay.[45]

Later in life Quakawoot would return to the workforce and apply the discipline, communication and study skills she acquired in the WRAAF. As was common practice for women in the 1960s, Quakawoot did not seek further employment because her husband did not want her to work. She had two children, but, after her youngest daughter was in school, Quakawoot slowly began to expand her labour beyond household duties. She first worked as a 'Girl Friday', doing odd jobs and running errands in a quarry office. Then, in 1979, Quakawoot became employed as a teacher at a special-needs school working with children with intellectual and learning disabilities. After the state closed special-needs schools and moved the students into the mainstream, Quakawoot taught special education in government schools. In her role as an educator, she always strove to better the lives of the disadvantaged, both Indigenous and non-Indigenous. Through this work, she was able to influence the lives of individual children and their families, serving as a role model. One anecdote reveals how significant her leadership as a black woman was to changing the attitudes of one particular white student:

> When I first went to teach at the high schools, this year eight boy came in, he was year eight that first year, and he came in and he looked at me and said, 'I just can't stand blackfellas,' and I just looked at him and I said, 'That's your problem, not mine.' And after that, and he was one of the special-needs kids that couldn't read properly, so I took him right through school. I took him right through, through grade ten or grade eleven and did all the things with him and taught him to spell, taught him to do his homework, taught him to write essays and do all those things and I'd completely forgotten about him after he left school. One day I was waiting for my husband [who was working] at TAFE and I saw him and he asked me if I came there every day and I said, 'Yes, I come to wait for my husband,' and, about a week later, he brought me a great big bunch of flowers with chocolates and everything in it and he said, 'If it wasn't for you, I wouldn't be where I am today,' and said, 'And thank you very much.'[46]

Since the 1980s Quakawoot has also participated in and initiated various non-profit projects, paralleling the post-service lives of many ex-servicewomen.[47] She has contributed to Aboriginal and South Sea Islander organisations in Mackay, particularly in relation to education. She has served as an Elder on the Murri Court in Townsville. She is a director of the Port Curtis Coral Coast Corporation, managing native title land and fighting to preserve the environment from development interests. In 2014 she was elected to the Working Party for the National Australian South Sea Islander People. She has also shown initiative by establishing simple programs that contribute to community morale and wellbeing. One such program is a tearoom at the Mackay Courthouse.

Quakawoot was giving evidence in court one day and saw a mother with two small children who were hungry with nothing to eat or drink. When she returned home, she rang the mayor, state and federal members of parliament, saying: 'I want something to be done about this ... I would like to have a room there that they could have a cup of tea and a couple of biscuits and sit down and have a chat if they want to.' A few years after the courthouse failed to follow through, the local member of parliament returned to Quakawoot to set it up. She says: 'Then [they] got a room at the courthouse for me ... put a table, a nice lounge and everywhere, where they could sit, have an urn and a fridge put in there. Now we have cups of tea. I put my face in the paper having a cup of tea, pretending [to drink] a cup of tea, and I got that much – that many people to come and help, but I only wanted them for Wednesdays and that was Children's Court days and the thing is up and running. That's been going for about four years now.'[48]

Quakawoot also founded the first Returned Servicewomen's League in Mackay in 1978, and it currently has approximately 37 members. She successfully lobbied for the construction of a memorial in Mackay dedicated to South Sea Islander military service, which is even more forgotten than Aboriginal and Torres Strait Islander service. Quakawoot shows no signs of slowing down either, as she continues to work for Aboriginal education while she studies a Certificate IV in Business and Governance. She states: 'I want to ask, can I go into the communities to find all the adult people who are illiterate and can I set up classes in those communities ... They should be looking at to teach the adult literacy into these places so as those mothers and fathers can understand what their children are learning now.'[49]

Mabel Quakawoot's post-service life, like those of the other women in this chapter, did not necessarily follow the same work she did in the armed forces. What is clear, though, is that the WRAAF furthered Quakawoot's education and provided the opportunity to escape domestic service. Other members of her family, too, have subsequently served in the military. One of Quakawoot's sisters also served in the WRAAF, and a brother served in the army and is a Vietnam veteran. Quakawoot's numerous roles as educator, lobbyist, advocate and fighter to improve the lives of the disadvantaged in Mackay demonstrates the many leadership contributions she has made in her local community. Reflecting on the position of military service in her and others' lives, Quakawoot says: 'But in reflection, it is a good thing to join … it is something that never leaves you and I think you become more proud of your country, joining the services than you do if you don't join.'[50]

No-nonsense advocate: Jacqueline Shaw

Aboriginal women had served in both the air force and army during the Second World War, but the first known Indigenous woman to serve in the navy is South Australian Marj Tripp, who joined in 1962. She recalls: 'My father was in the army, but I was going to join the police force or I was going to be an air hostess. But before we could even get in we had to get permission from the Protector of Aborigines to allow us to go into the services. So I actually was the first Aboriginal woman to join the WRANS.'[51]

Another early Aboriginal pioneer in the WRANS was Patricia Lees, a Stolen Generations survivor who grew up in a dormitory on Palm Island. She was one of 15 Aboriginal women from Palm Island who tried to enlist around the year 1966, and she was the only one admitted. She comments: 'It was soon found out that I was the first Indigenous female from Queensland, Aboriginal to go into the navy. The Department of Native Affairs – somebody in there identified that, and a fella … came and said, "We've got a great idea," he said, "for Aboriginal recruitment for the navy." He said, "Would you like to come, if the department arrange it, would you like to come and travel to all the Aboriginal communities – Cherbourg, Woorabinda, Yarrabah and Palm Island – and promote the navy?"'[52] Recruitment drives from individuals such as Lees meant that by the 1970s, the number of Indigenous women in the WRANS was on the rise. Among those new recruits was Jirrbal woman Jacqueline Shaw.

Shaw was born in Cairns in 1956. She was raised primarily by her grandparents but also maintained strong connections with her mother. Her grandmother worked as a housekeeper and her grandfather on the railway, and throughout Shaw's childhood they instilled in her and her brothers the value of education. Shaw does not consider herself to have been a target of prejudice in her youth, though she recalls that there were occasions when white parents expressed racist views at primary-school meetings. She thinks that she was not a target of racism because her 'grandparents, grandfather always worked. We were probably respected for that as any other, any other person. I didn't feel any racism.'[53]

After year ten Shaw began training as a nurse, but she did not like the profession. She wanted excitement and, as with the other women in this chapter, a chance encounter directed her to the armed forces. Shaw recalls: 'But one day I was sitting in the grade ten, high school, and careers week it was in Tully High School, and I saw this beautiful black woman walk in in a navy uniform, and I said, "Right, that's what I want to be." So I had an interview in Townsville … And then a year later to the day I got a telegram, come in. But in that meantime, I was at the Tully Hospital training to be a nurse, so that was a good little hospital, but when this came through this is what my dream was … So I thought maybe navy was my next best option, one of the services. It sounded safe and secure; that's why I did that.'[54]

The woman who inspired Shaw to join was a Torres Strait Islander who was the recruitment officer for HMAS *Moreton* in Brisbane. What sets Shaw's story apart from those of the other women in this chapter is that the inspiration to join came from another Indigenous woman. Like the other Indigenous ex-servicewomen, when presented with the idea to join the services, Shaw clearly saw it as an opportunity and an escape. Yet her testimony suggests that, without a clear inspiring example, Indigenous women still did not see the armed forces as an obvious career path. This was despite the fact that by the 1960s there was propaganda specifically targeting Indigenous women as prospective members of the forces. For instance, as mentioned in chapter 1, the New South Wales Native Welfare Department's monthly publication *Dawn* regularly reported on Indigenous people in the armed forces and even included an advertisement in August 1967 promoting careers in the women's services.[55] Indigenous communities on the whole still seemed to view the armed forces as men's work, and only a small number of women took the opportunity to enlist. In November 1973, at the age of 17, Shaw became one of those women and joined the WRANS.

Shaw went to HMAS *Cerberus* outside of Melbourne, where she underwent basic training with the other WRANS. She recalls being the only black WRANS candidate during training, but she later met other Aboriginal and Torres Strait Islander WRANS members – mostly from north Queensland – and became close friends with them. Shaw was assigned to work in the store at *Cerberus*, then later at HMAS *Harman* in Canberra as a victualler. Her role entailed dispensing kits to WRANS members, ordering food for the mess, arranging the menu and bookkeeping.[56] Until 1977 WRANS members were still not receiving seafaring training and still occupied roles that did not require trade training. Kathryn Spurling writes: 'The WRANS remained on the periphery of the Australian Navy. Members of the service were placed in unchallenging positions which best personified "feminine traits". Rather than challenge the social definition RAN administrators emphasised it.'[57]

Though Shaw's appointments fitted within the service's construct of 'feminine' work, her interactions with male servicemen had more complex gender dynamics. Unlike the other women in this chapter, Shaw does not recall male servicemen necessarily behaving chivalrously or gentlemanly. She instead says: 'If you worked down that area [galley], you know, you were expected to be one of the blokes if you were in their galley. That didn't worry me.'[58] Shaw's reflections suggest that by the 1970s women in the armed forces were developing into potential rivals for the men. The attitudes Shaw describes foreshadowed the difficult paths women would traverse from the time the ADF integrated women into the regular forces through to the present day.[59]

Shaw's testimony also differs from that of the other women in this chapter on the issue of race and racism in the navy. She indicates that for the most part her race was never an issue, but she recalls a few occasions when her Aboriginality was targeted. In one early instance she recollects: 'in Melbourne when we all got our uniforms, this Chinese girl turned around and said, "Oh, black fellow in a uniform," and I turned around and said, "Well, you ain't so white."' There were other instances when she was not the target of racial discrimination per se, but her position as an 'other' was clear. Shaw recalls early in her training when 'one girl came up to me and said, "I'm friends with an Aboriginal," something like that, to that effect, and I said, "Yeah, I have white friends too." But I did it as that was my whip – that was my defence was my mouth. But nicely, you know.' Shaw acknowledges that the woman did not have any malicious intent in her statement, but the exchange still marked Shaw as an outsider. Shaw also considers that there were times when the navy gave her tokenistic tasks to be a face for the public. She remarks: 'On the good side of things, if a group, scouts or anything came onto the base, "blacky" was picked [to tour them], you know, so in the end I thought it was like [a] token gesture.'[60] Shaw's assertions suggest that at times she was on show as a novelty, which, while not demeaning to her race per se, contributed to her sense of being an outsider. One way she coped, especially after she was stationed in Canberra, was to stay close to the other Aboriginal and Torres Strait Islander WRANS and to socialise with civilian Aboriginal Australians. That there were more Indigenous women in the services by the 1970s was a marker of the changing dynamics of race, gender and the armed forces. Shaw also had many white friends in the navy and found that she was usually treated as an equal to other women within the naval hierarchy.

By 1977 Shaw was tired of what had become a monotonous role in the WRANS. She reflects: 'And it just got too boring and it was no

Left: The March 1955 cover of *Dawn* featured Citizen Military Forces member Cecil Donovan. Image courtesy of NSW Aboriginal Affairs, Department of Education.

Below: Sergeant SKJ 'Len' Lenoy (far right) was an Aboriginal 3RAR serviceman killed on 24 April 1951 at the Battle of Kapyong, Korea. Image courtesy of AWM, HOBJ0116.

Three members of 3RAR with a North Korean interpreter (left). Lieutenant Reginald Saunders (second from right) was the highest profile Aboriginal soldier of the time, having also served in the Second World War. Image courtesy of AWM, P01813.866.

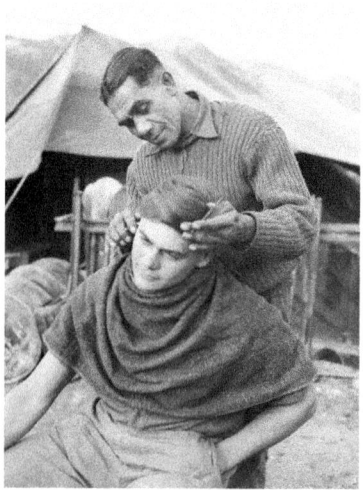

Private Richard (Dick) Hill (2RAR) of Cherbourg, Qld, doubles as a barber in Korea.
Image courtesy of AWM, HOBJ4732.

Private Steve Dodd photographed at Camp Casey, South Korea, 1953. Dodd would later lead the Adelaide Anzac Day march for many years. Image courtesy of AWM, P00969.049.

Torres Strait Islander Corporal Charles Mene (2RAR) receiving the Military Medal for bravery in Korea during Operation Blaze on 2 July 1952. Pinning the medal is the British High Commissioner to the Federation of Malay States, Sir Douglas MacGillivray. Image courtesy of AWM, HAL/57/0100/MC.

Lance Corporal Sarob Sambo, a Torres Strait Islander and ex-paratrooper, member of the 28th Commonwealth Infantry Brigade, photographed in Malaya in 1957. Image courtesy of AWM, FRE/57/0008/MC.

Lance Corporal Sue Giller (now Gordon, second from left) at the Women's Royal Australian Army Corps (WRAAC) graduating parade in 1961. For Indigenous personnel in the 1950–60s, military service was an egalitarian experience.

Gordon served in the WRAAC from 1961 to 1964. She credits the discipline instilled by the army for her success later in life. Both images on this page courtesy of Sue Gordon.

Four members of 3RAR on patrol in Borneo, 1965. The Torres Strait Islander section commander, Corporal Mial Bingarape (front row, centre), had just given directions to the forward scout. Image courtesy of Mial Bingarape and AWM, P00944.006.

Aboriginal serviceman Private Jim Molony (left) training with 7RAR for Vietnam at Shoalwater Bay, Qld, February 1967. Image courtesy of AWM, KEE/67/0020/NC.

Aboriginal soldier Bombardier John Burns (left) speaks with Gunner Bruce Morris during Operation Toan Thang, Vietnam, May 1968. Active combat cultivated strong bonds between the soldiers. Image courtesy of AWM, ERR/68/0474/VN.

Quartermaster Gunner Joseph Donovan (right), an Aboriginal sailor from Kempsey, NSW, spars on the HMAS *Parramatta*, 1970. A boxing champion, he represented Australia at the 1968 Olympics. Image courtesy of AWM, NAVYM0601/02.

Private Graeme M (Brownie) Brown, an Aboriginal member of 1RAR, on foot patrol in Baidoa, Somalia, March 1993. He served as part of the multinational Unified Task Force. Image courtesy of AWM, P01735.401.

An unidentified member of North-West Mobile Force (NORFORCE), c. 1999–2000, engaged in reconnaissance: sitting perfectly still for up to an hour to observe an area. Image courtesy of Ben Bohane.

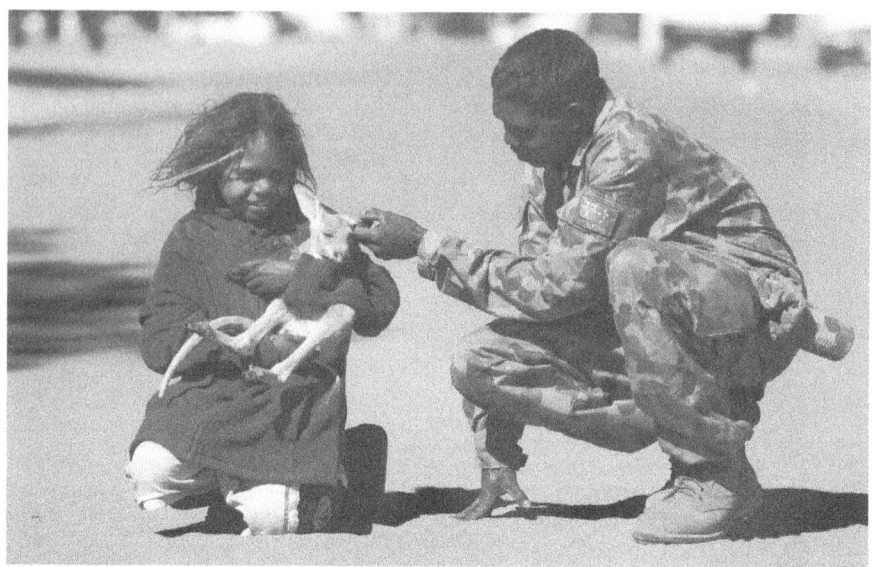

NORFORCE avoided criticism for its involvement in the controversial Northern Territory Intervention due to the goodwill it had already fostered in Aboriginal communities. Here Private Toby Cooper meets Soraya Rankin in Aputula, 2007. Image courtesy of Chris Crerar/Newspix.

NORFORCE 'green skins': Privates Elijah Appurryarnk, Leonard Lamilami and Allen Gebadi, c. 2009. Military service can be an empowering experience for young men and women. Image courtesy of David Hancock.

longer a challenge. Do you know what I mean? It was same old, same old clothing store and all that, and with … the area I was in, there was not much room for movement, you know, drafting and things like that.'[61] It is interesting that Shaw left the WRANS because of the limited job prospects just as the defence policies were opening up more opportunities for women, including sea service; even so, women's career options continued to be limited through the 1980s because policy reform did not mean an immediate change in practice.[62]

The new adventure that Shaw found was working for the National Aboriginal Conference, travelling around north Queensland and helping members of Aboriginal communities to register to vote in the representative body. She continued to do a similar role for the Aboriginal and Torres Strait Islander Commission (ATSIC) in the 1990s and has also done work for the Australian Electoral Commission for regular elections. In the mid-1980s Shaw returned to Canberra and took a position in the federal Department of Aboriginal Affairs. In that role, she recalls: 'we did question and answers. Every day we'd change the questions and answers on Aboriginal issues that concerned health, education mainly and normal mainstream. So copies of those had to go to the Minister for Health, Minister for Education, so they were asked questions in Aboriginal issues.'[63] Shaw performed that role for only about one year because she was frustrated with the culture associated with the bureaucracy. In particular, what she saw as the department's culture of secrecy contradicted Aboriginal interests, so she was uncomfortable in the position.

For the next 20 years Shaw raised a family while still helping out with ATSIC and general elections. She again became more involved in Indigenous affairs around 2009 when she joined the board of directors of the Wabubadda Aboriginal Corporation, representing the Jirrbal people. In that role she was involved in a recent native title determination and will be involved in negotiations with mining companies over mineral exploration. She also enrolled in a Bachelor of Applied Science in Indigenous Community Management and Development. She describes the course and her learning goals as such: 'So it's more or less approaching people, and we are called practitioners, that we can come in and be like mediators and work for what the Indigenous people want and really get that across to the non-Indigenous way of thinking. See, what's good for Cairns is not good for the Cape [York] where they put us all under one umbrella. So that is my idea of me having got radical. I'd rather do it in an intellectual way.'[64] Shaw finished the course in early 2015 and intends to work in teenage alcohol and drug education programs.

Jacqueline Shaw's reflections on her time in the WRANS are quite distinct from those of the other women in this chapter, possibly because she served during a time of change in Australian civilian and military society. The Whitlam and Fraser governments were in power, and issues such as self-determination, land rights and anti-discrimination statutes were on the public agenda. Shaw sees much of the reform of the 1970s to be tokenistic, and she wonders whether or not her position in the navy at the same time also represented a form of tokenism. She comments: 'I don't think really anyone understands what you really go through when you make a decision that you want to join the services. It is totally another world, and you don't think you're white, you don't think you're black, you think you're in the navy and that's the way you live. And to come out and debrief from that, the white people praise you up, the whitefellas go, "Well, why aren't you there [still in the navy] now," you know?'

Though Shaw appreciates the time she had in the navy and the way it transformed her life, she looks at it now as an experience that may have given her job skills as a *woman* but it did not empower her as a *black woman*. She says: 'There is an ex-WRANS association, and I have been getting letters and that from them. But I truly believe that I have another life because I am a black woman. I don't go, I don't want to be [at a] Tupperware party or, there's still too much to be done for our race, because we're not even under the Constitution, hey.'[65] Such sentiments question the nature of conformity within the armed forces. Whereas on one hand the WRANS and wider ADF represented an opportunity for Aboriginal women to be treated as equals, Shaw's reflections suggest that the conforming nature of military life limited expressions of Aboriginality as a positive point of difference. Jacqueline Shaw's sentiments reflecting on her 1970s time in the armed forces foreshadowed simmering issues, including racism, which the armed forces would have to confront in the 1990s.

Conclusion

The four women discussed in this chapter were not the only Aboriginal and Torres Strait Islander recruits to serve in the Australian armed forces during the period of separate women's services.[66] Though histories of the women's services have tended to focus on how they paradoxically challenged gender norms while attempting to prepare women for continued feminine lifestyles, for Aboriginal and Torres Strait Islander servicewomen the situation was different. While each of these Indigenous women had her own experiences of the forces, various themes still permeate their testimonies. Whether through acquiring new education opportunities and skills or through self-discipline, Aboriginal and Torres Strait Islander women took full advantage of the opportunities military employment provided to escape limitations imposed by assimilation policies, including careers in domestic service. Aboriginal women such as Sue Gordon and Jacqueline Shaw not only advanced themselves, but also used their skills to fight for the rights of other Indigenous people. Aboriginal women like Mabel Quakawoot stayed at home to raise their families, but later in life worked to educate Aboriginal and non-Indigenous youth. Torres Strait Islander women like Louise managed to raise a family and work part-time, and later in life upskilled to contribute to Indigenous health. Whether through chairing national inquiries, health work, tutoring young people, encouraging the use of the vote or serving in the judiciary, these ex-servicewomen have been role models, persons of influence and advocates for Aboriginal and Torres Strait Islander advancement. Their activities have adhered to conceptions of Indigenous women's leadership, including respect for all human beings, staying grounded in community, mentoring youth and fighting to improve the lives of the disadvantaged.

5

RACISM, INDIGENOUS PEOPLE, AND THE AUSTRALIAN ARMED FORCES

> But spending twenty years in the army you hear a lot of sort of anti-Aboriginal jokes, like people make jokes about the Irish and other people.[1]
>
> – Gerard Warber

Since 2007 the Department of Veterans' Affairs in conjunction with local Aboriginal organisations has hosted commemorative services in most Australian capital cities during Reconciliation Week, honouring Indigenous military service. The ceremonies have grown in popularity, bringing together a variety of Indigenous and non-Indigenous ex-service personnel, political leaders, celebrities and members of the Australian public. One of the recurring themes at each commemoration is military service as a historical and ongoing example of Reconciliation in practice. Guest speakers often discuss how, during the First and Second World Wars in particular, Aboriginal and Torres Strait Islander people were treated as equals in uniform, generally divorced from the racism they confronted in civilian society; once the uniform came off, they were again subject to prejudice.

There is ample historical evidence to support this conclusion, deriving from both Indigenous and non-Indigenous sources about the First and Second World Wars.[2] Historians, politicians and commentators alike often extrapolate from the experiences of the two world wars and assume that military service continued to represent a social paradigm free of racial prejudice. Yet interviews with Aboriginal and Torres Strait Islander ex-servicemen and women who served between the 1950s and 1990s suggest that the question of racism in the armed forces is not so simple. Ex-service personnel's commentaries vary dramatically, with some suggesting that they experienced no racism whatsoever, while others perceived that racism was widespread. The material derived from oral history interviews focuses primarily on individual *perceptions* and experiences of specific incidents of racial discrimination within the armed forces. It is less about structural, institutionalised forms of racism such as promotions, representation among ranks or even initiatives and policies that did not recognise or respect Indigenous culture.[3] The extent to which Aboriginal and Torres Strait Islander people perceived racism in the ADF and its predecessors is difficult to assess accurately, but the factors that seem to influence their experiences include: the era of service, the nature of the work, the specific branch of the ADF and their skin colour. Although previous chapters have touched on the question of racism and the ADF, this chapter analyses the topic in more depth thematically. Aboriginal and Torres Strait Islander perceptions of prejudice in the ADF seem to have increased as time went on, until finally in the 1990s the ADF stepped up efforts to quash racial discrimination.

The terms 'racism' and 'racial discrimination' are loaded with multiple connotations and meanings. This chapter accepts professor of sociology Christopher Bates Doob's basic definition of racism as an 'ideology contending that actual or alleged differences between different racial groups assert the superiority of one racial group'.[4] Racial discrimination can be either institutional – built into societal structures – or individual. This chapter focuses on individual racism, which Doobs defines as 'an action performed by one person or a group that produces racial abuse – for example, verbal or physical mistreatment'.[5] There are, of course, intersections between institutional and individual racism, and constantly shifting meanings and discourses about race mean that the notion of individual 'mistreatment' on racial grounds is sometimes in the eye of the victim and/or perpetrator. This chapter's focus on perceived individual racial discrimination accepts that different Aboriginal and Torres Strait Islander interviewees would attach different meanings to the terms 'racism' and 'racial discrimination'. The interviewees were specifically asked whether or not they experienced racism in the armed forces. The types of incidents that interviewees report comprise a variety of actions, including taunting, bullying, fighting or superiors inadequately addressing racial vilification claims. Some incidents are overtly discriminatory, whereas others represent examples of covert racism – where the non-Indigenous service personnel's actions reflected underlying racial prejudices.[6] The diversity of examples across the interviews provides insights into both individual and collective understandings of racial discrimination in the armed forces' recent history.

When examining perceptions of racial discrimination, as well as researching underlying causes for societal trends, there is never a precise answer because of the variations across individual circumstances. Even so, this chapter poses some preliminary arguments about how and why Indigenous perceptions of racism in the ADF have changed over time. It will hopefully contribute to larger conversations among Indigenous and non-Indigenous Australians about racism in the ADF.

Perceptions of racism over time

The most pronounced trend from Indigenous ex-service personnel's oral history interviews was that Aboriginal and Torres Strait Islander men and women who served in the 1950s–70s were less likely to perceive racism in the armed forces than those who served in the 1980s–90s. Noel Tovey, who served as a national serviceman in the RAAF in 1953, never mentions his race in his autobiographical account of national service. Instead, he comments: 'even though we all came from totally different backgrounds, once in uniform we were all the same'.[7] Among Korea and Vietnam veterans in particular, there were adamant statements that there was no racism. Korea veteran Ken Colbung describes it as 'quite a relief to get amongst other human beings in the army personnel, and be treated as one of them, an equal'.[8] Vietnam veteran Bob Blair declares: 'I could not even think of one incident with racism in the army, not one. I can't even ever recall anything about being sort of called black or whatever the case is.'[9] Ron Wenitong similarly affirms: 'No, I didn't find any at all. And, and your drill sergeants and everything they were straight down the line, yeah nothing.'[10] Torres Strait Islander Mial Bingarape, who served in the army from 1960 to 1966, including in the Indonesian Confrontation from 1963 to 1965, states: 'I think more or less, like I said, it's you as an individual, how you speak to people, how you respect people and it's your whole lifestyle, how you treat people. You know, I've never had that problem at all.'[11]

Aboriginal women who served in the women's services during the 1950s–60s similarly perceived racism to be minor, if at all present. WRAAF member Mabel Quakawoot firmly declares: 'No, no, no. None, none. There was no, no racism at all.'[12] Sue Gordon, who served as a signals operator in the WRAAC in 1961–63, recalls: 'I had no outright racism ... I had, you know, you've had name-calling all my life, so it was just more name-calling, but I didn't have a lot.'[13] These women acknowledge isolated incidents of name-calling but, given the prevalence of racism in wider Australian society, it did not impact on their psyches. The majority of their testimonies focus on memories of goodwill and mateship with other servicewomen. They perceived incidents of racial discrimination to be minor and isolated occurrences during their military careers.

One could argue that perhaps there was significant racial prejudice in the 1950s–60s armed forces but the Indigenous service personnel, growing up in a period during which racism was the norm, were so accustomed to it that they did not recognise it in the military. There is some merit to such a hypothesis to the extent that when questioned further about experiences in the armed forces, some ex-servicemen and women acknowledge occasional taunts. For instance, Sue Gordon states: 'I think there was some people who weren't sure why Aboriginal people, some still called us natives, were being allowed in [the armed forces].'[14] Yet to argue that these ex-service personnel simply did not recognise racism overemphasises their age as a factor. A review of 138 studies into self-reported racism found that age does not tend to skew self-reports of racism one way or another.[15] Assuming that older ex-service personnel simply did not recognise racism also overlooks their wider life histories. Those who served in the 1950s–60s grew up during the assimilation era when discrimination in Australia was rife; some service personnel had even been forcibly removed as children, and those who had not remember hiding from the welfare as children. They also freely discuss other examples of racism in their civilian lives before and after their military service, including confronting police harassment and being denied entry into pubs and clubs.[16] Essentially, these Indigenous men and women have clear understandings of what constitutes experiencing racial prejudice, and they are quite open about experiencing racism during their civilian lives. Consequently, their pronouncements that their times in the military were free of racial discrimination should not be discounted.

Whereas those who served in the 1950s–70s argue that the armed forces were mostly free of prejudice, those who served in the 1980s–90s present a history that does include racial discrimination. A 1993 report into the ethnic composition of the ADF found that one in five Aboriginal recruits feared they would experience racism in the ADF, and 7 per cent reported that their fears came to fruition.[17] Testimonies from ex-service personnel suggest that racism was usually in the form of taunts or name-calling from superior officers and fellow service members. Torres Strait Islander George Akee, who served in the Australian Army from 1988 to 1995, described the racism at Kapooka as 'shocking'. When asked whether racism was rare or common in the army, Akee answered: 'It's pretty common.'[18] Torres Strait Islander Ezra Anu, who served in the army from 1977 to 1999, similarly asserts that offensive language 'is a common thing ... and they would say stuff without even thinking about it. And I think that when people [became] more aware that these things offended me, they wouldn't say it in front of me. And if we're sitting in front of a group of people or in a meeting they wouldn't say derogative things until I turned my back. But I think whether I turn my back or not it shouldn't be said at all.'[19]

Akee's and Anu's assertions about pervasive racism are strong; other Aboriginal and Torres Strait Islander servicemen from the same time period acknowledge the existence of racism, but do not describe it as a widespread phenomenon. Ed Bailey, who served in the RAAF from 1990 to 1994, specifically recalls racial taunts as isolated incidents – albeit significant isolated incidents. One involved a supervisor calling him names, and the other a housemate serviceman making racist remarks behind his back.[20] Neil Macdonald, member of the RAN from 1988 to 1999, similarly describes racism as rare but noteworthy. He remarks: 'during my career I found that if you do something bad then race does come into it. And then they pick on your race. So if you accidently stuff up on something then your race will, you know, become an issue.'[21] Macdonald's testimony provides an example of covert individual racism, whereby denigrating attitudes towards Indigenous Australians were underlying but manifested only during particular types of situations. Linda McBride-Yuke, sister of deceased naval veteran Bill McBride who served from 1972 to 2004, indicates: 'I think in 32 years he probably had at least half a dozen probably one-on-one incidents that either wasn't taken any further in regards to just being fined on the spot, and handled internally.'[22] The pattern that emerges from these testimonies is that incidents of individual racism were not necessarily widespread, but there were indeed heightened perceptions of racism in the ADF in the 1980s–90s. Comparing and contrasting the 1980s–90s testimonies with those from the 1950s–70s presents several factors that account for the variations.

Patterns of racism (or lack thereof)

Nature of work: Combat vs peacetime

Those least likely to report racism are those men who served in active combat operations, especially in Korea or Vietnam. By virtue of being in combat, unity among the troops was vital, and there was little room for racial prejudice. Aboriginal Vietnam veteran Frank Mallard asserts: 'I think you'll find that in the Australian Army anyway, there's a professionalism of the soldiers that it's not your colour or your skin or whatever that makes you the person that you are, but it's the fact that we all trained together and we all rely upon one another for our safety and for someone to watch our back. So everyone sort of accepting that fact that it didn't matter where you came from or whatever.'[23] Mallard's statement aligns with historian Warren Young's assertions about the military-socialisation process creating a new social paradigm that does not necessarily reflect the same situation as civilian society.[24] What sets combat apart from peacetime military service in particular was the need to ensure unity against a common enemy. Historian James Westheider, who has written about American black–white race relations in Vietnam, has pointed to combat units as the main exception to what were otherwise often tense race relations. He writes:

> Survival in combat usually depends on teamwork and cooperation, and this forced blacks and whites in combat units to develop the cohesion often lacking in the support units ... Combat and the threat of death are great equalizers, and both white and black veterans who served in line companies have claimed there was a solidarity and camaraderie between the races.[25]

Michael Jeffery, former governor-general of Australia and a commanding officer (CO) in Vietnam, comments: 'in Vietnam it [racism] just didn't happen and it wouldn't have been tolerated. [There are] far more important things to think about, you know – supporting one another, staying alive, etc.'[26]

For Aboriginal and Torres Strait Islander servicemen, equality in combat operations represented an extension of the First and Second World War experiences. Describing the Second World War, historian Robert Hall writes: 'The cohesion of the small group in combat – the infantry section, the bomber crew, the tank crew – was sufficient to overcome the divisive effects of potential racism when the group contained both black and white servicemen.'[27] Vietnam veteran Dick Bligh similarly summarises: 'I think when we went to Vietnam, there wasn't any racism at all within the company or the battalion. Yeah, we were all there to do a job and everybody had an eye on each other.'[28] Among the testimonies of Aboriginal Vietnam veterans, notions of brotherhood with both Indigenous and non-Indigenous soldiers stand out. Veterans of more recent active operations have expressed similar sentiments. Steve Maloney, who served in East Timor as part of the multinational peacekeeping force INTERFET (International Force for East Timor) in 1999–2000, recalls experiencing racism in the army within Australia, but not while he was on active duty in East Timor. Similar to Vietnam veterans, Maloney asserts that all members of INTERFET shared common discomforts, as well as witnessed the horrors of a nation recovering from decades of war and genocide.[29]

Even among some Vietnam veterans, though, there was acknowledgement of one arena where racial taunting occurred, and that was during basic training. John Schnaars and George Bostock remember isolated incidents early in their training, such as officers using terms like 'black bastard'. They and other Aboriginal soldiers confronted these comments early on, and the taunting stopped.[30] Dick Bligh recalls racism being common during basic training at Kapooka, but that it disappeared after. He states: 'It was [common], it was. Even the instructors that were at Kapooka rac[ially] abuse [me], but yeah, you got used to [it]. Well, I wouldn't say that you got used to it; you had to accept it because if you didn't accept it, you would be out on your head. Because you couldn't punish people, particularly if they were NCOs or officers (ha, ha). But I guess once I left Kapooka and went to a place called Ingleburn to do my corps training, it was totally different. It was totally different. The people that were there were more professional than the instructors.'[31]

Vietnam veteran Kenny Laughton's fictionalised memoir *Not Quite Men, No Longer Boys* includes an instructor who is especially harsh on Laughton for being Aboriginal, and who makes statements including 'that's better than being a little black bastard nobody like you!'[32] The presence of race-based harassment during basic training echoes in the testimonies from the 1970s and 1980s. Ezra Anu states: 'I was called names in there as well … Being a recruit I had to swallow my spit and pride and just take it all in. They'd be shouting at your face and [there] was tears coming out of my eyes and I just couldn't do anything, you know.'[33] These testimonies suggest that racial epithets were part of the wider military-socialisation process. Basic training is a time when trainers target enlistees' vulnerabilities to shatter their confidence and then rebuild it under strict adherence to military principles. Targeting race would constitute another site of vulnerability. This is not to excuse such behaviour, but it does explain the prevalence of racial taunts in basic training.

Branch of service

In the most recent ADF census, taken in 2011, 1.7 per cent of army, 1.6 per cent of navy and 0.8 per cent of air force members identified as Aboriginal or Torres Strait Islander, constituting 1.4 per cent of the total ADF.[34] Traditionally the army has recruited more Aboriginal and Torres Strait Islander service personnel because of its larger size, the nature of the work and family traditions dating back to the First and Second World Wars. The different numbers of Indigenous members in the three services are by no means indicative of racial discrimination. Yet testimonies from members of the different branches do suggest varying degrees of prejudice across the services. In general, testimonies from navy ex-servicemen contain more stories of racism than their army or air force counterparts.

Historian Jason Sears argues that for 'many years the navy was regarded as the most difficult of the three Australian services for non-Europeans to enter'.[35] The 1993 inquiry into the ethnic composition of the ADF similarly concluded that air force recruits were the most tolerant and 'Navy recruits are somewhat more likely to support ethnocentrist opinions'.[36] These assertions have anecdotal support from Aboriginal testimonies of both the Second World War and immediate postwar era. Linda McBride-Yuke states that during the Second World War her father, Stan McBride, 'had tried for the navy, but the navy said they don't take Aboriginals, so he went to the army and it wasn't raised'. Testimony from an Aboriginal Korean War veteran suggests that similar racial discrimination prevented him from joining the navy. Vietnam veteran David Cook briefly served in the navy before being discharged for failing his examination on completion of the recruit disciplinary course.[37] Cook alleges, though, that his short time in the navy entailed regular confrontations with a racist officer. He asserts: 'And I was the only Aboriginal in the outfit, and there weren't many Aboriginals in the forces. And it didn't matter what I done, I just couldn't do it right. He just didn't want me in his outfit. He just – I was a blot on his outfit, being black.'[38] After his discharge from the navy, Cook enlisted in the army, where he encountered no racial prejudice.

The examples of name-calling and taunts increase in the testimonials of ex-sailors from the 1980s and 1990s; how they dealt with racist taunts varies, whether through personal confrontation or official channels. Torres Strait Islander Marsat Ketchell says that in the 1980s he developed clever ways to respond to racial abuse:

> So I've got comebacks. So every time they called me coon, I'd say, well, coon, to me, is an Australian word for cheese and cheese is yellow and I'm black. And coon to us, in the western Torres Strait

language, is flour as in bread flour and that's white. So you can't call me coon because I'm not white. And if they called me, sort of like, nigger, I'd say I'm not African, I'm not Afro-American. So I can't be a nigger. You have to find something else to call me. So I was happy with black bastard. But then I used to say black's not a colour. Black's a tone, so you can't call me black because I'm brown. So I got to be a smart-arse and that made them more upset and the more upset they got the more happier I was because I win. It's either that or a smack in the chops. No, it was good. If I didn't smack them in the chops one of my white mates would.[39]

Other ex-sailors indicate that they, too, sometimes responded to racial taunts by hitting the perpetrators. Individual servicemen often needed to confront racism on their own because, until the 1990s, there were no Defence regulations against racial vilification. Not all Aboriginal and Torres Strait Islander servicemen were as confident or brave. Aboriginal ex-sailor Dave Williams – who was quite assertive – recalls meeting a group of Torres Strait Islander ex-servicemen who said that they looked up to him for confronting racial abuse head-on.[40]

There is little indication that changes in Australian laws such as the *Racial Discrimination Act 1975* made the ADF more receptive to racial vilification claims. The 1993 report into the ADF's ethnic composition found that almost none of those Aboriginal and Torres Strait Islander personnel who indicated that they had experienced racism lodged formal complaints. Those who did challenge racial vilification through official means often came up against inadequate or improper responses and were unsatisfied with the outcomes.[41] In Neil Macdonald's case, one incident that stands out from the Gulf War involved a fellow sailor saying to him: 'you come to Tasmania and we'll show you what we did to the blacks there and the coons'. Macdonald complained to a CO, threatening to lodge an official complaint if the matter was not dealt with. He was upset not only over the comment, but also over the fact that several witnesses participated and did not challenge the racism. Describing the chief's response, Macdonald says: 'It was all kept like in-house, no official complaint was made … Our divisional officer, our weapons electrical engineering officer, got in there [regular departmental briefing] and said, "Look a few issues are happening about racism and blah, blah, blah." It didn't come out it was me but it was obvious it was me.'[42]

Bill McBride also tried to confront racial abuse through official channels. According to his sister, around the year 1990 he finally became fed up with the inadequate responses and took further action: 'And what he did was he lodged formal complaints internally, which of course didn't do anything for him. They either washed it under the carpet or they just ignored it, or they just said, "Oh, noted: your complaint's noted." So because nothing was done he went outside the system and went to the Human Rights and Equal Opportunity Commission [HREOC]. And the actual CEO … she took on his case personally … And the navy were not impressed. They were obviously quite angry that it had gotten external exposure.'[43] McBride's HREOC case was settled in arbitration. The fact that he felt the need to involve the HREOC suggests that the navy – and the ADF more widely – was not adequately equipped to handle racial vilification cases and preferred to avoid confronting the problem.

Though navy ex-servicemen's testimonies are more open about the presence of racism, this does not mean that the other branches were completely free of it, nor does it mean that all Aboriginal and Torres Strait Islander sailors experienced racism. Vietnam naval veteran Brian White states: 'No matter what walk of life you came from or what your background was you found brotherhood in the Navy.'[44] What stands out about the navy, though, is more open discussions about individual encounters with racial prejudice across the testimonies and historical records.

Skin colour

One contentious matter that also factors in the ex-servicemen and women's experiences of racism is skin colour. This issue is problematic because of the history of white authorities legislating Aboriginality based on skin colour and/or blood quanta. It was not until the early 1970s that the Commonwealth and state governments moved towards a 'definition' of Aboriginality based on culture rather than physical appearance. Formalised in the 1983 High Court ruling *Commonwealth v. Tasmania*, the national 'definition' of Aboriginality is in three parts: 1. One must be of Aboriginal or Torres Strait Islander descent; 2. Have an Indigenous community with which to identify; and 3. Be identified as a member by that Indigenous community. Many Australians are either ignorant of this official 'definition' or do not accept it, preferring to determine Aboriginality based on physical appearance.[45] One recent high-profile example is the racial vilification case surrounding *Herald-Sun* columnist Andrew Bolt. Bolt argued first in a newspaper column and then in court that several prominent Aboriginal people of mixed descent should not really be considered Aboriginal.[46] Legal considerations of Bolt's trial aside, what his column and case highlight is a common sentiment in Australian society – namely, that 'real' Aboriginal people have dark skin. Such false suppositions have impacted on the lives of all Aboriginal and Torres Strait Islander people, and they have resonated in the ADF as well. Those Indigenous service people with darker skin were more likely to report being victims of racial taunts than those individuals with fairer skin, who may not have been recognised as or targeted as Indigenous.

All of the men and women who reported racial prejudice in the armed forces, including name-calling and other comments, are people who are 'visibly Indigenous'. Their facial features and skin colours are such that most Australians would not question their Aboriginality or Torres Strait Islander identity. It makes sense that persons who are noticeably black would be targeted for comments such as 'black bastard'. Ezra Anu, for instance, notes that common comments in the 1970s–80s thrown at him and other Indigenous servicemen included being described as 'blacksey' or 'niggersey'.[47] By contrast, several of the ex-servicemen who indicated that they did not experience any racism in the armed forces could be mistaken in appearance as non-Aboriginal. Among those men is RAAF ex-serviceman Mick Pittman, who served from 1969 to 1989; he vociferously insisted: 'Never. It [race] absolutely never came up. I didn't witness, experience any racism whatsoever.'[48]

Indigenous servicemen and women such as Pittman were not necessarily hiding their Aboriginality. Rather, by virtue of the service personnel's fairer skin, sometimes non-Indigenous and even Indigenous colleagues assumed they were white.[49] Among those men is Frank Mallard, who served from 1962 to 1985, including a tour in Vietnam and then subsequent service in the Army Reserve until 1999. He recalls witnessing racism while serving in Townsville:

> I said, 'Well, you know, I'm of Aboriginal descent,' and that sort of stopped everybody in their tracks. They sort of looked at me and said, 'You're pulling my leg.' I said, 'No, I'm not pulling your leg,' and I said, 'I don't like the way that you talk about these sort of things, you know. You have to have respect for people.' So you know, after that everyone was a little bit careful about what they were saying, and when they said it in front of me they didn't make those sort of remarks anymore. But yeah, that's the sort of racism that I saw but it was directed at other people. It was not directed at me because of the colour of my skin, you see, and that's where people can get things, as I said before, so wrong. They can be making remarks about somebody and not knowing exactly who that person is and what his relationship is to a different nationality or a different culture.[50]

Sometimes Aboriginal service personnel were quite conscious that they were being mistaken for another race and were content with this because it made their daily routines easier. Former major Jo West recalls:

> it still happens today, where you cross paths with people who aren't particularly well educated or know how to deal with Aboriginal

Racism, Indigenous people, and the Australian armed forces

people. You know, when I was going through RMC [Royal Military College, Duntroon] it was easier for me to not mention that I was Indigenous and for people to just assume that I was Islander descent because they handled the Fijians and PNG cadets particularly well.[51]

Some similar intriguing testimony on the topic of physical appearance and racism in the ADF comes from Stan Phoenix, who served in the army from 1973 to 1999 and later worked in a civilian capacity at the weapons training Singleton Range in the Hunter Valley. Phoenix grew up not knowing he was Aboriginal until his father revealed it to him in 1978 – after he had already been serving for five years. Being fair-skinned and not even knowing about his Aboriginality, Phoenix by his own admission has been able to pass as non-Aboriginal and has wound up in situations witnessing racism as an insider-outsider. He says: 'you sit on the fence a lot and listen to what people say. And I think that's, when you're saying before touching raw nerves, that's the thing that hurts the most … That you have mates who say the things they say about Aboriginal people without really having no knowledge of them.' Phoenix cites several examples of witnessing other soldiers making derogatory comments about Aboriginal people; when he revealed his Aboriginality, some stopped speaking to him. Reflecting on racism in the army in general, he comments:

> In the army there are certain times with certain people, and they're not all like that, I'd say, 1 per cent, they were really racist and they think they're in the army to kill, to do a bit of ethnic cleansing and to show that people, the Australian soldiers, the bronze Anzac and all that sort of stuff. And you used to listen to those blokes at the bar run them down, call them black bastards and I never said nothing, you know, but depending on what they were saying it's, I'd move off, you know. See, you see a lot of that. I'm sure the same people, if I stood there with a bone in my nose, wouldn't have said anything, but you know, people just don't know.

Phoenix mentioned that he witnessed darker Aboriginal soldiers being referred to in terms such as 'that stupid black prick'. Similar to Neil Macdonald's comments about covert individual racism, Phoenix says: 'so it's not that you hate them because they're black but because you're pissed off, you just say something'.[52] Phoenix's testimony is enlightening about the treatment darker versus fair-skinned Aboriginal people received in the ADF. In particular, his reflections about race, skin colour and non-Indigenous servicemen's attitudes indicate the fundamental principle underlying racial attitudes in the Australian military: they reflect the sentiments, knowledge and ignorance that permeate civilian Australia.

Wider Australian society

Warren Young argues that the relationship between minority participation in military versus civilian societies may follow one of three patterns: continuous, discontinuous or parallel. Continuous patterns signify the 'deliberate projection of the minority-societal relationship onto the military organization';[53] discontinuous means that the minority's relationship within the military differs from its status within civilian society; and parallel patterns suggest that the relationship mostly mirrors that of civilian society, but with some discontinuity. Young asserts that the continuous or parallel patterns are most common,[54] and the Australian case aligns with his argument because Indigenous people's status and treatment within the post–Second World War military were not dissimilar to their position in civilian society. The non-Indigenous servicemen and women who served alongside Aboriginal and Torres Strait Islander personnel came to the armed forces with their own personal experiences and biases as shaped by Australian society. As such, it is not surprising that their attitudes to race, and Indigenous people in particular, would reflect the trends of the wider population.

The question of whether Australian society has grown more racist since the Second World War is contentious, and a handful of historians have attempted to address it through various analytical prisms. Historian Russell McGregor effectively summarises the difficulty of addressing such a question: 'Acceptance, it must be conceded, is a rather amorphous achievement, and it is impossible to precisely calibrate the degree of acceptance at a particular point in time.'[55] Notwithstanding the difficulties of such a task, the works of McGregor, Tim Rowse, Murray Goot, Steve Mickler and Scott Bennett suggest that contrary to popular assumptions – that Australian society has grown more accepting and tolerant of Australian Indigenous people and their cultures – since the 1980s there has been a polarisation of popular opinion and an entrenchment of anti-Indigenous biases. Such sentiments would also resonate among non-Indigenous members of the armed forces.

The expansion of civil rights to Indigenous Australians in the 1960s–70s complemented rising public support for formal Indigenous equality. Much of this success is due to the campaigns of activist groups such as FCAATSI and international pressure to abolish the White Australia Policy.[56] The 1967 referendum, when 90.77 per cent of Australians voted to amend the constitution to grant federal jurisdiction over Aboriginal people and to count Aboriginal people in the census, is generally considered to represent an overwhelming vote for Aboriginal equality. Yet, as McGregor, Goot and Rowse argue, the vote for equality was a vote for abstract principles rather than a vote for interpersonal acceptance. They point to surveys conducted in the 1960s suggesting that most Australians were willing to recognise Aboriginal people as part of society at large, but not to admit them within their own social circles. As Bennett highlights, areas with larger Aboriginal populations registered higher levels of 'no' votes.[57] Even among 'yes' voters, surveys about why they voted 'yes' indicate 'that some of those who were to vote for constitutional reform harboured negative perceptions of Aborigines'.[58] This research implies that perhaps Australian society was not as accepting in the 1960s as one would think the referendum vote indicated.

Yet the ex-servicemen and women who served in the 1960s are those who perceived low levels of racism. This has much to do not only with the combat factor in Vietnam, but also it suggests that ignorance and unfamiliarity did not necessarily mean contempt for Indigenous people. The majority of Australians in the 1960s had little personal experience or exposure to Aboriginal people, culture or living conditions. Historian Jennifer Clark has documented the limited coverage Aboriginal people received in the media, such as an average of less than one story a month on the then Australian Broadcasting Commission (ABC) from 1960 to 1969. Steve Mickler's analysis of the scant newspaper coverage during the 1960s reveals that reports tended to romanticise Aboriginal people as primitives, promoted the assimilation cause, held government primarily responsible for resolving Indigenous disadvantage or played on images of Aboriginal suffering to garner support for causes such as the referendum.[59] This lack of media coverage meant middle Australia was generally ignorant of Indigenous concerns and experiences. Essentially, in the 1960s, there were not so many negative images bombarding middle Australia with a sense of Indigenous culpability for their disadvantage. Consequently, white service personnel could interact with Indigenous servicemen and women with a naivety that did not necessarily reflect racial prejudice.

In the decades that followed the referendum, as the federal government took a larger role in Indigenous affairs, so too did the media report more on Indigenous issues. However, much of the media coverage by the 1980s was negative and served to fill the ignorance of many non-Indigenous Australians with myths, stereotypes and a sense of Indigenous idleness. The impact of skewed coverage, as academic Sarah Maddison notes: 'often reporting in an uncritical manner on government policy or replicating the racist views sometimes evident in the wider community ... combined with the minimal reporting offered to critics of current government policy and the inadequacy of Australian curricula, contribute to a poorly informed population'.[60] The rise of media coverage in the 1980s heightened misunderstandings about so-called special privileges, and by 1985 even the Department of Aboriginal Affairs was warning that latent racism among the Australian public was becoming more blatant.[61] Negative and/or misleading media reports do not necessarily cause racism, but unchallenged they may fuel ignorance and misunderstandings. Lee Sigelman and Susan Welch theorise in the American context that:

> whites' perceptions and expressions of racial hostility should be materially affected by personal contact with blacks, because such contact is a key source of positive information about blacks; in the absence of this source, whites must fall back on other information sources, including long-standing racial stereotypes and media reports, which are more likely to be negative.[62]

During the 1990s, Australian society seemed to polarise around the topic of Indigenous affairs. While many Australians supported the Reconciliation movement, others expressed vocal opposition through support for politicians such as Pauline Hanson and the One Nation Party. Goot and Rowse have demonstrated that by the year 2000, 'research showed non-Indigenous Australians to be divided about some Aboriginal grievances; and on those aspects of the Aboriginal agenda that required reform to law and order and the greater expenditure of money, Aboriginal sympathisers were clearly in the minority'.[63] Given these trends of more vocal anti-Indigenous sentiments, it is not surprising that such sentiments filtered into the ADF. Consequently, it makes sense that Indigenous ADF members in the 1980s–90s would perceive more racism than those who served in the 1950s–70s.

Towards a time of Reconciliation?

The subject of racism is always complex, particularly when analysing historical trends and individual perceptions. Former federal race discrimination commissioner Irene Moss wrote in a 1994 opinion piece in *The Age*: 'How many racists does it take to condemn a society as racist? A question that does not allow an objective, quantified response will provoke widely varying replies depending on who is asked. For Aboriginal and Torres Strait Islander people, the answer to the question must surely be an overwhelming "Yes, Australians are racist."'[64] Moss's assertion about Aboriginal and Torres Strait Islander perspectives was generalised, but she was certainly correct that the question 'Are Australians racist?' never goes away. Just as civilian Australia regularly questions the extent of racial discrimination in society, so too has the ADF and its predecessors confronted the presence of racism.

Aboriginal and Torres Strait Islander servicemen and women have reported varying degrees and manifestations of racism within the armed forces over time. The testimonies in this chapter have shown the diversity of issues at play in the recent history of racism in the ADF. Such factors include the branch of service, combat versus peacetime work and skin colour of those personnel targeted for racial abuse. Though reports of racial discrimination in the ADF have risen since the 1980s, so, too, have servicemen and women been more assertive in their condemnations of prejudice. Moreover, in the 1990s the ADF adopted policies against racial vilification and, as the next chapter outlines in more detail, took active steps to promote Reconciliation and Indigenous service. Training for all service personnel now includes education courses designed to combat ignorance among new recruits. Brigadier Nagy Sorial, CO of the Pilbara Regiment between 2004 and 2006, says of his experience with new recruits: 'The odd person that had come in, you found out pretty quickly if they were not tolerant of people different to themselves, and generally you worked on them to try to educate them in the first instance, because most people it's just a lack of education … You got the odd one that you just weren't going to change their mind. Pull them in and say, look this is not for you.'[65]

Racism, Indigenous people, and the Australian armed forces

Even interviewees who described racism in the armed forces are satisfied with their times of service and would recommend the ADF as a career opportunity for Indigenous Australians. Continuing such a proud tradition of Indigenous service is perhaps the best ammunition for the ADF in the ongoing struggle against racism.

6

A CHANGING DEFENCE FORCE AND RECONCILIATION

I enjoyed the Army, I made some great friends. I believe that a lot of our young, unemployed people should join the Army for discipline and friendship wise, and you can earn a living in there. It was one of my greatest times, I think.[1]

– Japarta Maurie Ryan

Bringing people of NESB [non-English speaking background] and Aborigines and Torres Strait Islanders into the ADF may help to give the ADF a broader appreciation of other cultures and the way they may respond to Australian strategic and security planning.[2]

– 'The Ethnic Composition of the Australian Defence Force', 1993

In his landmark 1992 Redfern address, Prime Minister Paul Keating asked all Australians to imagine themselves in the position of Indigenous Australians. He reflected on the long history of Aboriginal and Torres Strait Islander dispossession, discrimination and erasure from Australia's national consciousness. He also declared: 'Imagine if non-Aboriginal Australians had served their country in peace and war and were then ignored in history books.'[3] Keating's Redfern address is considered one of the most significant markers of the Reconciliation movement of the 1990s. The formal Reconciliation process grew out of recommendations from the 1991 Royal Commission into Aboriginal Deaths in Custody. Subsequently, the Commonwealth government established the Council for Aboriginal Reconciliation in 1991 with the ten-year aim to promote: better relationships between Indigenous and non-Indigenous Australians, knowledge of shared histories, understandings of Indigenous disadvantage, appreciation of Indigenous cultures and a document expressing new relationships between Indigenous and non-Indigenous Australians. The nebulous nature of the term Reconciliation was always open to interpretation, leaving what many consider unfinished business at the end of the formal process in 2001.[4]

Throughout the Reconciliation movement, public and private institutions were all encouraged to participate by thinking about what they as organisations could do to promote the ideals of Reconciliation. As Keating's Redfern address suggested, the ADF was not immune from this process. Given the long history of Aboriginal and Torres Strait Islander participation in the armed forces, it is not surprising that the ADF, the Department of Defence and the Department of Veterans' Affairs had the potential to play significant roles to promote Reconciliation. The defence community responded to the call for Reconciliation in numerous ways – some well before Reconciliation became a popular term, and others more recently. The success of Reconciliation within the defence community stems from organisations' willingness to work at the grassroots level with local Indigenous communities, whether they are in remote or urban areas. Some of the more pronounced examples discussed in this chapter include the special role of Indigenous defence networks in remote Top End units, anti-racism and Reconciliation Action Plans across the ADF and the Department of Defence, and special programs promoting Indigenous service in the ADF. These new initiatives also align with the changing strategic and operational dynamics of the ADF since the late 1980s.

Regional Force Surveillance Units

In 2001 the then chief of army (now governor-general of Australia), Peter Cosgrove, wrote that in the decade after the end of the Vietnam

War, 'planners were attempting to redefine the role and purpose of the Australian Defence Force'. Eventually, according to Cosgrove, 'the concept of forward defence was abandoned in favour of a policy of defence of the Australian mainland'.[5] One might question (as military historian Jeffrey Grey has, for instance) whether in fact the ADF totally abandoned forward defence, but Cosgrove's next point illustrates the greater emphasis placed on mainland security at this time.[6]

In the 1980s the ADF recognised the need to create regional force surveillance units, 'which would be recruited, trained and operate … in their own areas of influence'.[7] Thus the army established North West Mobile Force (NORFORCE) in Darwin in July 1981, followed by the Pilbara Company in January 1982 (known as the Pilbara Regiment after 1985), and in 1985 the 51st Battalion, Far North Queensland Regiment (51 FNQR). Subsequent policy initiatives such as the Dibb Report of 1986 and the 1987 white paper *The Defence of Australia* meant, among other matters, the transfer of many regular units north, and the incorporation of these new surveillance units into an army structure with an expanded presence in the Top End of the country. Dibb had identified Southeast Asia as an 'area of direct military interest' for Australia. Thus the defence of northern Australia, including its surveillance, was regarded as a high priority.[8] Given the location of these units, there was the opportunity for them to work closely with remote Aboriginal and Torres Strait Islander communities. These units wound up not only working with communities, but also specifically targeting local Indigenous Australians for recruitment. Due to the relatively high proportion of Indigenous members, and unusual roles within the ADF, the Top End surveillance units reveal new possibilities for Indigenous–non-Indigenous relationships in the services, and an opportunity for Reconciliation on a local but significant scale.

The three Regional Force Surveillance Units (RFSUs), formerly part of the army's 6th Brigade, responsible for 'intelligence surveillance target acquisition', were relocated to the 2nd Division at the end of 2014.[9] They are reserve units with small components of regulars. As reserve units, members can serve anywhere between 14 and 200 days per year and must meet minimum fitness and education requirements. Their areas of operation are gigantic: NORFORCE's responsibilities include all of the Northern Territory and the Kimberley in Western Australia; the Pilbara Regiment's zone is equal to about one-sixth of continental Australia; while 51 FNQR has 640,000 square kilometres to look after. The significance for this project of the geographical spread is that simple statements such as 'the RFSUs have a high number of Indigenous members' are more complex than they look, given the range of communities that participate in these forces. In terms of the overall army structure, the RFSUs are unique, not just because of their large percentage of Indigenous soldiers, but also because their entrance requirements are varied to account for the social situation of many Aboriginal or Torres Strait Islander people. Finally, within the Army Reserve, the RFSUs have major responsibilities not normally associated with that part of the defence forces, which has sometimes struggled to assert a clear purpose and identity. As Jeffrey Grey notes, the RFSUs 'make extensive use of Aboriginal people and Torres Strait Islanders … a telling example of what the Army reserve might do if properly resourced and given a clearly defined role'.[10]

Former governor-general Michael Jeffery played a crucial role in the establishment of NORFORCE and spreading the doctrine of northern surveillance, and both he and the current governor-general, Peter Cosgrove, take pride in their roles establishing and working with the RFSUs. The then Lieutenant Colonel Jeffery became CO of the SAS in January 1976 and soon was investigating the possibility of his unit assuming some of the roles that the North Australian Observer Unit (NAOU) had performed during the Second World War. In the post-Vietnam era there was a renewed sense of a 'vulnerable' northern area of Australia and, as one of Jeffery's officers noted, the new CO 'discussed the idea of land surveillance operations as a viable and realistic role for the Regiment'.[11] When Jeffery was promoted to colonel and became the first director of the Special Action Forces in 1979, he was in the right position to develop the surveillance scheme for northern Australia.

As NORFORCE's historian states, in peacetime the unit, like the other RFSUs, is responsible for surveillance operations intended to 'detect change to the environment, which could range from the presence of physical evidence (suggesting some form of an incursion or activity) to disruptions in normalcy patterns'. Such unusual patterns might then result in some form of military response. Close relationships with local communities are understandably crucial to the success of the wide range of activities that comprise the RFSU charter. Therefore, Indigenous participation in the three RFSUs is not only welcome but essential.[12] It is not a matter of tapping into some mysterious 'innate skills' but of using something more tangible – local knowledge. As a former commander of 51 FNQR stated:

> For the things we were doing in that environment, it wasn't just innate skills or particularly developed skills in any function. More importantly, it was an understanding of the country around them and the people who lived in that country and the patterns of life that happen in that part of the world. Because there was a view that this knowledge was very important, not only just for the border protection side of the house but if we ever had to fight a war in the northern part of Australia then having that home ground advantage of understanding the territory, the people, the weather patterns ... and how all that interacted was gold and would be something that an adversary would never, ever have.[13]

The Indigenous component of each of the three RFSUs varies between each regiment and within each regiment over time. It has been claimed in the past that NORFORCE is predominantly Aboriginal – approximately 60 per cent or more. This figure may be seriously overstated. The 2013 Senate Estimates hearings figures provided by the army established that 30.9 per cent of NORFORCE was Indigenous, while 23 per cent of 51 FNQR was Indigenous, both Torres Strait Islander and Aboriginal. The figure for the Pilbara Regiment is lower – 3.2 per cent – which is unsurprising as the Aboriginal proportion of the region's population is much lower than in NORFORCE areas of operation such as Arnhem Land. In 2011 it was claimed that 8 per cent of the Pilbara Regiment was Indigenous, though the composition of all reserve units can vary over relatively short periods of time.[14] The differences among the RFSUs are the result of several factors including the size of the Indigenous populations in different areas of the country, the history of Indigenous–non-Indigenous relations in those regions and traditions of military service. In this the RFSUs are a microcosm of their particular segments of Australian society.

In the Pilbara, for example, a former CO described the revealing state of affairs he encountered between 1994 and 1995:

> The Pilbara Regiment, in my time ... had very few self-identified Aboriginals. The difference in societies of 'Desert Aborigines' across the Pilbara and the east is a very interesting comparison with northern, coastal Indigenous society ... That said, I did actively pursue a number of traditional communities in the area (Jigalong, in particular) and the non-traditional environment at Carnarvon. Neither initiative was successful for interesting reasons, essentially beyond my control ... In Karratha to 'make a point' the local WA Police Superintendent, the Head of the WA Department of Aboriginal Affairs (responsible for the Pilbara and the Kimberley) and I met quite publicly in uniform ... to have a couple of drinks together. This had the advantage of letting people know that the Army, Police and Indigenous Affairs were linked.[15]

What the CO found was that suspicion, ingrained institutional responses, discrimination and exclusion all inhibited his ability to recruit

Aboriginal members into the Pilbara Regiment. No amount of goodwill and the offer to participate in the defence forces could overcome these problems quickly. Yet over time these issues could be resolved, as direct approaches to Indigenous groups and gaining their trust paid off in terms of increased involvement in RFSUs. Thus, by the time Brigadier Nagy Sorial was CO of the Pilbara Regiment (2004–06), he found that his recruiting efforts were successful and the Indigenous proportion of his unit was about the same as the proportion of Indigenous people in the whole region: '8 or 9 per cent I think is where we were sitting, which I was happy with because it was a reflection of the society, which is all you can really be.'[16]

The situation with NORFORCE is different in a number of ways. For a start, Aboriginal Australians constitute a significant proportion of its members. Secondly, relationships between the formal army structure and several local communities are unusually close in numerous cases. Much of this stems from the goodwill generated between the Australian Army and Northern Territory Aboriginal communities during the Second World War.[17] Finally, both the Indigenous and non-Indigenous media have frequently portrayed NORFORCE, the first of the surveillance units, as an Aboriginal success or good news story in print, television and electronic media. One example of a feel-good piece on NORFORCE published in *Australian Geographic* in 2009 also reveals some dubious assumptions about 'inherited' skills given a modern coat of paint. The journalist accompanying a NORFORCE detachment wrote:

> I'm on patrol along the Daly River, one of northern Australia's largest and most pristine waterways. Around me are 10 men from Norforce Regiment: all indigenous and mostly from Arnhem Land, NT. Dressed in fatigues and their faces camouflaged, they move through the bush effortlessly and silently, hugging the shaded areas, at times unseen. The few words of command are spoken in Yolngu Matha, the

native tongue of north-east Arnhem Land ... While the soldiers carry guns, a radio and medical supplies, their easy movement and silent observations are skills that cannot be taught by even the best military instructors; their talents are instinctive, a product of thousands of years accumulated knowledge. It's expertise the Australian Army is putting to good use to protect the remote north of the country.[18]

Knowledge of country is one thing, but the assumptions and stereotypes of instinctive trackers with warrior traits actually constitute false constructs of the martial race stereotype. Such language follows a long history of employing Aboriginal people for their bushcraft, such as 'trackers' in Australia's police forces, the last of whom retired in Queensland in July 2014.[19] Though many NORFORCE members do possess essential surveillance skills, they learned them as part of their upbringing, rather than these skills being inherent to their race. Perhaps this depiction is partly an attempt to graft a warrior image onto more passive representations of Aboriginal people, as the myth was already well established in the nineteenth century that 'Aborigines did not resist the occupation of Australia by the British'.[20]

The RFSUs are reserve forces, but with some adjustments. Several qualifications for reserve service have been relaxed in the case of the RFSUs, chiefly in terms of health and prior educational background. There is also some flexibility in criminal background checks when candidates committed lesser offences as minors; those who have committed violent crimes or repeated theft are still not eligible. Attendance patterns may be determined in part by an Indigenous member's community responsibilities, and unlike other reserve units they train in the Top End, often in their own communities.[21] In whatever roles RFSUs have been engaged, their COs are anxious to ensure that these activities are 'real', that they contribute meaningfully to the army's work. Former RFSU COs interviewed for this project stressed the high performance of their units and the military capabilities of their members, Indigenous and non-Indigenous. This also provided their COs with a high sense of job satisfaction. For example, Brigadier Nagy Sorial of the Pilbara Regiment said that he had 'loved the job' for several reasons. Firstly, there was 'the work aspect of it ... the ability to actually take soldiers on operational duties'. Then there was 'the ability to actually see parts of the country that you otherwise wouldn't see'.[22] The former COs also emphasise that, with rare exceptions, relationships between Indigenous and non-Indigenous soldiers were cooperative and professional. Racial distinctions disappeared under the common 'green skin' of the army uniform. This experience of equality is similar to that of veterans from earlier periods. As Colonel Clay Sutton, former CO of NORFORCE, stated: '[we] didn't care if you were a blackfella or a whitefella, the stink come up, you were green, you were in a green uniform'.[23]

Recruitment for the RFSUs is conducted via the traditional processes followed by the Army Reserve. In addition the RFSUs have more proactive policies, establishing closer links with remote communities and attempting to earn the trust of their leaders. For Brigadier Mal Rerden, CO of 51 FNQR between January 1996 and December 1997, it was crucial to talk to 'the community Elders' about 'providing their people with some training and experience' that 'would help build leaders for the community'.[24] Or, as Lieutenant Colonel Simkin expressed it: 'you'd talk to the Elders and say ... "We're looking for good young men who ... want to come and work in NORFORCE," and the Elders love it; they ... would hold their own little selections within their tribe and find the best guys and only want to send them off ... and do some service in NORFORCE 'cos the tribal Elders saw it as a way of keeping their better young kids in the community gainfully employed so they didn't go off track doing something else ... They would get some experience, some training and come back better able to be leaders within the community.'[25]

The RFSU leaders stress the positives for Indigenous Australians of their continued participation in these defence units. Both the army and soldiers have benefited from this relationship. Michael Jeffery referred to his son's experience commanding a NORFORCE company from Alice Springs, where 'he established such a close relationship with his soldiers ... he was made a member of the tribe'. The concept of Indigenous involvement was both 'strategically and tactically sensible' and 'having Aboriginal soldiers fulfil the roles was terrific'.[26] It is a 'win–win situation', as Colonel Sutton, a former commander of NORFORCE, declared: advantageous for the participants and 'we needed the Aboriginal soldiers as part of our concept'.[27]

Aboriginal and Torres Strait Islander responses to RFSUs

The RFSUs thus provide a positive image to Australia of contemporary Indigenous Australians. Media articles have highlighted the invaluable skills and knowledge of Aboriginal and Torres Strait Islander soldiers, as well as discussing how their reserve service has made a positive impact on the lives of some young men and women. As one newspaper article stated in December 2011: '[a] unique army unit patrols our top end, on watch for smugglers and poachers, and prepared for battle should conflict erupt but ... Norforce's greatest legacy may be its empowerment of Indigenous locals'. This article stressed how some lives had been turned around by the discipline and camaraderie of the RFSU. For example, Private Desmond Lightning from the Kimberley region told the journalist that before he joined NORFORCE he was 'running amok, getting drunk and fighting'. The article added that virtually 'all the indigenous soldiers' had similar stories, as have other members of the RFSUs who have talked about their reasons for joining up.[28] Similarly, in an ABC documentary, another member of NORFORCE, Barak Sambono from Darwin, hoped his example was catching because he saw 'a lot of young boys back in the community where I stay and I thought it would be a great opportunity for me to get them involved in NORFORCE' and 'it would also be employment for them and get them off drinking and that sort of thing'.[29]

This generalisation, of course, needs to be treated cautiously. Lieutenant Colonel Gunder recalls what he described as his '"aha" moment' when he realised some of his prior assumptions about his Indigenous soldiers might be incorrect. Shortly after taking over command of 51 FNQR in 2000, Gunder was conducting a recruit course in Cooktown with Torres Strait Islanders, Aboriginal people and 'white blokes from the Gulf'. The recruits were learning navigation and map reading. Gunder asked one Torres Strait Islander if he was following what he was being taught: 'And he just looked at me and he said, "I should fucking hope so. I'm a cartographer by trade."'[30]

Commanders have also learned important lessons over three and a half decades in how to recruit Indigenous Australians successfully. According to one of the chief instructors at the first Aboriginal Recruit Course for NORFORCE, held at Kimbolton station in Western Australia in October 1981, it had 'been proven that traditional Australian Aboriginals can be selected and basically trained for military service'. This was despite teething problems with different communities interacting, inexperience on the part of the people running the course, and some disappointing early retention rates. In a significant assessment Warrant Officer Class One Reg Davies concluded:

> What reassurance has he [i.e. the new recruit] that he has chosen an appropriate test? Partly the knowledge that his 'traditional' skills, that his Aboriginality is *for the first time in his life* an asset in the interaction between cultures … his capacity to accommodate the change is his warrant for success on our terms, while satisfying his own curiosity about an experience which is as exciting as it is daunting, as intimidating as it is reassuring, as unusual as it is formal.[31]

Throughout the RFSUs' history and across their various tasks, Aboriginal and Torres Strait Islander men and women have reported favourably on their participation in the units. They see it as an opportunity to continue practising their bush culture as well as to learn other skills. Torres Strait Islander Corporal Mary Ware, a member of Charlie Company in 51 FNQR, says: 'I joined up the Reserves in 1997, and since June 2004 I've been on continuous full-time service … Basically, I haven't sort of gone anywhere beyond Australia, so I did a clerk course and I basically just run the orderly room on Thursday Island and Charlie Company.'[32] Patrick Puruntatameri, an artist from Melville Island, is another example of a NORFORCE member who had a troubled alcoholic past. He re-evaluated his life, gave up the grog and prioritised his art practice and also joined NORFORCE. Describing his pride, Patrick states: 'When I got my uniform here, I think everyone all look up to me. We got this bloke, he's protecting us … I sometimes feel proud of myself because when I'm talking to people and I'm telling them stories and they really enjoy my story, and it makes me feel really good.'[33]

Two themes permeate many RFSU members' testimonies: the sense of colourblind mateship and the RFSUs representing a continuation of traditions. Torres Strait Islander Private Nathaniel Tyson of Charlie Company remarks: 'Being in the Army Reserve, particularly with Charlie Company, there's a bond of brotherhood that everyone knows each other and we sort of learn all together. We're all one mind, one heart, and one strength. That's what it's like and that's what I like about it.' Patrol Commander Chris Torenbeek similarly states: 'It's all working together as a big team because with the brotherhood that we have here and the mateship, I just really love it. All these boys that we have here in Charlie Company are real good soldiers, excellent. They know the sea, they know the land real well. We all grew up together and that mateship is real strong.'[34] James Wood of NORFORCE states: 'Once the uniform comes on, we're all just one colour and that's green. No matter what race you are – black or white, or even Indigenous – wherever they come from, we're all just one colour, just one brothers.'[35] The notion of there being no black or white but only green is an expression commonly used across the RFSUs. Referring to Aboriginal and Torres Strait Islander kinship patterns of 'skins', another expression is that in the RFSUs everyone is 'green skin', bringing together various non-Indigenous, Aboriginal and Torres Strait Islander mobs.

Like many Aboriginal and Torres Strait Islander service personnel in other parts of the ADF, the idea of continuing traditions of family service also permeates the members' reasons for joining. Torres Strait Islander Lance Corporal Eccles Newie of Charlie Company, 51 FNQR, states: 'I've been in the unit for eight years now. My mum's brother was in the army, so was his dad. And I have older brothers that was in the army when I was still in school that wanted me to join … They were happy for me, like me joining up, but they always worry about me when I go out.'[36] James Wood of NORFORCE comments: 'I'm a modern warrior but I keep my traditional values: self-esteem, more independence, confidence, making yourself a better person.'[37] Summarising the sense of pride and links between community and the RFSUs, Private Nathaniel Tyson of 51 FNQR states: 'Being in the RFSU, I feel really proud because I'm giving something back to the community, a sense of service, and also doing something to sort of honour our forefathers because they've paved the way for us and in a way we're giving thanks and doing our part in the army as well in defence.'[38]

Changing roles of RFSUs

NORFORCE and 51 FNQR foster historical links with earlier units in their areas of operation. In the case of the latter, the original 51st Battalion was raised in 1916 as part of the 1st AIF, with the 'Far North' identification coming in 1936 when a part-time unit was raised at Cairns. NORFORCE traces its antecedents to the 2/1st NAOU (or 'the Nackeroos'), which was tasked with similar surveillance and reconnaissance tasks when Japan appeared to threaten northern Australia during the Second World War. NORFORCE's historian

A changing defence force and Reconciliation

spends considerable time discussing the Nackeroos, their heritage and the precedent they set for NORFORCE, and this link between the Nackeroos and NORFORCE forms part of the popular discourse surrounding the two units. NORFORCE has even adopted the colours of the NAOU as its own. Thus Rachael Maza, introducing a documentary on NORFORCE airing on *Message Stick* on ABC television in 2004, stated: 'NORFORCE is the army that looks after our northern borders, and its history stems from the original "Nackeroos" of World War II, a community of army forces and Indigenous communities working together to protect our coastlines.'[39] Drawing the historical connections is meant to emphasise the participation of a range of Aboriginal peoples, as well as to position NORFORCE as part of a longer tradition of Top End Aboriginal defence.

Over time the original role or set of roles of the RFSUs has been modified, which is scarcely surprising as the ADF as a whole has grappled with Middle Eastern commitments, peacekeeping initiatives – most famously INTERFET in East Timor – border protection and, controversially, the Northern Territory Intervention in 2007–08. Border protection, including the detection of so-called suspected illegal or irregular entry vessels (SIEVs), developed significantly as a political issue during the last two terms of the Howard government (2001–07). For the ADF this became Operation Resolute in July 2006. With the establishment of Border Protection Command later in 2006, NORFORCE and the Pilbara Regiment became part of the effort to detain and/or deter such vessels and their human cargo. Such roles continued under the Abbott government's Operation Sovereign Borders, although the army plays only a small part in this ongoing program, which is chiefly conducted by the navy and Australian Border Force (previously Customs).[40] Even so, monitoring for unauthorised boat arrivals and drug smugglers is central to the RFSUs' mission today.

In June 2007 Prime Minister Howard initiated the Northern Territory Intervention. The army had a major role in the early stages of this program under the title of Operation Outreach. A recent historian of the Australian Army describes the Intervention as 'an attempt to break the cycle of violence and abuse against Aboriginal children'. Although those are the stated aims, there are significant debates over the politics of the Intervention, including questions about it serving as a wedge issue in the 2007 election or as an attempt to reimpose assimilation in remote Aboriginal communities. Though the same historian described the army as the 'most trusted national institution', many opponents of the Intervention regarded the deployment of the army into remote Aboriginal communities as a politicisation of the ADF role.[41] It was possibly inevitable that NORFORCE (with some members from the Pilbara Regiment) was used extensively during the Intervention to win the trust of Aboriginal Elders to implement medical, logistical and communications measures.[42] NORFORCE supplied 400 of the 600-plus defence force personnel, their assignments ranging from support of the Child Health Check teams to installing new police stations. In these tasks NORFORCE appears to have been successful, primarily because of the goodwill remote Aboriginal communities already felt for the unit. Operation Outreach ceased in late 2008, though the Intervention as a whole was maintained by the new Labor government. NORFORCE escaped the criticism some have made of the Intervention and its perceived failures, with the new Labor minister for defence science and personnel claiming in 2008 that the 'role of the indigenous soldiers of Norforce in the implementation of the operation was critical to its success'.[43]

The ADF has recognised the success of the RFSUs not only for their contributions to Australia's defence, but also for their positive impact on education and employment in remote Aboriginal and Torres Strait Islander communities. It also realised that there were many young men and women with potential to join the RFSUs but who did not have minimum education requirements. Consequently, in 2009, the Australian Army piloted a bridging course to help up to 20 Aboriginal men meet the minimum entrance requirements for NORFORCE.

A changing defence force and Reconciliation

The seven-month course introduces recruits to the army and also includes training in basic literacy, numeracy and first aid. It also inculcates important skills such as endurance, problem solving and commitment. Passing the course gives graduates a Certificate II in Adult Education and Rural Operations and may lead to entry into NORFORCE. While some of the men wanted to join NORFORCE, others wanted to apply their new skills in other ways in their home communities. For instance, Leon Gumbala said that he 'could be a bookkeeper or manager, police aide, teacher'.[44] Nineteen-year-old recruit Anthony Baker certainly improved his self-esteem through participating in the course, stating: 'All my mates and all my relations look up to me now and even older people, they see me walk past, and say g'day to you and they ask you, "Are you in NORFORCE?" and you're proud to say you are.'[45]

Another important outcome of the bridging course is the mentoring role that recruits play for young people. Anthony's father, Frazer Baker, remarks: 'Coming back to community as a young man hopefully it will change other young people in the community, more or less look for a different goal in life, because there's not much opportunities out there.' Anthony states: 'You show up in a uniform, and to see a difference in a community where all the young people want to join up. I tell them to give it a go and tell them it's what you need.' As of 2010, the pilot program was scheduled to expand to recruit Indigenous women as well.[46] Such an initiative, in conjunction with the continuing good work of the RFSUs, shows just how effective the ADF has been in promoting Reconciliation at the grassroots level since before it was on the national agenda. It is perhaps surprising the ADF's activities are not better known generally, not because they make a good story but because they are important.

A changing defence force

The creation and evolution of the RFSUs was one manifestation of wider shifts in the operation of the ADF; by the 1990s, with the end of the Cold War, there was a growing recognition that Australia's defence needs and strategic circumstances were changing. The ADF had already been involved in peacekeeping operations since the end of the Second World War, and through the course of the 1990s, peacekeeping within international coalitions would become even more common. Though the numbers of Australian troops sent into these conflict zones were smaller than in previous conflicts such as Vietnam, still Aboriginal and Torres Strait Islander men and women were among the ranks. In the 1990s three conflicts stood out, and three ex-servicemen relate their roles and perspectives.

Gulf War, 1990–91

On 2 August 1990 the Iraqi Army under direction of President Saddam Hussein invaded neighbouring Kuwait. Within days there was a condemnatory United Nations Security Council resolution, followed shortly by a United States–led coalition sent to protect Saudi Arabia and blockade Iraq in the Persian Gulf. Australian forces were among the first to join the coalition. Between August 1990 and January 1991, coalition forces were on standby in the Gulf region. A new Security Council resolution gave 15 January 1991 as a deadline for Iraqi forces to withdraw from Kuwait. On 17 January, with the deadline passed, coalition forces began an aerial bombardment of Iraqi targets, driving most of the forces out of Kuwait within a matter of days. On 24 February 1991 ground troops began an assault on remaining Iraqi positions in Kuwait as well as within Iraq. Within two days Iraqi forces finally withdrew from Kuwait and on 28 February the coalition declared both a ceasefire and a victory.

Australia provided approximately 1800 of the 40,000 troops drawn from 30 nations. Though Australia despatched members of all three services, the RAN played the largest role. It sent two frigates, two replenishment ships and four warships: HMAS *Sydney* (IV), HMAS *Adelaide*, HMAS *Brisbane* and HMAS *Darwin*. The warships were responsible for providing anti-aircraft protection for carrier battle groups of the US

A changing defence force and Reconciliation

Navy.[47] Serving on board HMAS *Sydney* was Gumbaynggirr sailor Neil Macdonald, who had joined the navy in 1988 for the opportunity it provided him to learn a trade in electronics. He worked with the naval-combat data systems, essentially maintaining the weapons systems. The *Sydney* was in Hawai'i at the time of the invasion of Kuwait, and it was quickly sent back to Australia and then deployed to the Middle East. Macdonald remembers lots of waiting at sea in the 48 days before the January 1991 war began. His vessel was responsible for protecting oil platforms and performing other tasks assigned by the Americans.[48]

Popular memory of the Gulf War often focuses on the psychological impacts of the months of waiting for the war to begin. Macdonald and the Australian sailors, too, had to cope with the months of suspense and anticipation: 'You'd see the task force going up with the US Marines that were supposed to invade Kuwait, but they didn't … During the day, because of mines, the ship would go travel and be able to move, but at night all engines would be switched off and we'd float with the tide because you couldn't see the mines at night.' Macdonald remembers that the night before the war started, everyone knew, even though it was supposed to be a secret. Once it did start, the routine on HMAS *Sydney* changed little for Macdonald and his colleagues, as they continued to perform the tasks they had been doing for months. Remembering the end of the war, Macdonald comments: 'When the war ended, we came in for port at Dubai and we were having fun. You had drinks and all that over and done with. And then we went back to sea and it was just a real anti-climax. And then after that it was like, okay, what's going to happen next?'[49]

Though figures are unavailable for the total number of Indigenous Australians who served in the Gulf War, Macdonald believes that there were only about 30 Aboriginal and Torres Strait Islander service personnel. Given the relatively small overall deployment and that the majority of personnel were navy, this seems a reasonable estimate. Indeed, the 1993 inquiry into the ethnic composition of the ADF reported only 44 Aboriginal or Torres Strait Islander members of the navy.[50] As mentioned in the previous chapter, Macdonald's identity as an Aboriginal man did sometimes cause tensions during his naval career, yet his testimony also suggests that little distinguished Aboriginal servicemen's and women's experience of the Gulf War from that of their non-Indigenous comrades.

Somalia, 1992–94

In July 1992 the United Nations authorised peacekeepers to enter wartorn Somalia to monitor a ceasefire between rival militias. In November the United States agreed to join these peacekeepers, who were providing support to humanitarian relief agencies unable to distribute food free from harassment. Australia sent 990 personnel mostly from infantry (1RAR), but also from engineers, signals and intelligence. Based at Baidoa, west of Mogadishu, the Australian contingent's responsibilities were to secure Baidoa, to protect distribution of aid and to disarm aggressive local groups. After the United Nations mission changed from protecting food distribution to nation-building, 1RAR was withdrawn from Baidoa in May 1993 and returned to Australia. A small Australian Movement Control Unit remained in Somalia. After the American 'Black Hawk Down' incident in October 1993, most countries withdrew from Somalia, but Australia's small force remained and even received support from the SAS from April 1994. Australia withdrew its final troops in November 1994.[51]

Among those infantry troops who served with 1RAR was Torres Strait Islander Chris Townson. Townson remembers the shock of arriving in Mogadishu and then immediately being flown to Baidoa, where the Australians had recently relieved French troops. Describing their work, Townson states: 'We'd get deployed out and provide security for other communities or villages so that they'd get their food … You've only got a platoon, which is about 30 men, and you have about a couple of hundred people. When they storm and rush to get, when they see the food, that's what we'd deliver.' Townson's unit also went on regular patrols, which were challenging given the hot weather conditions and the heavy gear that the men had to wear and carry. He remembers that as early as his first patrol, there was a recurring putrid stench. By the time the patrol returned to base, they realised what it was: 'What had happened was that this ground, they just shoved a body and they just threw rocks over the body, and they didn't cover everything. You might have an arm coming out or a leg; the locals just weep. They're just rotten, they're dead. We were sitting on these things. We'd probably been soiled with dead people. That's the smell. I'll never forget that smell; it was bad.'[52]

In addition to the difficult conditions and the language and cultural barriers, patrols faced real danger from Somali bandits. On one occasion Townson's armoured patrol vehicle narrowly missed an anti-armour round, similar to what are now known as improvised explosive devices (IEDs). On other occasions the patrols came across recently killed corpses, indicating that the enemy was nearby. In one situation Townson encountered a hostile and nearly killed him during the engagement, and this incident had a profound psychological impact on him. He suffered post-traumatic stress disorder upon his return to Australia. He drank heavily and had tendencies towards violence, and he noticed similar problems among other Indigenous and non-Indigenous men who had served in Somalia. In October 1994 Townson left the army with a TPI (totally and permanently incapacitated) pension because of his post-traumatic stress disorder. Fortunately for him, about ten years later he found peace through returning to Torres Strait and undergoing traditional healing rituals. He remarks: 'I tried all that traditional medicine. It grows up there on the land; my father showed me this stuff. I take it in and listen. I know salt water's good for me and that's my culture. I would go down the rock pool and dip my body in there a couple of times, relax, come out. I told my boys that: "That's a medicine, mate. Because my blood's in you, you're gonna go in there."'[53]

Townson recalls serving with at least one other Torres Strait Islander in Somalia, as well as knowing of other Aboriginal and Torres Strait Islander men who served there. Like Macdonald's testimonies about the Gulf War there is little distinction between the Indigenous and non-Indigenous experience in the active field of operations. Even so, Townson's Somalia and post-Somalia experiences show ways that Torres Strait Islander service personnel may find their cultural connections to be a source of healing from the trauma they witnessed overseas as peacekeepers.

INTERFET (East Timor), 1999

Arguably Australia's most high-profile military engagement of the 1990s came at the end of the decade. Australian peacekeepers were despatched to East Timor in September 1999 as the leading component of INTERFET. Following the overwhelming success of an independence referendum on 30 August 1999, Timorese anti-independence militias instigated violence that consumed the country. A United Nations Security Council resolution authorised the formation of INTERFET under the leadership of Australian Major General Peter Cosgrove, and the first Australians landed in East Timor on 20 September 1999. INTERFET's mission was to secure control of East Timor's infrastructure, then the capital Dili, and to extend security to other parts of East Timor while patrolling to ensure that militia violence stopped. There were few active engagements, and INTERFET formally ended in February 2000 when Australia handed over the operation to the United Nations. Though Australian troops have gradually reduced in number since East Timor was formally recognised as an independent nation in 2002, some Australian peacekeepers are still present. At its peak in November 1999, about 5700 Australians were serving in East Timor out of the 11,000-strong, 22-nation coalition.[54]

Among the Australians who arrived on day one in East Timor was 22-year-old Quandamooka and Noonuccal soldier Steve Maloney, who had been serving in the Army Reserve since he was 17 and the regular army since he was 19. Maloney served in the Signals Corps as an operator of information systems and radios. In 1997 he was deployed to Cambodia for a Service Assisted Evacuation, meaning the evacuation of

A changing defence force and Reconciliation

Australian and Canadian nationals from the Australian Embassy, due to the civil war. Maloney's deployment in East Timor was longer, lasting from the very beginning of INTERFET in September 1999 until a few weeks before the United Nations took over in February 2000. Maloney vividly remembers arriving in the country that had been torn apart by 25 years of occupation: 'This is day one; it's kind of like after the scene of the crime. You could always smell the fires in the air – that nasal smell where you've got that heavy stench. It's hot, humid and sticky, and there's always an orange haze, the thickness of the smoke in your lungs and that dense air you're breathing in all the time.'[55]

Though Maloney travelled to different parts of East Timor, his unit was not on regular patrols; rather, it was based at the heliport and was known as the 'Response Force', being the first to respond to any incidents. Many of Maloney's memories of East Timor are of the Timorese people, and particularly of seeing the scars of the trauma they had lived through while they tried to rebuild their lives. He reflects: 'There were also a lot of internally displaced people. Up and down the roads there were thousands of families without homes. Sometimes you would see children who didn't appear to have parents. We sometimes collected all the candy and chocolates from our ration packs and then threw them out of the back of vehicles when we drove around Dili and into the mountains. The children were happy with this gesture.'[56] Maloney is proud of his service in East Timor and the role Australia played both protecting the Timorese people and helping to rebuild.

Though Maloney did not engage in active combat while in East Timor, he still found it to be a confronting experience. This is not dissimilar from other soldiers who served there, as trauma can also come from seeing the aftermath of violence. When he returned from East Timor, Maloney requested a discharge from the army because, as he states: 'I didn't want to see any more destruction and death. I really couldn't face it anymore. I had experienced first-hand the depth of what conflict can bring out in humanity … there was no future in just going from war zone to war zone for the rest of your life.' Maloney's comments reflect the challenges confronting the ADF's increasing role in peacekeeping missions in the post–Cold War era. Service personnel train to protect themselves and others, but it is not just the battlefield that can mentally wound. Maloney remarks: 'It's taken me perhaps, I'd say, a good ten years to understand what I went through and I think that I'm only now picking up the pieces, in the last couple of years and especially after I received my first degree.'[57]

Maloney's manner of coping with the distressing sights he saw in East Timor – including mass graves – has been through education. He has completed an arts degree majoring in peace and conflict studies at the University of Queensland and is also completing a Bachelor of Laws. Peace and conflict studies have helped Maloney to put his own personal experiences in Cambodia and East Timor into a wider historical and geopolitical context. He is also interested in Aboriginal and Torres Strait Islander politics and legal issues, particularly the movement to reform the Australian Constitution to recognise Indigenous Australians. Reflecting on his time in the army and the changing dynamics of defence at the turn of the century, Maloney states: 'I'd like to think the army's evolving and getting better. Nobody ever looks at the military and believes they were bigger than the military, not even a general. The army is a larger institution than any one individual, and I hope it's adapting to the twenty-first century.'[58]

Aboriginal and Torres Strait Islander men and women also served as part of Australia's commitment in Iraq (2003–09; 2015–present) and Afghanistan (2001–14), but none were available for interviews for this book.

Defence and Reconciliation

Changes to the ADF in the 1990s occurred not only as a result of the 1987 white paper or post–Cold War geopolitics. By the 1990s Australians had

A changing defence force and Reconciliation

undergone massive shifts in attitudes towards gender, sexuality, multi-culturalism and, for our purposes, race and Indigenous Australians.[59] Though practical efforts to work with remote Indigenous communities had already been ongoing since the 1980s, in the 1990s the Department of Defence and the ADF implemented policy changes to address the position of Aboriginal and Torres Strait Islander personnel in regular units and across the department. In 1993, at the request of the minister for defence science and personnel, the ADF commissioned the Australian Defence Studies Centre at the Australian Defence Force Academy to investigate ethnic participation in the ADF, focusing on people from non-English speaking backgrounds and Aboriginal and Torres Strait Islander people. The report was the first Defence-commissioned investigation into race and ethnicity and also represented the first opportunity to examine the current situation for Aboriginal and Torres Strait Islander service personnel.

The report found that on one hand some of the military norms clashed with Aboriginal and Torres Strait Islander traditions, including the emphasis on discipline, punctuality and separation from kin for large periods of time. On the other hand, though, the report identified the pride that Aboriginal and Torres Strait Islander communities had in their previous military service, particularly in the Second World War, and noted that as a result there was strong support for the ADF among Indigenous communities. Aboriginal and Torres Strait Islander people were under-represented within the air force and navy but slightly over-represented within the army. This pattern was a continuation of the long history since the First and Second World Wars of Indigenous Australians being more likely to join the army. While their numbers were relatively strong in the army, even there they were 'severely under-represented' among officer ranks. The report did not suggest any discriminatory barriers to Indigenous Australians becoming officers, but rather emphasised that their lower education levels were a major factor. Approximately 21 per cent of Aboriginal and Torres Strait Islander enlistees had a post–secondary school qualification upon enlistment, the majority being trade qualifications. After joining, only a small number of Indigenous recruits took advantage of qualification opportunities within the ADF, increasing the percentage with qualifications to 34 per cent.[60] While there has been some increase in the number of Aboriginal and Torres Strait Islander officers over the last 20 years, still they are under-represented. Retired Aboriginal officer Jo West, formerly a major, considers that this ongoing under-representation is due not so much to racial discrimination but to 'a factor of people not getting … enough talent getting to the start line and then showing to get that. So it's an Australian issue, not a Defence issue.'[61]

The core of the report focused on ways that the ADF could alter its recruitment practices to create a defence force more reflective of multicultural Australia. The report identified recruitment barriers including literacy skills, possible cultural biases within psychological tests, and height and weight requirements that may also unintentionally discriminate against particular ethnic groups. For all obstacles, the report recommended proactive steps to educate recruiters about cultural diversity, as well as to target and work with Indigenous communities. This meant, for instance, providing information about education programs to help applicants who did not meet literacy requirements, as well as to support recruits' families who did not have high literacy levels. Working with Indigenous communities could have the snowball effect of informing more potential candidates about ADF employment opportunities, bringing in more qualified individuals. The report even advocated establishing an Aboriginal and Torres Strait Islander recruitment cell in Townsville, if possible staffed by an Indigenous person. Setting targets, as distinct from quotas, would encourage the ADF to follow through on its commitment to recruitment diversity. The report also recommended that, for the first time, the ADF recruitment process capture data that included both the applicants' parents' country of birth and whether or not the recruit was Aboriginal or Torres Strait Islander.[62]

A changing defence force and Reconciliation

The ALP government welcomed the report's findings, with the minister for defence science and personnel, Senator John Faulkner, describing them as proof that 'on the whole, the recruiting process appeared free of discrimination on the basis of either race or culture'.[63]

Faulkner gave a vague commitment to increasing diversity in the ADF, without promising to implement any of the report's specific findings. In the short term, while there were reforms to data collection and some of the testing regimes in the recruitment process, there was little action on the recommendations for targeted recruitment of Indigenous Australians. Even so, in the 20-plus years since that report, there has been a gradual implementation of programs and initiatives akin to what was recommended in 1993. In 1996 the ADF launched its first Aboriginal and Torres Strait Islander recruiting strategy, sending Aboriginal service personnel to regional and remote communities to advise Indigenous youth about defence employment possibilities.[64] The Department of Defence launched its first Reconciliation Action Plan in 2007; its 2010–14 plan pledged that 'Defence will be genuinely committed to a broadened membership base and actively involved in realising strategies that encourage and foster Indigenous participation and potential'.[65] In 2008 the Department of Defence established a Defence Directorate of Indigenous Affairs as part of its Indigenous Employment Strategy. The directorate's job is to work with Indigenous communities and to provide advice on Defence Indigenous personnel and policy matters. The Indigenous Employment Strategy also promises: 'Each Commanding Officer has the responsibility to ensure that his/her personnel have access to an environment that is genuinely committed to diversity in the workplace and accepts the differences that set each person apart from the next.'[66]

Like the bridging course for entry into NORFORCE, the ADF has established pre-entry courses for Indigenous Australians across the country to assist them to meet ADF entry requirements. In 2009 the ADF partnered with TAFE South Western Sydney Institute to deliver the Indigenous Pre-Recruitment Course (IPRC) to eligible Aboriginal and Torres Strait Islander people aged between 17 and 54. The six-week course runs across six months, combining intensive week-long residential schools with other study in between. The emphasis of the course is on improving candidates' fitness, and their literacy and numeracy skills so that they can meet the required year-ten literacy, numeracy and science standards. Now the IPRC works with the Australian Army's 9th Brigade to introduce participants to the basic drill instruction, military norms, culture and discipline required to succeed in the ADF, while also embedding Aboriginal and Torres Strait Islander culture within the curriculum. The course does not guarantee participants a position within the ADF, but it has been successful at recruiting Aboriginal and Torres Strait Islander men and women since 2009. The ADF has run the IPRC in sites across Australia including Sydney, Tasmania, the Torres Strait, Adelaide, Cairns and Western Australia.[67] One recent graduate, Tylisha Pitt, describes the commonalities between military and Indigenous cultures: 'There's a sense of family and the need to be loyal to one another. For our people, being through the struggles of the past, family keeps us together. It's exactly the same with the military.'[68] The Department of Defence also has expanded the five-month intensive NORFORCE bridging course to other parts of Australia as the Defence Indigenous Development Program (DIDP).[69]

Other initiatives to increase Indigenous employment have come from within the specific branches of the ADF. The army, for instance, now employs eight Indigenous recruitment officers across Australia, as well as two Indigenous mentors stationed at Kapooka to help recruits through basic training. In 2012 the RAAF appointed Harry Allie as its inaugural Air Force Indigenous Elder, representing the air force at functions and playing a role in recruitment and mentoring of Indigenous RAAF recruits. The army followed suit in April 2015, appointing Roy Mundine its inaugural Indigenous Elder. In 2012 the RAAF inaugurated its own RAAF Indigenous Youth Program, introducing small groups of years 10–12 Aboriginal and Torres Strait Islander students to the different trades and other opportunities available through a career in the RAAF. In 2014 the navy ran its own DIDP in Cairns, with 23 Indigenous men and women graduating, most of whom will pursue careers in the RAN. Recruit Allan Anderson said of the program: 'When we went to *Cerberus* we were given a glimpse at what is to come in our future training, but with the last five months in the Defence Indigenous Development Program I feel like I am ready to take on the challenge.'[70]

Besides looking to bring Indigenous Australians into the armed forces as members, the ADF has also contributed to Reconciliation through partnerships with Indigenous Australian communities, particularly in remote Australia. For instance, when the Australian Army runs its 'Survival School' to prepare members to live in harsh bush conditions without rations or gear, Aboriginal women from remote communities teach participants about bush tucker, bush medicine and hunting and gutting wild turtles.[71] In September 2012 RAN crew members of the HMAS *Warramunga* spent a week with the Warramunga people of Tennant Creek, 500 kilometres north of Alice Springs in the Northern Territory. The intent of the visit was to strengthen ties between the two groups sharing the same name, while allowing the navy members to learn more about Aboriginal culture. Sailors visited the local primary school to learn about bush tucker from the children, played a friendly Australian Rules football match against the local team, travelled up-country, shared stories and feasted with the locals. Both the sailors and the traditional owners found it a valuable experience, with one of the latter, Anthony Crafter, remarking: 'that's the way we show respect – by teaching them about land stuff'.[72]

In another example of communities welcoming ADF members, soldiers from 9th Battalion, the Royal Queensland Regiment, travelled on a 117-kilometre trek with 37 Indigenous teenagers to commemorate a group of Aboriginal people forcibly removed to Cherbourg in 1905. Along the walk, soldiers learned from Cherbourg Elders about their culture and history while also organising training exercises for the young people. The Army Aboriginal Community Assistance Program, a joint project supported by the army and the Department of Prime Minister and Cabinet, has visited remote communities since 1997. It has undertaken engineering projects, such as construction of infrastructure, and health and training initiatives to improve living standards in remote communities.[73] These are just some of the ways in which the ADF has taken an active role promoting better understanding between Indigenous and non-Indigenous Australians – the very central message of the Reconciliation process.

Efforts within the ADF to include more Aboriginal and Torres Strait Islander service personnel – whether through RFSUs or in regular units – have mirrored growing interest in Reconciliation across Australia. As this book has demonstrated, it is not that Indigenous membership in the ADF is new per se, as it has been going on throughout the post–Second World War era and indeed as far back as the Boer War. What has changed, though, is the role of Aboriginal and Torres Strait Islander personnel, whether because of changing defence missions overseas or because of Indigenous-specific initiatives within the ADF. What is remarkable about the ADF is not the number of programs it has that promote Aboriginal and Torres Strait Islander participation. Rather, what is remarkable is how successful these programs have been at providing training, education and employment within the ADF. Indigenous service in the ADF has been hailed as an example of bridge-building and of the successful use of local skills and knowledge.

EPILOGUE

COMMEMORATING INDIGENOUS SERVICE

> ... after 1945, as nearly always after 1918, any Aboriginal name on a [war memorial] pedestal could be identified only by somebody who was looking for it.[1]
>
> – Ken Inglis

The centenary of the First World War includes public commemorations of Aboriginal and Torres Strait Islander military service, of which the play *Black Diggers*, discussed in the preface, forms a part. Much of the impetus for remembrance has come from Indigenous veterans themselves. The first effort at organising an Indigenous veterans' group was in the 1980s. The short-lived Victorian-based National Aboriginal and Islander Ex-Services Association wanted to organise a group of Aboriginal veterans to participate in the Anzac Day march. The group met vocal opposition from Victorian RSL President Bruce Ruxton on the grounds that if they were permitted to march, then soon other 'special' interest groups such as lesbian and gay service personnel would want to march. In 1985 the group planned its own march through the Melbourne suburb of Northcote; about 15 Koorie veterans and another 15 European supporters participated in the march, while a festival followed. The organisers determined that the march was not sustainable because in Victoria most veterans were older, and most Aboriginal veterans were content to participate with their units in the larger Melbourne Anzac Day march. The National Aboriginal and Islander Ex-Services Association also staged an Aboriginal Memorial Service at the Shrine of

Remembrance during NAIDOC Week in 1985. The service included the raising of the Aboriginal flag (much to the dismay and disapproval of Bruce Ruxton). A small contingent of representatives of the three services, including retired generals, attended the service, as well as a handful of Koorie ex-servicemen and women.[2] In 1993 as well, a group of about 50 Aboriginal people under the leadership of the Kombumerri Aboriginal group led the Gold Coast Anzac Day march. Among the marchers were Oodgeroo Noonuccal and the widow of Captain Reg Saunders.[3] Although the NAIDOC service and Anzac Day marches did not become annual events, they were a preview of Indigenous ex-service commemorations to come.

By the new century, new groups of ex-service personnel were emerging in the major capital cities. In 2000 the recently formed WA Aboriginal and Torres Strait Islander Veterans and Services Association approached the Western Australian RSL for permission to march as a contingent in Perth's Anzac Day march. As the Victorian Aboriginal group had found over a decade earlier, traditionally Anzac Day contingents were for military units only. In the end the Western Australian RSL not only supported the Aboriginal organisation, but also invited them to lead Perth's 2001 Anzac Day parade. The contingent of about 90 received loud applause, and this was the first time an Aboriginal or Torres Strait Islander group led an Anzac Day march in a capital city. Aboriginal Vietnam veteran and group organiser Phil Prosser stated: 'It is quite important for the indigenous people of Australia to be able to go public and show that we did actually represent our people and the whole of Australia.'[4] In 2007 members of the Aboriginal community in Redfern, Sydney, organised the first annual Coloured Diggers March on Anzac Day. At least 300 people turned out for it; since then its popularity has grown, drawing local politicians and culminating in a commemorative ceremony and festival at a park in Redfern.[5] This is held in the afternoon so that ex-service personnel can also join their units in the large Sydney Anzac Day march. The Australian War Memorial, too, now hosts an Anzac Day ceremony to commemorate Aboriginal and Torres Strait Islander service just after the main Dawn Service. The Aboriginal and Torres Strait Islander Veterans and Services Association of Australia has held the ceremony since 2004 at the Aboriginal Memorial plaque on Mount Ainslie, behind the Australian War Memorial.[6] These high-profile Anzac Day commemorations complement smaller services undertaken in Aboriginal and Torres Strait Islander communities across Australia.

Commemorations have also expanded beyond just Anzac Day, particularly to National Reconciliation Week in May/June and NAIDOC Week in July. In 2006, at the encouragement of Koorie Elder Aunty Dot Peters, the Victorian RSL organised a commemorative service at Melbourne's Shrine of Remembrance during National Reconciliation Week. Supporting this initiative, in 2007 the Department of Veterans' Affairs began sponsoring similar services in the other Australian capitals except Hobart and Darwin. NAIDOC Week services honouring Indigenous military participation have been held sporadically since the 1990s, and in 2014 the NAIDOC Week theme was 'Serving Country: Centenary & Beyond'.[7] Grassroots organisations also coordinate commemorative services, the best example being the Perth-based Honouring Indigenous War Graves, founded in 2003. The founder and president, Aboriginal Vietnam veteran John Schnaars, describes the organisation's work: 'We look at working with the families of Indigenous veterans to put a war grave – or a headstone on their grave if they haven't got one – and also to do a ceremony and that if somebody has got a headstone on, we'll still do a ceremony to get some closure for the families – healing.'[8] Honouring Indigenous War Graves performs about a dozen ceremonies each year, primarily in Western Australia, and also marches as a contingent in Perth every Anzac Day.

There has also been a new surge in memorials dedicated to Aboriginal and Torres Strait Islander service. As historian Ken Inglis documents comprehensively, war memorials to all military conflicts and various particular units or public figures dot the Australian landscape; until recently none were dedicated to Aboriginal and Torres Strait Islander service. Some early examples in Indigenous communities include the Narungga War Memorial in Point Pearce, South Australia (1999), and a Thursday Island memorial dedicated to the TSLI (2001). One intriguing example is the 2000 Anzac Day rededication of a memorial, originally constructed in 1937, commemorating Cape Barren Islanders from Tasmania who served in the First World War.[9] The planning and construction of Indigenous war memorials in major capital cities have received more attention, though. Canberra's memorial to Aboriginal and Torres Strait Islander service, at Mount Ainslie, is a simple brass plaque affixed to a stone. It was originally constructed by private citizens in 1988, and it was not until the late 1990s that Canberra's Indigenous community embraced it as a site of significance. The Australian War Memorial has also embraced the Mount Ainslie site since its refurbishment in 2004, even hosting the abovementioned Anzac Day and National Reconciliation Week ceremonies there.[10]

The first state capital city to complete a memorial to Aboriginal and Torres Strait Islander military service was Adelaide in November 2013. The construction of the memorial followed years of lobbying and fundraising with the support of the South Australian state government and South Australian branch of the RSL. At the dedication ceremony, Frank Lampard, the deputy chair of the Aboriginal and Torres Strait Islander War Memorial Committee, delivered an impassioned speech in which he declared, to resounding applause: 'I'm proud to say that lack of recognition ends today!'[11] In Sydney, the Coloured Diggers Project had lobbied for a memorial to Aboriginal and Torres Strait Islander military service since at least 2008. The City of Sydney eventually agreed to the proposition and held a competition to design a commemorative artwork. The sculpture was completed and dedicated before Anzac Day 2015.[12] These initiatives, and ongoing pushes for similar memorials in other major urban centres, including on Anzac Parade in Canberra, demonstrate both the twenty-first century's growing call for recognition of Indigenous service history and the receptiveness of non-Indigenous Australia to honour those voices.

Recognising and commemorating the experiences of Aboriginal and Torres Strait Islander servicemen and women widens our understanding of Australian military history. It also helps us to understand how Australians have constructed their national identity across the twentieth century and the position of Indigenous people within that identity. James Wood, member of NORFORCE, effectively encapsulates the significance of Indigenous military service: 'First World War, Second World War, Vietnam, Korea – Indigenous soldiers were there, and it's good because we're defending our country, which has always been our country.'[13]

ACKNOWLEDGEMENTS

Conducting the research, drawing out the key themes and putting this book together was no easy task, and many people have helped along the way. First and foremost we must thank all of the interview participants from across Australia, who were generous to share their time and life stories with us. The history of Aboriginal and Torres Strait Islander military service is not just about facts, figures and events, but about people. Those people have contributed to the defence of their kin and country, continuing a long tradition going back thousands of years.

Several colleagues read and commented on portions of this manuscript and other research over the years: Shurlee Swain, Nell Musgrove, Maggie Nolan, Ellen Warne, Patty O'Brien, Bart Ziino, Melissa Bellanta, Hannah Forsyth and Cath Bishop. Over the course of the project we employed several research assistants, who provided valuable help both editing interview transcriptions and conducting archival research: Sari Braithwaite, Christin Quirk, Kirstie Close-Barry and Rachael Lorenz-Stockdale. For providing critical cultural advice and connections with community, a very special thanks to the staff at Australian Catholic University's Jim-baa-yer Indigenous Unit, especially the former academic coordinator Naomi Wolfe.

Acknowledgements

Funding for this project came from several sources: an ARC Discovery grant (2011–13), Army History Research Grant (2010), the National Library of Australia (2010) and an Australian Catholic University Faculty of Arts and Sciences Early Career Research Incentive Award (2009). Australian Catholic University and the Australian Academy for the Humanities provided much-needed funds to subsidise the publication. We also thank the staff at University of Queensland Press, particularly Madonna Duffy, Cathy Vallance and Nikki Lusk, for their hard work on this book.

Finally, of course, thank you to our families and friends, who have supported us both over the years. They have endured our research trips, distractive nights typing away and endless babble about the people we have met. From Noah, thank you to the Riseman clan in the United States and the Smith clan in Melbourne, especially partner Michael. From Richard, thank you, as always, to Anne Marie and the steadily expanding family.

Source acknowledgements

Portions of chapter 1 about Reg Saunders were originally published in Noah Riseman, 'Aboriginal Military Service and Assimilation', *Aboriginal History*, 38, 2014, pp. 155–78, and is republished here with the permission of the *Aboriginal History* board.

Portions of chapter 3 were originally published in Noah Riseman, 'Equality in the Ranks: The lives of Aboriginal Vietnam veterans', *Journal of Australian Studies*, 36, no. 4, December 2012, pp. 411–26, reprinted by permission of the publisher (Taylor & Francis Ltd, tandfonline.com); and Noah Riseman, 'The Curious Case of Mervyn Eades: National service, discrimination and Aboriginal people', *Australian Journal of Politics and History*, 59, no. 1, 2013, pp. 64–80, *Australian Journal of Politics and History* © 2013 School of History, Philosophy, Religion and Classics, School of Political Science and International Studies, The University of

Queensland and Wiley Publishing Asia Pty Ltd.

Portions of chapter 4 were originally published in Noah Riseman, 'Escaping Assimilation's Grasp: Aboriginal women in the Australian women's military services', *Women's History Review*, 24, no. 5, 2015, pp. 757–75, reprinted by permission of the publisher (Taylor & Francis Ltd, tandfonline.com).

Portions of chapter 5 were originally published in Noah Riseman, 'Racism, Indigenous People and the Australian Armed Forces in the Post–Second World War Era', *History Australia*, 10, no. 2, 2013, pp. 159–79, reprinted by permission of the *History Australia* editors.

LIST OF ABBREVIATIONS

1RAR	1st Royal Australian Regiment
2RAR	2nd Royal Australian Regiment
3RAR	3rd Royal Australian Regiment
ABC	Australian Broadcasting Corporation
ADF	Australian Defence Force
AIF	Australian Imperial Force
ATSIC	Aboriginal and Torres Strait Islander Commission
AWAS	Australian Women's Army Service
AWM	Australian War Memorial
BCOF	British Commonwealth Occupation Force
CO	commanding officer
DIDP	Defence Indigenous Development Program
DLNS	Department of Labour and National Service
FCAATSI	Federal Council for the Advancement of Aborigines and Torres Strait Islanders
FNQR	Far North Queensland Regiment
HREOC	Human Rights and Equal Opportunity Commission
INTERFET	International Force for East Timor

IPRC	Indigenous Pre-Recruitment Course
IWM	Imperial War Museum
NAIDOC	National Aboriginal and Islander Day Observance Committee
NAOU	North Australian Observer Unit
NORFORCE	North West Mobile Force
NTSRU	Northern Territory Special Reconnaissance Unit
RAAF	Royal Australian Air Force
RAANC	Royal Australian Army Nursing Corps
RAN	Royal Australian Navy
RFSU	Regional Force Surveillance Unit
RSL	Returned and Services League
SAS	Special Air Service Regiment
TSLI	Torres Strait Light Infantry Battalion
WAAAF	Women's Auxiliary Australian Air Force
WRAAC	Women's Royal Australian Army Corps
WRAAF	Women's Royal Australian Air Force
WRANS	Women's Royal Australian Naval Service

NOTES

PREFACE

1   Gordon Briscoe, *Racial Folly: A twentieth century Aboriginal family*, ANU E Press and Aboriginal History Incorporated, Canberra, 2010, p. xxiv.
2   Heather Goodall, 'Too Early Yet or Not Soon Enough? Reflections on sharing histories as process', *Australian Historical Studies*, vol. 33, no. 118, 2002, p. 24.

INTRODUCTION

1   Noah Riseman, 'The Stolen Veteran: Institutionalisation, military service and the Stolen Generations', *Aboriginal History*, vol. 35, 2011, pp. 57–77; David Cook, interview with Noah Riseman, Raymond Terrace, NSW, 20 January 2010.
2   Jeff McCormack, interview with Noah Riseman, Monarto, SA, 9 July 2012.
3   Jeffrey Grey, *A Military History of Australia*, 3rd edn, Cambridge University Press, Melbourne, 2008; John Connor, *The Australian Frontier Wars: 1788–1838*, UNSW Press, Sydney, 2002; Henry Reynolds, *Forgotten War*, NewSouth Publishing, Sydney, 2013.
4   Matt Peacock, 'War Memorial Battle over Frontier Conflict Recognition', *The 7.30 Report*, Australian Broadcasting Corporation (ABC), 26 February 2009, abc.net.au/7.30/content/2009/s2502535.htm, accessed 22 August 2012; Ken Inglis, *Sacred Places: War memorials in the Australian landscape*, 3rd edn, Melbourne University Press, Melbourne, 2008, pp. 501–4.
5   Fiona Nicoll, 'War by Other Means? Sovereignty and the Aboriginal Tent Embassy', in Gary Foley, Andrew Schaap & Edwina Howell (eds), *The Aboriginal Tent Embassy: Sovereignty, black power, land rights and the state*, Routledge, Abingdon, 2014, pp. 267–83.
6   Henry Reynolds, *The Other Side of the Frontier: Aboriginal resistance to the European invasion of Australia*, 3rd edn, UNSW Press, Sydney, 2006; Henry Reynolds, *Fate of a Free People: The classic account of Tasmanian wars*, 2nd edn, Penguin, Melbourne, 2000; Connor, *The Australian Frontier Wars*.

7   Marcia Langton, 'They Made a Solitude and Called It Peace', in Rachel Perkins & Marcia Langton (eds), *First Australians: An illustrated history*, The Miegunyah Press, Melbourne, 2008, pp. 25–37; Howard Pederson & Banjo Woorunmarra, *Jandamarra & the Bunuba Resistance*, 3rd edn, Magabala Books, Broome, 2011.
8   John Maynard, '"Let Us Go" … It's a "Blackfellows' War": Aborigines and the Boer War', *Aboriginal History*, vol. 39, 2015, pp. 143–62.
9   Australia, *Defence Act* (as amended 1909), section 61(h).
10 Cited in Timothy Winegard, *Indigenous Peoples of the British Dominions and the First World War*, Cambridge University Press, Cambridge, 2012, p. 87.
11 Winegard, *Indigenous Peoples of the British Dominions and the First World War*, p. 230. See also Rod Pratt, 'Queensland's Aborigines in the First Australian Imperial Force', in P Whitney Lackenbauer, R Scott Sheffield & Craig Leslie Mantle (eds), *Aboriginal Peoples and Military Participation: Canadian & international perspectives*, Canadian Defence Academy Press, Kingston, ON, 2007, pp. 222–4.
12 Winegard, *Indigenous Peoples of the British Dominions and the First World War*, p. 237. See also pp. 135 and 212–5; Noah Riseman, 'Enduring Silences, Enduring Prejudices: Australian Aboriginal participation in the First World War', in David Monger, Katie Pickles & Sarah Murray (eds), *Endurance and the First World War: Experience and legacies in New Zealand and Australia*, Cambridge Scholars Publishing, Newcastle upon Tyne, 2014, pp. 178–95; Philippa Scarlett, *Aboriginal and Torres Strait Islander Volunteers for the AIF: The Indigenous response to World War One*, Indigenous Histories, Canberra, 2011, pp. 31–53; David Huggonson, 'The White Australia Ideal and Australia's Defence Policy', *Journal of the Royal Historical Society of Queensland*, vol. 17, no. 8, November 2000, pp. 373–9.
13 Pratt, 'Queensland's Aborigines in the First Australian Imperial Force', pp. 231–3; Winegard, *Indigenous Peoples of the British Dominions and the First World War*, pp. 248–9; David Huggonson, 'Aborigines and the Aftermath of the Great War', *Australian Aboriginal Studies*, vol. 11, no. 1, 1993, pp. 5–7; Simon Flagg & Sebastian Gurciullo (eds), *Footprints: The journey of Lucy and Percy Pepper*, National Archives of Australia (NAA) and Public Record Office of Victoria, Canberra, 2008, pp. 57–78; Doreen Kartinyeri, *Ngarrindjeri Anzacs*, Aboriginal Family History Project, South Australian Museum and Raukkan Council, Adelaide, 1996, pp. 30–1.
14 Memorandum from Comptroller, Department of Repatriation, Melbourne, to Department of Repatriation, Sydney, 12 April 1919, in series A2487, item 1919/3202, NAA, Canberra.

Notes

15 Throughout this book we use 'RSL' to refer to the organisation whose name has changed several times since its foundation in 1916 as the Returned Sailors and Soldiers Imperial League of Australia. Since 1990 it has been the Returned and Services League of Australia Limited.

16 Scarlett, *Aboriginal and Torres Strait Islander Volunteers for the AIF*, pp. 22–3, 61–9; Rod Pratt, '"By Cripes! I'll Fight for White Australia!": Queensland Aborigines in the First AIF', Thesis for Master of Literary Studies, University of Queensland, 1990, pp. 6–7, 60.

17 Prime Minister Robert G Menzies, to Secretary, Departments of the Army and Navy, 25 February 1940, in series A2671, item 45/1940, NAA, Canberra.

18 Robert Hall, *The Black Diggers: Aborigines and Torres Strait Islanders in the Second World War*, 2nd edn, Aboriginal Studies Press, Canberra, 1997, chapter 2 and p. 60.

19 Hall, *The Black Diggers*, chapter 3; Robert Hall, *Fighters from the Fringe: Aborigines and Torres Strait Islanders recall the Second World War*, Aboriginal Studies Press, Canberra, 1995, pp. 135–53, 173–91; Elizabeth Osborne, *Torres Strait Islander Women and the Pacific War*, Aboriginal Studies Press, Canberra, 1997, pp. 103–22.

20 Noah Riseman, *Defending Whose Country? Indigenous soldiers in the Pacific War*, University of Nebraska Press, Lincoln, 2012, chapters 1 and 2; Hall, *The Black Diggers*, pp. 85–99; Donald Thomson, *Donald Thomson in Arnhem Land*, revised edn, compiled and introduced by Nicolas Peterson, The Miegunyah Press, Melbourne, 2005, final chapter.

21 Hall, *The Black Diggers*, chapter 4; Hall, *Fighters from the Fringe*, pp. 61–133, 155–72; Alick Jackomos & Derek Fowell, *Forgotten Heroes: Aborigines at war from the Somme to Vietnam*, Victoria Press, Melbourne, 1993, pp. 13–63.

22 *No Bugles, No Drums*, produced by Debra Beattie-Burnett, directed by John Burnett, Seven Emus Productions in association with Australian Television Network, 49 mins, videocassette, 1990; Riseman, *Defending Whose Country?*, chapter 2; Hall, *The Black Diggers*, chapters 7 and 8; Ronald M Berndt & Catherine H Berndt, *End of an Era: Aboriginal labour in the Northern Territory*, Australian Institute of Aboriginal Studies, Canberra, 1987, chapter 8.

23 John Chesterman, *Civil Rights: How Indigenous Australians won formal equality*, University of Queensland Press, Brisbane, 2005, pp. 61, 125–34; Tamara Hunter, 'The Myth of Equality: The denial of citizenship rights for Aboriginal people in Western Australia', *Studies in Western Australian History*, vol. 22, 2001, pp. 76–80.

1 DEFENCE REFORMS AND OPPORTUNITIES: 1946–64

1 Len Ogilvie in 'Book Shines Light on Indigenous Soldiers', *Stateline WA*, 22 October 2010.
2 'Aboriginal Paratrooper: Australia's first', *Dawn*, vol. 1, no. 4, April 1952, p. 13.
3 *Dawn*, vol. 4, no. 3, March 1955, p. 1.
4 Anna Haebich, *Spinning the Dream: Assimilation in Australia, 1950–1970*, Fremantle Press, Perth, 2008, p. 12.
5 Russell McGregor, *Indifferent Inclusion: Aboriginal people and the Australian nation*, Aboriginal Studies Press, Canberra, 2011, pp. 50–4, 101–12; Rani Kerin, *Doctor Do-Good: Charles Duguid and Aboriginal advancement 1930s–1970s*, Australian Scholarly Publishing, North Melbourne, 2011, pp. 15–60; Haebich, *Spinning the Dream*, pp. 110–4; Morris Janowitz, 'Military Institutions and Citizenship in Western Societies', *Armed Forces and Society*, vol. 2, no. 2, 1976, pp. 185–204.
6 Grey, *A Military History of Australia*, pp. 201–3.
7 See Robin Gerster, *Travels in the Atomic Sunshine: Australia and the occupation of Japan*, Scribe, Melbourne, 2008.
8 Cited in Cameron Forbes, *The Korean War: Australia in the giants' playground*, Macmillan, Sydney, 2010, pp. 285–6.
9 Hall, *The Black Diggers*, p. 193; Robin Gerster, *Big-noting: The heroic theme in Australian war writing*, Melbourne University Press, Melbourne, 1987, p. 152.
10 Abala was of Khungarakung descent and was a pioneer rugby league player in Darwin. He was tragically killed while playing that game in 1956. See 'Steve Abala' at Monument Australia, monumentaustralia.org.au, accessed 6 April 2015.
11 Christine de Matos, 'A Very Gendered Occupation: Australian women as "conquerors" and "liberators"', *US–Japan Women's Journal*, vol. 33, 2007, pp. 87–107, found in University of Wollongong Research Online, ro.uow.edu.au/cgi/viewcontent.cgi?article=1186&context=artspapers, accessed 12 September 2015.
12 *The Sunday Times* (Perth), 17 March 1946, p. 4.
13 See, for example, the photograph of Ned Egglestone, an Aboriginal member of the Salvage Unit in the British Commonwealth Occupation Force (BCOF), AWM P01795.001, Australian War Memorial (AWM), Canberra.
14 'Ken Colbung', *Message Stick*, produced and directed by Kelrick Martin, produced by the ABC, 2004, abc.net.au/tv/messagestick/stories/s1070887.htm, accessed 27 January 2015. See also Private Kenneth Colbung, Royal Australian Infantry Corps, interviewed by Bill Bunbury for ABC Radio

Notes

National Hindsight for program 'Korea, 1950–1953, The Forgotten War', S01906, AWM, Canberra.

15 'EX-DX516', *The Daily News* (Perth), 22 March 1946, p. 5. Also see *The Daily News*, 5 April 1946, p. 5.
16 *The Daily News*, 26 March 1946, p. 6.
17 *The Advertiser* (Adelaide), 23 March 1946, p. 8.
18 *The Daily News*, 28 March 1946, p. 6. For more on postwar rehabilitation services, see Stuart Macintyre, *Australia's Boldest Experiment: War and reconstruction in the 1940s*, NewSouth Publishing, Sydney, 2015.
19 For an example of this, see the story of Arthur Farrell in *The Daily News*, 12 March 1947, p. 1. Farrell, ex–9th Division, 2nd AIF, qualified for BCOF through his service on Tarakan in 1945.
20 Lieutenant Colonel MH McArthur, Joint Secretary, Principal Administrative Officers Committee (Personnel), 29 August 1950, series A816, item 72/301/23, NAA, Canberra; Australian Military Forces Minute Paper, 'Enlistment of Aborigine in ARA', 20 May 1949, in series MP742/1, item 275/1/696, NAA, Melbourne.
21 'Enlistment of Aborigine in ARA', 20 May 1949.
22 Unsigned document, May 1949, in series MP742/1, item 275/1/696, NAA, Melbourne.
23 Memo from APA to Captain Esdailo, Navy Department, 19 May 1949, and memo from APA to Captain Costello, Air Force Department, 19 May 1949, in series MP742/1, item 275/1/696, NAA, Melbourne.
24 W Funnell, chair, War Manpower Resources and Planning Committee, 'Service of persons of non-British descent under the National Service Scheme', 21 May 1951, series A816, item 72/301/23, NAA, Canberra.
25 'Minute by Defence Committee at meeting held on Thursday, 7th September, 1950', in ibid.
26 *Defence Legislation Amendment Act 1992*, no. 91, 1992.
27 In May 1950 Australia sent air transports and bombers to Malaya. In 1955, after the end of the Korean War, they also sent ground troops. See Peter Dennis & Jeffrey Grey, *Emergency and Confrontation: Australian military operations, Malaya and Borneo, 1950–1966*, Allen & Unwin in association with the AWM, Sydney, 1996.
28 *The Argus* (Melbourne), 6 March 1956. See also the website of the Maryborough (Queensland) Military and Colonial Museum, maryborough-museum.org/malayan.html, accessed 27 January 2013. For a detailed account of this soldier's career, see garriehutchinson.com/2013/11/13/sgt-cecil-anderson-indigenous-soldier-in-three-wars/, accessed 8 February 2015.

29 For the Korean War generally, see Robert O'Neill, *Australia in the Korean War 1950–1953, volume 1, strategy and diplomacy*, AWM and the Australian Government Publishing Service, Canberra, 1981; *volume 2, combat operations*, AWM and the Australian Government Publishing Service, Canberra, 1985; Richard Trembath, *A Different Sort of War: Australians in Korea 1950–53*, Australian Scholarly Publishing, Melbourne, 2005. The bugle reference is taken from the title of a memoir of the Korean War: Jack Gallaway, *The Last Call of the Bugle: The long road to Kapyong*, University of Queensland Press, Brisbane, 1994.

30 Cedric 'Ned' Egglestone and Don McLeod, Royal Australian Infantry Corps, interviewed by Bill Bunbury, 3 September 1998, for the ABC Radio National *Hindsight* program 'Korea, 1950–1953, The Forgotten War', S01907, AWM, Canberra; Leonard Ogilvie, interviewed by John Bannister, 10 February 2004, 26869, Imperial War Museum (IWM), London; Ken Colbung, interview with Lily Kauler, 22 October 2001, *Bringing Them Home Oral History Project*, TRC 5000/336, National Library of Australia (NLA), Canberra.

31 Ken Colbung, interview with Kerrie Jean Ross, *Awaye!*, ABC Radio National, 27 August 2007, nma.gov.au/exhibitions/first_australians/resistance/yagan/awaye_audio_program_transcript, accessed 27 January 2015. See also Private Kenneth Colbung, Royal Australian Infantry Corps, interviewed by Bill Bunbury, for the ABC Radio National *Hindsight* program 'Korea, 1950–1953, The Forgotten War', S01906, AWM, Canberra; Leonard Ogilvie, interviewed by John Bannister, 10 February 2004, 26869, IWM, London.

32 Leonard Ogilvie, interviewed by John Bannister, 10 February 2004, 26869, IWM, London; Leonard Ogilvie, interviewed by John Bannister, 25 May 2001, *Bringing Them Home Oral History Project*, TRC 5000/274, NLA, Canberra.

33 This at least is the story told in Gina Lennox, *Forged by War: Australians in combat and back home*, Melbourne University Press, Melbourne, 2006, p. 162, an account based largely on family reminiscences.

34 Saunders cited in Harry Gordon, *The Embarrassing Australian: The story of an Aboriginal warrior*, Lansdowne Press, Melbourne, 1965, p. 142.

35 Forbes, *The Korean War*, p. 269.

36 Gordon, *The Embarrassing Australian*, p. 17.

37 For the patchy Australian coverage of 'our' Korean War, see Fay Anderson & Richard Trembath, *Witnesses to War: The history of Australian conflict reporting*, Melbourne University Press, Melbourne, 2011, pp. 209–22.

38 'Aboriginal Tells Army Why He Quit', *The Herald* (Melbourne), 12 March

Notes

1956, in series B2458, item 337678, NAA, Canberra. See also Gordon, *The Embarrassing Australian*, pp. 160–2.

39   Cecil Fisher Papers, PR 91/163, AWM, Canberra; Trembath, *A Different Sort of War*, p. 169; Christobel Mattingley & Ken Hampton (eds), *Survival in Our Own Land: 'Aboriginal' experiences in 'South Australia' since 1836*, Hodder & Stoughton, Sydney, 1992, p. 288.

40   *The West Australian* (Perth), 4 March 1952, p. 3; *The Morning Bulletin* (Rockhampton), 24 April 1952, p. 6; 'Trooper Gets Medal', *Dawn*, August 1957, p. 19.

41   In a Cinesound newsreel from 1950, for example, an Aboriginal soldier at Ingleburn in New South Wales was filmed in a slow close-up in a feature showing the first Australian troops leaving for Korea. See *Cinesound News*, no. 985, FO1992, AWM, Canberra. On international criticism, see *Vote Yes for Aborigines*, written and directed by Frances Peters-Little, produced by Ronin Films, 2007, DVD; and Chesterman, *Civil Rights*.

42   FO7535, AWM, Canberra.

43   *Townsville Daily Bulletin*, 30 September 1947, p. 5. See another north Queensland newspaper for a similar judgement of the wartime Torres Strait Light Infantry as 'a body of excellent soldiers': *The Cairns Post*, 4 May 1946, p. 5.

44   Alistair Thomson, 'Anzac Stories: Using personal testimony in war history', *War & Society*, vol. 25, no. 2, October 2006, pp. 1–21; Alistair Thomson, *ANZAC Memories: Living with the legend*, 2nd edn, Monash University Publishing, Melbourne, 2013.

45   Cedric 'Ned' Egglestone and Don McLeod, Royal Australian Infantry Corps, interviewed by Bill Bunbury, 3 September 1998, for the ABC Radio National *Hindsight* program 'Korea, 1950–1953, The Forgotten War', S01907, AWM, Canberra.

46   See Trembath, *A Different Sort of War*, pp. 145–82, for a detailed discussion of the 'forgetting' of the Korean War.

47   Private Kenneth Colbung, Royal Australian Infantry Corps, interviewed by Bill Bunbury, 3 September 1998, for the ABC Radio National *Hindsight* program 'Korea, 1950–1953, The Forgotten War', S01906, AWM, Canberra. See also Leonard Ogilvie, interviewed by John Bannister, 10 February 2004, 26869, IWM, London; Cedric 'Ned' Egglestone and Don McLeod, Royal Australian Infantry Corps, interviewed by Bill Bunbury, 3 September 1998, for the ABC Radio National *Hindsight* program 'Korea, 1950–1953, The Forgotten War', S01907, AWM, Canberra.

48   'Billabong' in *The West Australian*, 25 October 1952, p. 9.

49 See *The West Australian*, 4 November 1952, p. 4; *Townsville Daily Bulletin*, 5 November 1952, p. 3; *The Northern Standard* (Darwin), 7 November 1952, p. 7.

50 'Aboriginal Unit Proposed', *The Cairns Post*, 5 November 1951, p. 1; 'Aboriginal Battalion', *The Morning Bulletin*, 5 November 1951, p. 4; 'Aboriginal Battalion Suggested', *The Advertiser*, 5 November 1951, p. 2.

51 Haebich, *Spinning the Dream*, p. 152; McGregor, *Indifferent Inclusion*, p. 74; Julie Wells & Michael Christie, 'Namatjira and the Burden of Citizenship', *Australian Historical Studies*, vol. 31, no. 114, 2000, pp. 113–17.

52 *The Herald* cited in Paul Pottinger, 'The Unknown Soldier', *The Australian Magazine*, 4 November 2000, p. 34. See also 'Hero's Kiddies Meet Santa', *The Argus*, 21 December 1950, p. 4; 'Revue Company for Portland', *The Portland Guardian*, 13 January 1947, p. 2; 'Home from Korea', *The Portland Guardian*, 10 March 1952, p. 2; '"Daddy's Safe Home Again!" – with Geisha Dolls, Too', *The Argus*, 18 January 1952, p. 3; 'Spencer St Stopped Work to Cheer Him', *The Argus*, 18 January 1952, p. 3.

53 Haebich, *Spinning the Dream*, p. 152 and see also pp. 118–21, 137–54; McGregor, *Indifferent Inclusion*, p. 74; Wells & Christie, 'Namatjira and the Burden of Citizenship', pp. 113–17.

54 Glenda Hume cited in Pottinger, 'The Unknown Soldier', p. 34. See also Gordon, *The Embarrassing Australian*, pp. 165–8.

55 Gordon, *The Embarrassing Australian*, pp. 138–9.

56 Typed note in series B337, item 664, NAA, Melbourne.

57 Gordon, *The Embarrassing Australian*, p. 172.

58 Kerin, *Doctor Do-Good*, p. 152.

59 *The Cairns Post*, 4 November 1952, p. 5. Also see *The Northern Standard*, 7 November 1952, p. 7; *Townsville Daily Bulletin*, 5 November 1952, p. 3; *The West Australian*, 4 November 1952, p. 4.

60 *The Cairns Post*, 18 April 1951, p. 3.

61 'Aborigines Discover Advantages in Army Life', *Dawn*, May 1964, pp. 9–11.

62 *Dawn*, August 1967, p. 12.

63 *One People*, prepared by the Department of Territories, for use by the National Aborigines' Day Observance Committee on the celebration of National Aborigines' Day, 14 July 1961, p. 27. For analysis of these pamphlets see Haebich, *Spinning the Dream*, pp. 137–58; McGregor, *Indifferent Inclusion*; Steve Mickler, *The Myth of Privilege: Aboriginal status, media visions, public ideas*, Fremantle Arts Centre Press, Fremantle, 1998, pp. 94–101.

64 *One People*, p. 30.

65 *One People*. Emphasis added.

Notes

66 Kim Scott & Hazel Brown, *Kayang & Me*, Fremantle Arts Centre Press, Fremantle, 2005, p. 153.
67 Kerin, *Doctor Do-Good*, p. 116.
68 Phil Prosser, in *The Forgotten*, directed by Glen Stasiuk, originally aired as an episode of *Message Stick* on the ABC, 27 April 2003, videocassette.
69 Phillip Prosser, interview with John Bannister, Perth, 22 January 2000, *Bringing Them Home Oral History Project*, TRC 5000/183, NLA, Canberra.
70 Cecil Fisher to Mike O'Sullivan, Australian War Memorial, c. 1991, Cecil Fisher Papers, PR 91/163, AWM, Canberra.
71 'Anzac Day: Living with Granny (Cherbourg)', Cecil Fisher Papers, PR 91/163, AWM, Canberra.
72 For court cases involving the punishment of Indigenous veterans for drinking in this period, see '"Rotten" Legislation for Coloured Australians', *The West Australian*, 5 November 1952, p. 3; *The West Australian*, 21 January 1953, p. 10, where the magistrate apologised for his hands being tied though the defendant was 'good enough to fight for us'; *The Barrier Miner* (Broken Hill), 22 January 1953, p. 3; *The Argus*, 21 January 1953, p. 1; *The Argus*, 22 January 1953, p. 2.
73 *The West Australian*, 2 December 1952, p. 3.
74 *The Sunday Times*, 14 December 1952, p. 5.
75 *The Daily News*, 24 October 1953; *The Sunday Times*, 1 November 1953, p. 13; Charles Duguid, *No Dying Race*, Rigby, Adelaide, 1963, pp. 180–3.

2   THE RSL AND AUSTRALIAN INDIGENOUS VETERANS

1 *The West Australian*, 26 July 1952.
2 CW Joyce, secretary, Victorian Branch, RSL to JC Neagle, federal secretary, RSL, 16 April 1946, RSL papers, series 1, MSS 6609, box 158, file 2248c, NLA, Canberra.
3 The quote comes from Michael McKernan's entry on the RSL in Graeme Davison, John Hirst & Stuart Macintyre (eds), *The Oxford Companion to Australian History*, Oxford University Press, Melbourne, 1998, pp. 556–7. See also Carina Donaldson & Marilyn Lake, 'Whatever Happened to the Anti-war Movement?' in Marilyn Lake & Henry Reynolds (eds), *What's Wrong with Anzac? The militarisation of Australian history*, NewSouth Publishing, Sydney, 2010, pp. 71–93. The RSL badly needs a wide-ranging and critical history. GL Kristianson, *The Politics of Patriotism: The pressure group activities of the Returned Servicemen's League*, ANU Press, Canberra, 1966, is invaluable but is now out of date, as is Peter Sekuless & Jacqueline Rees, *Lest We Forget: The history of the Returned Services League 1916–1986*, Rigby, Sydney, 1986.

4   McKernan in Davison, Hirst & Macintyre, *The Oxford Companion to Australian History*, pp. 556–7.
5   It is not surprising that women were overlooked. In the period immediately after the Second World War, the Commonwealth government and the services were tepid at best about the role of women in the peacetime forces. After the war the women's auxiliaries were abolished and it took several years before they were re-established. Grey, *A Military History of Australia*, pp. 206–7.
6   Quoted in Hall, *The Black Diggers*, p. 26.
7   See assistant federal secretary, RSL, to CW Joyce, secretary, Victorian branch, 17 April 1946; assistant federal secretary, RSL, to Frank Strahan, secretary, Prime Minister's Department, 17 April 1946; Frank Strahan, secretary, Prime Minister's Department, to assistant federal secretary, RSL, 26 April 1946; JC Neagle, federal secretary, RSL, to Frank Strahan, 25 June 1946; Frank Strahan to JC Neagle, 28 June 1946, and JC Neagle to Frank Strahan, 30 July 1946, all in RSL papers, series 1, MSS 6609, box 158, file 2248c, NLA, Canberra.
8   Frank Strahan, secretary, Prime Minister's Department, to JC Neagle, federal secretary, RSL, 1 August 1946, in ibid.
9   General secretary, RSL, to JB Chifley, prime minister, 20 November 1946, in ibid. Also see *The Argus* (Melbourne), 2 November 1946.
10 CW Joyce, secretary, Victorian branch RSL, to JC Neagle, federal secretary, RSL, 28 March 1947 in ibid.
11 *The Argus*, 25 March 1947.
12 *Morwell Advertiser*, 17 February 1949.
13 JB Chifley to general secretary, RSL, 14 August 1947 in RSL papers, series 1, MSS 6609, box 158, file 2248c, NLA, Canberra. Also see *Centralian Advocate* (Alice Springs), 25 October 1947.
14 General secretary, RSL, to prime minister, 7 October 1947 and 17 November 1948, in ibid.
15 JB Chifley to general secretary, RSL, 23 February 1949; assistant secretary, RSL, to JR Lewis, secretary NSW branch, RSL, 26 July 1949; and FC Green, clerk of the House of Representatives, to assistant secretary, RSL, 28 July 1949, in ibid. Also see *The Age*, 4 March 1949.
16 Richard Broome, *Aboriginal Australians: A history since 1788*, Allen & Unwin, Sydney, 2010, p. 208. See also *The Age*, 1 September 1948.
17 JE Hammond, *Winjan's People: The story of the South-West Australian Aborigines*, edited by Paul Hasluck, Imperial Printing Co., Perth, 1933; Paul Hasluck, *Black Australians: A survey of native policy in Western Australia, 1829–1897*, Melbourne University Press in association with Oxford University Press,

Notes

Melbourne, 1942; Paul Hasluck, *Native Welfare in Australia: Speeches and addresses*, Paterson Brokensha, Perth, 1953; Paul Hasluck, *Shades of Darkness, Aboriginal affairs 1925–1965*, Melbourne University Press, Melbourne, 1988.

18 PA McBride, for the prime minister, to the general secretary, RSL, 20 January 1950, in RSL papers, series 1, MSS 6609, box 158, file 2248c, NLA, Canberra.
19 In a speech to the Native Welfare Council reported in *The Argus*, 30 September 1952.
20 *The Argus*, 1 October 1952.
21 General secretary, RSL, to RG Menzies, prime minister, 17 September 1951, in RSL papers, series 1, MSS 6609, box 158, file 2248c, NLA, Canberra. Also see *The West Australian*, 29 October 1951.
22 *Centralian Advocate*, 14 December 1951. Until 1968 the MHRs for the Northern Territory and the Australian Capital Territory also had limited voting powers and influence within parliament.
23 *The Cairns Post*, 25 February 1952.
24 Resolution no. 105, 13th Annual Congress of the RSL, 7 December 1928, RSL papers, series 1, MSS 6609, box 38, file 4219b, NLA, Canberra.
25 See *Mufti*, journal of the Victorian branch of the RSL, March 1950, pp. 18–19; May 1950, p. 8; July 1950, p. 20; August 1950, p. 28. See also Trembath, *A Different Sort of War*, pp. 21–2.
26 *The Sydney Morning Herald*, 28 May 1951; *The Advertiser*, 28 and 29 May 1951.
27 *The Sydney Morning Herald*, 5 June 1951.
28 *The Bulletin*, 12 February 1951.
29 *The Canberra Times*, 2 July 1951. Also see *The Sydney Morning Herald*, 6 December 1951. The issue did not go away, though, for in August 1952 the New South Wales branch raised it again. See *The Sydney Morning Herald*, 16 August 1952.
30 Kingsley Martin, *The Magic of the British Monarchy*, Little, Brown and Company, Boston and Toronto, 1962, p. 116.
31 'The Coronation Contingent of 1953' at awm.gov.au/blog/2009/03/11/the-coronation-contingent-of-1953/, accessed 17 December 2013.
32 *The Sunday Herald* (Sydney), 8 February 1953.
33 *The Courier-Mail* (Brisbane), 12 February 1953.
34 RSL papers, series 1, MSS 6609, box 240, file 3894c, NLA, Canberra. See also *The Courier-Mail*, 12 February 1953, and *The Barrier Miner*, 14 February 1953, where the strong statements of the Victorian RSL are attributed to the state president, ND Wilson, which is almost certainly correct. See on this

point *The Mail* (Adelaide), 14 February 1953, and *The Argus*, 14 February 1953.
35 The description used in *The Sydney Morning Herald*, 8 February 1953.
36 *The Sunday Times*, 17 February 1953. Also see *The Sunday Herald*, 15 February 1953.
37 *The Portland Guardian*, 19 February 1953.
38 *The Courier-Mail*, 27 February 1953.
39 *The Advertiser*, 27 February 1953. See also *Townsville Daily Bulletin*, 28 February 1953; *The West Australian*, 28 February 1953; and *The Argus*, 28 February 1953. In this period Australia maintained a cumbersome bureaucratic structure whereby the Department of Defence theoretically exercised oversight of three separate service ministries (army, navy and air) and related portfolios such as supply, defence production, etc. Not until the advent of the Whitlam government were all defence-oriented departments located within the one ministry. See Grey, *A Military History of Australia*, pp. 225–6, 255–6.
40 *The West Australian*, 5 March 1953, and *The Advertiser*, 5 March 1953. For McBride's firm, rather uncompromising personality, which did not help Saunders's chances, see David Lee, 'McBride, Sir Philip Albert (1892–1982)', *Australian Dictionary of Biography*, National Centre of Biography, Australian National University, adb.anu.edu.au/biography/mcbride-sir-philip-albert-15051/text26249, accessed 31 December 2013.
41 *The Mail*, 7 March 1953.
42 *The Advertiser*, 3 March 1953. Also see *The Mail*, 7 March 1953.
43 See *The Advertiser*, 9 March 1953; *The Argus*, 9 March 1953; *The Barrier Miner*, 10 March 1953; and *The Advertiser*, 11 March 1953.
44 Mrs Evelyn Rowland in *The West Australian*, 29 July 1953. Her suggestion for a suitable means of commemoration reflected contemporary opinion that such things should be 'useful', i.e., a hospital, school or park rather than a monument such as a sculpture. See Inglis, *Sacred Places*, pp. 352–8.
45 *The Advocate*, 21 March 1953.
46 *The West Australian*, 28 May 1953.
47 Mrs Ellen Berger of Hawthorn, Victoria, in *The Argus*, 15 April 1953.
48 General secretary, RSL, to Josiah Francis, minister for the navy, 20 September 1955, in RSL papers, series 1, MSS 6609, box 158, file 2248c, NLA, Canberra.
49 Incorporated in RSL circular no. 78/55, 10 October 1955, in ibid.
50 Sir Philip McBride, minister for defence, to general secretary, RSL, 14 February 1956, in ibid.
51 Queensland branch motion for RSL federal executive meeting, August 1956, in ibid.

Notes

52 *The Argus*, 11 December 1954. The capitals are in the original.
53 ND Wilson to Sir George Holland, 14 December 1954, RSL papers, series 1, MSS 6609, box 201, file 3089c, NLA, Canberra. See also *The Mirror* (Sydney), 11 December 1954; *The Argus*, 13 December 1954; *The Age*, 13 December 1954.
54 Extract from the 43rd annual report of the national executive of the RSL for year ending 31 December 1958, RSL papers, series 1, MSS 6609, box 201, file 3089c, NLA, Canberra.
55 National secretary, RSL, to AR Browning, sergeant-at-arms and clerk of committees, federal parliament, 29 May 1961, RSL papers, series 1, MSS 6609, box 310, file 4797c, NLA, Canberra.
56 Resolution no. 258 of the national congress of the RSL, 21 December 1961, in ibid.
57 Hall, *The Black Diggers*, p. 191.
58 Ruxton was president of the Victorian branch between 1979 and 2002. For his friendly relationship with Indigenous soldiers during the Second World War, see Anne Blair, *Ruxton: A biography*, Allen & Unwin, Sydney, 2004, pp. 31, 40.
59 *The Australian*, 12 August 1981, on the occasion of the league's records being donated to the NLA.
60 *Toorak Times*, February 1982, exact date unknown, in Bruce Ruxton papers, MSS 9904, box 11, folder 36b, NLA, Canberra.
61 *The Age*, 27 February 1982.
62 *The Sydney Morning Herald*, 26 September 1984. This theme preoccupied Ruxton throughout much of 1984. See also *The Standard* (Warrnambool), 7 June 1984; *Sunday Observer* (Melbourne), 17 June 1984; *The Age*, 18 July 1984; *The Standard*, 8 August 1984; *The Advertiser*, 26 September 1984. The interest of the Warrnambool newspaper in the issue is due to the proposal of the state Labor government to compulsorily acquire land at nearby Lake Condah for development as an Aboriginal tourist park.
63 *Australian Playboy*, April 1988, p. 36.
64 *The Age*, 10 September 1988.
65 Michael Mummery, former South Australian president of the RSL and a strong supporter of the recognition of Indigenous service, claimed that the 'media had got it 180 degrees wrong'. Alf Garland had laughed at the idea of blood tests as 'that would only prove whether they were A+ or B-'. Michael Mummery, interview with Richard Trembath, Adelaide, 17 September 2012.
66 *The Canberra Times*, 10 September 1988.
67 *The Sun* (Melbourne), 10 September 1988.

68 *The Sydney Morning Herald*, 10 September 1988.
69 *The Australian*, 1–2 June 1991.
70 Grey, *A Military History of Australia*, p. 2.
71 See 'Canberra: A Special Ceremony on the Slopes of Mount Ainslie Has Marked the Involvement and Achievements of Australia's Indigenous Soldiers', WINTV, Canberra, news broadcast, 4 July 2000, title no. 452926, National Film and Sound Archives, Canberra.

3   INDIGENOUS SERVICE AND VIETNAM

1 Kenny Laughton, *Not Quite Men, No Longer Boys*, Jukurrpa Books, Alice Springs, 1999, p. 296.
2 Glenn James, interview with Ina Bertrand, Templestowe, Vic, 23 January 2001, available from *Victorians at War – Oral history project*, victoriansatwar. net/archives/james.html, accessed 18 February 2013.
3 David Cook, interview with Noah Riseman, Raymond Terrace, NSW, 20 January 2010.
4 Colonel OM (Max) Carroll (RL), '"They Were Foremost Australian Soldiers": An oral account of Aboriginal and Thursday Island soldiers who served in Malaya and Vietnam: 1957 to 1967', *Aboriginal History*, vol. 16, no. 1, 1992, p. 99.
5 See Peter Edward, *Australia and the Vietnam War*, NewSouth Publishing, Sydney, 2014; John Murphy, *Harvest of Fear: A history of Australia's Vietnam War*, Allen & Unwin, Sydney, 1993; Paul Ham, *Vietnam: The Australian war*, HarperCollins, Sydney, 2007.
6 There is, of course, the story of the female Aboriginal singers who travelled to Vietnam to perform. This story was adapted into the play *The Sapphires* in 2004 and the popular film *The Sapphires* in 2012. See 'The Sapphires: Where are they now?', *Australian Geographic*, 5 September 2012, australiangeographic. com.au/topics/history-culture/2012/09/the-sapphires-where-are-they-now/, accessed 8 September 2014.
7 See Thomson, 'Anzac Stories'; Thomson, *ANZAC Memories*.
8 John Schnaars, interview with Noah Riseman, Perth, 23 November 2010, ORAL TRC 6260/1, NLA, Canberra; Frank Mallard, interview with Noah Riseman, Perth, 24 November 2010, ORAL TRC 6260/2, NLA, Canberra; Bob Blair, interview with Noah Riseman, Rockhampton, 22 June 2010; Dianne Gage, interview with Noah Riseman, Brisbane, 1 June 2011.
9 Phillip Prosser, interview with John Bannister, Perth, 22 January 2000, *Bringing Them Home Oral History Project*, TRC 5000/183, NLA, Canberra.
10 See Noah Riseman, 'The Stolen Veteran', pp. 57–77; Sue Gordon, interview

Notes

with John Bannister, Perth, 12 October 1999, *Bringing Them Home Oral History Project*, TRC 5000/52, NLA, Canberra; Australia, Senate, Community Affairs Reference Committee, *Forgotten Australians: A report on Australians who experienced institutional or out-of-home care as children*, 2004, p. 161, aph.gov.au/Parliamentary_Business/Committees/Senate/Community_Affairs/Completed_inquiries/2004-07/inst_care/report/index, accessed 12 September 2015.

11   Dick Bligh, interview with Noah Riseman, Perth, 25 November 2010, ORAL TRC 6260/4, NLA, Canberra.
12   Ron Wenitong, interview with Noah Riseman, Cairns, 23 June 2010.
13   Frank Mallard, ORAL TRC 6260/2, NLA, Canberra.
14   Phil Prosser, in *The Forgotten*, directed by Glen Stasiuk. See also Phillip Prosser, TRC 5000/183 NLA, Canberra.
15   Geoff Shaw, in *I Hope the War Will Be Over Soon*, directed by John Ruane, produced by Juniper Films, 1988, DVD; Dick Bligh, interview; George Bostock, interview with Noah Riseman, Brisbane, 18 June 2010.
16   Bob Blair, interview.
17   Max Gardner, interview with George Bostock, 28 April 1991, BOSTOCK_G01-016546, Australian Institute for Aboriginal and Torres Strait Islander Studies (AIATSIS), Canberra.
18   Frank Mallard, ORAL TRC 6260/2, NLA, Canberra.
19   Dianne Gage, interview.
20   Commonwealth of Australia, *National Service Act 1951*, section 18.
21   Noel Loos & Koiki Mabo, *Eddie Koiki Mabo: His life and struggle for land rights*, University of Queensland Press, Brisbane, 1996, pp. 83–4.
22   Commonwealth of Australia, *National Service Act 1964*, section 18(e).
23   HA Bland, secretary, Department of Labour and National Service, to secretary, Prime Minister's Department, 7 May 1965, in series K38, item 1971/3551, NAA, Perth. Document also appears in series A463, item 1962/3685 part 1, NAA, Canberra.
24   See Ann-Mari Jordens, 'An Administrative Nightmare: Aboriginal conscription 1965–72', *Aboriginal History*, vol. 13, no. 2, 1989, pp. 124–34.
25   'Native Call-up Demand', *The Canberra Times*, 29 January 1965, in series AWM263, item D/2/6, AWM, Canberra.
26   Sue Ping, Kempsey, NSW, fourth-form history student, to minister for the interior, 1 October 1971, in series A2354, item 1968/1, NAA, Canberra.
27   David Michael, 'Exemption of Natives from Conscription', *The West Australian*, 8 February 1965, in series 2030, item 1965/0317, State Records Office of Western Australia (SRO), Perth. See also SK Randell, 'Platform', *The West Australian*, 15 February 1965; SK Randell, 'Equality for Aborigines',

The West Australian, 17 February 1965; Miss Barbara Stewart, Gnowangerup, WA, to minister for labour and national service, no date, c. early 1969, in series K38, item 1971/3551, NAA, Perth; Miss Sharyn Capewell, Grenville, NSW, to minister for labour and national service, 15 March 1971, in series A2354, item 1968/1, NAA, Canberra.

28   'N.S. Urged for Natives', *The West Australian*, 17 July 1967, in series 2030, item 1965/0317, SRO, Perth; Mrs NG Moir, to officer-in-charge, National Service Training, 28 September 1965, in series K38, item 1971/3551, NAA, Perth; BG Dexter, director, to the secretary, Department of Labour and National Service, 29 February 1972, in series A2354, item 1968/1, NAA, Canberra.

29   Stan Davey, hon. general secretary, Federal Council for the Advancement of Aborigines and Torres Strait Islanders, to the Hon. AJ Forbes, minister for the army, 2 November 1965, in series AWM263, item D/2/6, AWM, Canberra. For other Indigenous organisations, see FE Gare, commissioner of native welfare, WA, to the director, Department of Labour and National Service, 17 March 1969, in series 2030, item 1965/0317, SRO, Perth; document also appears in series K38, item 1971/3551, NAA, Perth, and series A2354, item 1968/1, NAA, Canberra.

30   'Aborigines Wanted in Call-up', *The West Australian*, 4 July 1967; FJ Martin to secretary, Federal Parliamentary Country Party, 29 March 1971, both documents appear in series K38, item 1971/3551, NAA, Perth; 'Libs Urge Aborigines for Call-up', *The Daily News*, 3 July 1967, in series 2030, item 1965/0317, SRO, Perth; series A452, item NT1964/7194, NAA, Canberra; series A452, item NT1967/2081, NAA, Canberra; BG Dexter, director, to the secretary, Department of Labour and National Service, 29 February 1972, in series A2354, item 1968/1, NAA, Canberra.

31   Graham Atkinson, interview with George Bostock, April 1991, BOSTOCK_G01-016549, AIATSIS, Canberra.

32   David Williams, interview with Noah Riseman, Merrylands, NSW, 4 November 2011.

33   John Schnaars, ORAL TRC 6260/1, NLA, Canberra. See also John Schnaars, in 'The Last Post', *Message Stick*, directed by Adrian Wells, produced by the ABC, 2006, DVD.

34   Frank Lampard, interview with Noah Riseman, Adelaide, 28 November 2013.

35   Commonwealth of Australia, *National Service Regulations 1964*, regulation 18.

36   'Aboriginal Welfare Conference 1965, Liability of Aborigines to register for national service', submitted by the Department of Territories, 22 July 1965,

Notes

    in series AWM263 D/2/6, AWM, Canberra; document also appears in series A452, item NT1964/7194, NAA, Canberra.

37 HA Bland, secretary, Department of Labour and National Service, 6 December 1965, series K38, item 1971/3551, NAA, Perth. See also HA Bland, secretary, Department of Labour and National Service, to secretary, Prime Minister's Department, 7 May 1965, series A463, item 1962/3685 part 1, NAA, Canberra; reply to CWA WA letter, 9 March 1966, series AWM263, item D/2/7, AWM, Canberra.

38 Pam Maclean, 'An Almost Universal Scheme of National Service in Australia in the 1950s', *Australian Journal of Politics and History*, vol. 52, no. 3, 2006, p. 394.

39 Numerous documents in: series A2354, item 1968/1, NAA, Canberra; series AWM263, item D/2/6, AWM, Canberra; series AWM263, item D/2/7, AWM, Canberra; series A452, item NT1964/7194, NAA, Canberra; memo from CE Reseigh, for secretary, Department of Territories, to the secretary, Prime Minister's Department, 15 January 1968, series A463, item 1968/3222, NAA, Canberra; document also appears in series A2354, item 1968/1, NAA, Canberra.

40 PH Cook, secretary, Department of Labour and National Service, to director, Office of Aboriginal Affairs, 19 February 1970, series A2354, item 1968/1, NAA, Canberra.

41 PE Felton, superintendent of Aborigines welfare, Aborigines Welfare Board, to director, Department of Labour and National Service, Melbourne, 11 August 1965, in series AWM263, item D/2/6, AWM, Canberra.

42 CJ Millar, director, Department of Aboriginal Affairs, Adelaide, to BG Dexter, director, Office of Aboriginal Affairs, Canberra, 24 March 1969, series A2354, item 1968/1, NAA, Canberra.

43 PE Felton, superintendent of Aborigines welfare, Aborigines Welfare Board, to director, Department of Labour and National Service, Melbourne, 11 August 1965; RA Smee, regional director, NSW, Department of Labour and National Service, to Dr PH Cook, first assistant secretary, Department of Labour and National Service, 16 December 1965; A Gibson, regional director, Queensland, Department of Labour and National Service, to Dr PH Cook, first assistant secretary, Department of Labour and National Service, 10 December 1965; GE McGregor, assistant registrar, Perth, 19 January 1966, 'Memo for File'; FH Moy, for secretary, Department of Territories, to the secretary, Department of Labour and National Service, 10 May 1966. All documents appear in AWM263, item D/2/6, AWM, Canberra.

44 G Sutcliffe, Department of Labour and National Service Minute, 'Liability of

Aborigines for national service', 2 March 1966, series AWM263, item D/2/6, AWM, Canberra.
45 BG Dexter, director, Office of Aboriginal Affairs, to the minister, 1 May 1968, in series A2354, item 1968/1, NAA, Canberra.
46 CJ Millar, director of Aboriginal affairs, Department of Aboriginal Affairs, Adelaide, to BG Dexter, director, Office of Aboriginal Affairs, Canberra, 24 March 1969, series A2354, item 1968/1, NAA, Canberra.
47 Glenn James in Alick Jackomos & Derek Fowell, *Forgotten Heroes*, p. 67.
48 Documents in series K38, item 1971/3551, NAA, Perth.
49 Department of Labour and National Service News Release, 'National Service – Eric J. Simms', 6 October 1970, series AWM263, item D/2/7, AWM, Canberra.
50 James, *Victorians at War*.
51 Bob Blair, interview.
52 David Cook, interview.
53 James, *Victorians at War*.
54 Sandy MacGregor, as told to Jimmy Thomson, *No Need for Heroes*, CALM Pty Limited, Sydney, 1993, pp. 89–90.
55 Bob Blair, interview.
56 ibid.
57 Hewitt Whyman, interview with George Bostock, 26 April 1991, available from BOSTOCK_G01-016548, AIATSIS, Canberra.
58 James, *Victorians at War*.
59 Dick Bligh, interview.
60 Geoff Shaw, in *I Hope the War Will Be Over Soon*, directed by John Ruane.
61 Frank Mallard, interview.
62 David Williams, interview.
63 John Schnaars, interview.
64 Frank Mallard, interview.
65 ibid.
66 George Bostock, interview.
67 Dick Bligh, interview.
68 Frank Mallard, interview.
69 Various service records of Vietnam veterans, accessed through the Central Army Records Office (CARO).
70 Dick Bligh, interview.
71 Darryl 'Rocky' Wallace, interview with George Bostock, 11 April 1991, BOSTOCK_G01-016549-50, AIATSIS, Canberra.
72 Frank Mallard, interview.

Notes

73 George Bostock, interview.
74 David Cook, interview. See also MacGregor, *No Need for Heroes*, p. 85.
75 Frank Mallard, interview.
76 Ron Wenitong, interview.
77 David Cook, interview.
78 James E Westheider, *The African American Experience in Vietnam: Brothers in arms*, Rowman and Littlefield, Lanham, MD, 2008; James E Westheider, *Fighting on Two Fronts: African Americans and the Vietnam War*, New York University Press, New York and London, 1997.
79 David Cook, interview.
80 Billy Coolburra, in MacGregor, *No Need for Heroes*, pp. 82–3; Graham Atkinson, BOSTOCK_G01-016549, AIATSIS, Canberra; Frank Mallard, interview.
81 Darryl 'Rocky' Wallace, BOSTOCK_G01-016549-50, AIATSIS, Canberra.
82 George Bostock, 'Black Veterans of Vietnam', unpublished manuscript, pp. 11–12, MS 3012, AIATSIS, Canberra.
83 ibid., p. 12.
84 Hewitt Whyman, BOSTOCK_G01-016548, AIATSIS, Canberra.
85 Graham Atkinson, BOSTOCK_G01-016549, AIATSIS, Canberra. See also Graham Atkinson, in Jackomos & Fowell, *Forgotten Heroes*, p. 72.
86 Geoff Shaw, in *I Hope the War Will Be Over Soon*, directed by John Ruane.
87 Commonwealth of Australia, *National Service Regulations 1964*, regulation 18.
88 'At the Court of Petty Sessions Held at Albany Before H.J. Ryan, Esq., S.M. This 22nd Day of November, 1971; Date of Decision: 13 December, 1971, Between: Nigel Frederick Spitz, Commonwealth Police, Complainant, and Mervyn Eades, Defendant', in series A2354, item 1968/1, NAA, Canberra.
89 ibid. See also various newspaper articles in: series A2354, item 1968/1, NAA, Canberra; item 1862902, NLA, Canberra; series A1734, item NT1972/23, NAA, Canberra.
90 'Is Mervyn Eades Black or White?', *The Australian*, 15 December 1971. Document appears in: series A2354, item 1968/1, NAA, Canberra; item 1862902, NLA, Canberra; series A1734, item NT1972/23, NAA, Canberra; Roberta B Sykes, *Black Majority*, Hudson Publishing, Melbourne, 1989, pp. 10–12.
91 'Marking the Color Line', *The Australian*, 16 December 1971. Document appears in: series A2354, item 1968/1, NAA, Canberra; series A1734, item NT1972/23, NAA, Canberra.
92 JE Cooper, senior research officer II, Office of Aboriginal Affairs,

'National Service Act', 15 March 1972, in series A2354, item 1968/1, NAA, Canberra.

93 'Marking the Color Line', in series A2354, item 1968/1, and series A1734, item NT1972/23, NAA, Canberra.

94 A Stephen, to Mr Kangan, 1st assistant secretary, 'Departmental Definition of "Aboriginal"', 31 August 1972, in series AWM 263, item D/2/6, AWM, Canberra.

95 Michael Hamel-Green, 'The Resisters: A history of the anti-conscription movement 1964–1972', in Peter King (ed.), *Australia's Vietnam: Australia in the Second Indo-China War*, Allen & Unwin, Sydney, 1983, p. 117. See also PH Cook, secretary, Department of Labour and National Service, to director, Office of Aboriginal Affairs, 3 March 1972, in series A2354, item 1968/1, NAA, Canberra.

96 PH Cook, secretary, Department of Labour and National Service, to director, Office of Aboriginal Affairs, 3 March 1972, in series A2354, item 1968/1, NAA, Canberra.

97 JE Cooper, senior research officer II, Office of Aboriginal Affairs, 'National Service Act', 15 March 1972, in series A2354, item 1968/1, NAA, Canberra.

98 FEA Bateman, SM, 'Hearing of a Charge under Section 48 1(b) – National Service Act – Stanley Robert WARD', Perth Court of Petty Sessions 21 June 1972, in series AWM263, item D/2/7, AWM, Canberra.

99 'An Aboriginal May Not Wear a Suit', *Truth* (Sydney), 1–8 July 1972, in series AWM263, item D/2/7, AWM Canberra. See also: 'SM – Remark Not Meant to Offend', *The Daily News*, 22 June 1972, p. 3; 'Aboriginal Should Get Benefit of Doubt', *The Daily News*, 22 June 1972, p. 3; 'Remarks Were Compliment, Not Insult, Says SM', unclear newspaper or date; 'Call-up Fine for Well Dressed Quarter-caste', *The Sun*, 22 June 1972; 'N.S. Case: Defence of part-native rejected', *The West Australian*, 22 June 1972. Articles all appear in series AWM263, item D/2/7, AWM, Canberra; '"Black or White" Court Riddle', *The Sun*, 22 June 1972, in series A2354, item 1968/1, NAA, Canberra.

100 'When is an Aboriginal Not One? When He's a Conscript', *The Australian*, 24 June 1972, in series AWM263, item D/2/7, AWM, Canberra.

101 Secretary, Department of Labour and National Service minute, 'National Service; Robert MUNTZ', 30 June 1972, in series AWM263, item D/2/6, AWM, Canberra.

102 Denis Freney, *A Map of Days: Life on the left*, William Heinemann Australia, Melbourne, 1991, p. 267.

103 Bobby Baker in Kevin Cook & Heather Goodall, *Making Change Happen:*

Black and white activists talk to Kevin Cook about Aboriginal, union and liberation Politics, ANU E Press, Canberra, 2013, p. 33.
104 MD Robertson, regional director, Department of Labour and National Service minute, to secretary, Melbourne, Attention Mr Watcher, 20 December 1972, in series AWM263, item D/2/7, AWM, Canberra.
105 Graham Atkinson in Jackomos & Fowell, *Forgotten Heroes*, pp. 71–2.
106 See Australia, *Morbidity of Vietnam Veterans: A study of the health of Australia's Vietnam veteran community: volume 1 – male Vietnam veterans*, Department of Veterans' Affairs, Canberra, 1998–99.
107 Geoff Shaw, in *I Hope the War Will Be Over Soon*, directed by John Ruane.
108 Phil Prosser, in *The Forgotten*, directed by Glen Stasiuk.
109 David Cook, interview; Riseman, 'The Stolen Veteran', pp. 66–72.
110 Graham Atkinson, in Jackomos & Fowell, *Forgotten Heroes*, p. 72. See also Graham Atkinson, BOSTOCK_G01-016549, AIATSIS, Canberra; George Bostock, interview; Hewitt Whyman, BOSTOCK_G01-016548, AIATSIS, Canberra; Darryl 'Rocky' Wallace, BOSTOCK_G01-016549-50, AIATSIS, Canberra.
111 Geoff Shaw, in *I Hope the War Will Be Over Soon*, directed by John Ruane.
112 Max Gardner, BOSTOCK_G01-016546, AIATSIS, Canberra; Ron Wenitong, interview; John Schnaars, interview; Frank Mallard, interview; Dianne Gage, interview; George Bostock, interview; Dick Bligh, interview; Bob Blair, interview; Glenn James, in Jackomos & Fowell, *Forgotten Heroes*, p. 69; James, *Victorians at War*.
113 George Bostock, interview; Dick Bligh, interview; John Schnaars, in 'The Last Post', *Message Stick*, directed by Adrian Wells.
114 Bob Blair, interview.
115 Frank Mallard, interview.

4 SKILLING INDIGENOUS WOMEN: ABORIGINAL AND TORRES STRAIT ISLANDER PEOPLE IN THE WOMEN'S SERVICES

1 Jacqueline Shaw, interview with Noah Riseman, Cairns, 27 September 2012.
2 Judy Costello, '"Why Would a Woman Want a Job Like That?" A personal reflection', in Peter Dennis & Jeffrey Grey (eds), *A Century of Service: 100 years of the Australian Army. The 2001 chief of army's military history conference*, Army History Unit, Department of Defence, Canberra, 2001, p. 3.
3 Dale Spender, foreword, in Ann Howard, *Where Do We Go from Here?*, TARKA Publishing, Sydney, 1994, p. ix. See also Lorna Mill, *Been There – Done That*, L. Mill, Melbourne, 1984, p. 10.

4   See Haebich, *Spinning the Dream*; Tim Rowse (ed.), *Contesting Assimilation*, API Network, Perth, 2005; McGregor, *Indifferent Inclusion*.
5   Jan 'Kabarli' James, *Forever Warriors*, Scott Print, Perth, 2010.
6   See Sue Hardisty (ed.), *Thanks Girls and Goodbye! The story of the Australian Women's Land Army 1942–45*, Viking O'Neil, Melbourne, 1990. See also M Buckley, L Irwin & H Kinsella, *We Also Served*, MJ Buckley, Goonellabah, NSW, 1995, pp. 115–30.
7   Sàmantha Joseph, in 'Strong Indigenous Women Speak on Leadership', *Indigenous Law Bulletin*, vol. 7, no. 1, November 2007, p. 2.
8   Jackie Huggins, 'Indigenous Women and Leadership: A personal reflection', *Indigenous Law Bulletin*, vol. 6, no. 1, March/April 2004, pp. 5–6.
9   For numbers see Department of Veterans' Affairs, *Study of Returned Servicewomen of the Second World War*, Australian Government Publishing Service, Canberra, 1985, p. 11. The most comprehensive histories of the Second World War women's services are: AWAS: Lorna Ollif, *Women in Khaki*, Ollif Publishing Company, Sydney, 1981; Grace Johansen, 'The AWAS: A social history of the Australian Women's Army Service during the Second World War', BA (Honours) Thesis, History Department, Central Queensland University, 1996; Ann Howard, *You'll Be Sorry!*, TARKA Publishing, Sydney and Melbourne, 1990; Jean Beveridge, *AWAS: Women making history*, Booralong Publications, Chevron Island, Qld, 1988; WAAAF: Joyce Thomson, *The WAAAF in Wartime Australia*, Melbourne University Press, Melbourne, 1991; Clare Stevenson & Honor Darling (eds), *The WAAAF Book*, Hale & Iremonger, Sydney, 1984; WRANS: Shirley Fenton Huie, *Ships Belles: The story of the Women's Royal Australian Naval Service in war and peace 1941–1985*, The Watermark Press, Sydney, 2000; Kathryn Leslie Spurling, 'The Women's Royal Australian Naval Service: A study in discrimination 1939–1960', MA thesis, History Department, The University of New South Wales at the Australian Defence Force Academy, 1988; Margaret Curtis-Otter, *WRANS*, 2nd edn, The Naval Historical Society of Australia, Sydney, 1996. Other good overviews include: Patsy Adam-Smith, *Australian Women at War*, 2nd edn, Penguin, Melbourne, 1996; John Moremon, 'After "the Girls" Came Home: Ex-servicewomen of Australia's wartime women's auxiliaries', in Martin Crotty & Craig Barrett (eds), *When the Soldiers Return: November 2007 conference proceedings*, RMIT Publishing in association with the School of History, Philosophy, Religion and Classics, University of Queensland, Melbourne, 2009, pp. 203–11. There have also been several memoirs published by ex-servicewomen.
10 The most comprehensive histories of the post–Second World War women's

Notes

services are: WRAAF: Janette Bomford, *Soldiers of the Queen: Women in the Australian Army*, Oxford University Press, Melbourne, 2001; Lorna Ollif, *Colonel Best and Her Soldiers: The story of 33 years of the Women's Royal Australian Army Corps*, Ollif Publishing Company, Sydney, 1985; WRANS: Huie, *Ships Belles*; Spurling, 'The Women's Royal Australian Naval Service'. Whereas there have been several published memoirs of Second World War ex-servicewomen, this is not the case for the postwar servicewomen.

11   Hugh Smith & Ian McAllister, 'The Changing Military Profession: Integrating women in the Australian Defence Force', *Australian and New Zealand Journal of Sociology*, vol. 27, no. 3, November 1991, pp. 371–5, 377–9; Ollif, *Colonel Best and Her Soldiers*, pp. 129, 160–1, 197–8, 202, 214–15, 221; Bomford, *Soldiers of the Queen*, p. 122; Huie, *Ships Belles*, p. 308; Spurling, 'The Women's Royal Australian Naval Service', p. 385; Kathryn Spurling, 'From Exclusion to Submarines – The integration of Australian women naval volunteers', *Australian Defence Force Journal*, vol. 139, November/December 1999, pp. 37–8; Katerina Agostino, 'Women in Uniform: Challenging feminisms', in Kathryn Spurling & Elizabeth Greenhalgh (eds), *Women in Uniform: Perceptions and pathways*, School of History, University College, UNSW, Australian Defence Force Academy, Canberra, 2000, p. 77; Katerina Agostino, 'Femininities and Masculinities in the Royal Australian Navy: Workplace discourses', PhD thesis, Department of Psychology and Sociology, James Cook University, 1997, p. 77; Thomson, *The WAAAF in Wartime Australia*, p. 2; Jeremy Thompson, 'Women Cleared to Serve in Combat', *ABC News*, 27 September 2011, abc.net.au/news/2011-09-27/women-on-the-frontline/2946258, accessed 30 December 2011.
12   See Osborne, *Torres Strait Islander Women and the Pacific War*, pp. 15–86.
13   'Louise', interview with Noah Riseman, Canberra, 12 April 2012.
14   ibid.
15   Ellie Gaffney, in Sally S Goold & Kerrynne Liddle (eds), *In Our Own Right: Black Australian nurses' stories*, eContent Management, Maleny, Qld, 2005, p. 99. See also Ellie Gaffney, *Somebody Now: The autobiography of Ellie Gaffney, a woman of Torres Strait*, Aboriginal Studies Press, Canberra, 1989, especially pp. 25–42; Doris Pilkington (Nugi Garimara), *Under the Wintamarra Tree*, University of Queensland Press, Brisbane, 2002, pp. 146–53.
16   Goold & Liddle (eds), *In Our Own Right*; Sue Forsyth, 'Telling Stories: Nurses, politics and Aboriginal Australians, circa 1900–1980s', *Contemporary Nurse*, vol. 24, no. 1, February 2007, p. 39.
17   'Louise', interview.
18   ibid.

19 Jan Bassett, *Guns and Brooches: Australian Army nursing from the Boer War to the Gulf War*, Oxford University Press, Melbourne, 1992, pp. 186–7.
20 'Louise', interview. On nurses in Japan and Korea, see Bassett, *Guns and Brooches*, pp. 178, 182–4; Rupert Goodman, *Our War Nurses: The history of the Royal Australian Army Nursing Corps 1902–1988*, Boolarong Publications, Brisbane, 1988, pp. 250–8; Rupert Goodman, *Queensland Nurses: Boer War to Vietnam*, Boolarong Publications, Brisbane, 1985, pp. 255–62.
21 'Louise', interview.
22 Margie Richter, 'WRAAC Girl', in Bill & Margie Richter, *Radio Operator: Vietnam War; School of Signals; healing journey*, Bill & Margie Richter, Maleny, Qld, 2013, pp. 109–10. Rules allowing married women to remain in the forces were brought into WRAAC in 1968, WRANS in 1969 and at a similar time in the other forces. See Bomford, *Soldiers of the Queen*, p. 15; Ollif, *Colonel Best and Her Soldiers*, p. 3; Curtis-Otter, *WRANS*, p. 75; Spurling, 'The Women's Royal Australian Naval Service', p. 289; Huie, *Ship's Belles*, pp. 273, 287.
23 'Louise', interview.
24 ibid.
25 ibid.
26 See Goold & Liddle (eds), *In Our Own Right*, pp. 16, 29–31, 52, 86 and 101; Gaffney, *Somebody Now*, pp. 44–8.
27 'Louise', interview.
28 Sue Gordon, interview with Noah Riseman, Perth, 25 November 2010, ORAL TRC 6260/5, NLA Canberra. For a history of Sister Kate's Home, see Anna Haebich, *Broken Circles: Fragmenting Indigenous families*, Fremantle Arts Centre Press, Fremantle, 2000, pp. 280–7. For another personal perspective on Sister Kate's Home, see Quentin Beresford, *Rob Riley: An Aboriginal leader's quest for justice*, Aboriginal Studies Press, Canberra, 2006.
29 See Victoria Haskins, *One Bright Spot*, Palgrave Macmillan, Basingstoke, 2005; Margaret Tucker, *If Everybody Cared: Autobiography of Margaret Tucker MBE*, Ure Smith, Sydney, 1977; Ruth Hegarty, *Is That You, Ruthie?*, University of Queensland Press, Brisbane, 1999; Doreen Kartinyeri & Sue Anderson, *My Ngarrindjeri Calling*, Aboriginal Studies Press, Canberra, 2008.
30 Sue Gordon, interview with Noah Riseman. See also Sue Gordon, JP, in Roberta Sykes (ed.), *Murawina: Australian women of high achievement*, Doubleday, Sydney and New York, 1993, p. 79.
31 Gordon, in Sykes (ed.), *Murawina*, p. 80. See also Sue Gordon, interview with Noah Riseman.
32 See Noah Riseman, 'The Stolen Veteran', pp. 57–77. Non-Indigenous

Notes

Australians who went to boarding schools also found themselves well-prepared for military discipline and regimentation. See Suellen Murray, John Murphy, Elizabeth Branigan & Jenny Malone, *After the Orphanage: Life beyond the children's home*, UNSW Press, Sydney, 2008, pp. 132–3; Robin Levett, *The Girls*, 2nd edn, Hudson Publishing, Newstead, Vic, 2005, pp. 195–6.

33 Sue Gordon, interview with Noah Riseman.
34 ibid.
35 Gordon, in Sykes (ed.), *Murawina*, p. 80.
36 Sue Gordon, interview with Noah Riseman.
37 ibid. See also Gordon, in Sykes (ed.), *Murawina*, p. 80. For more information about Noonkanbah, see Steve Hawke & Michael Gallagher, *Noonkanbah: Whose land, whose law*, Fremantle Arts Centre Press, Fremantle, 1989; Erich Kolig, *The Noonkanbah Story*, University of Otago Press, Dunedin, 1987.
38 Sue Gordon, interview with Noah Riseman. See also Gordon, in Sykes (ed.), *Murawina*, p. 81.
39 Sue Gordon, interview with Noah Riseman.
40 ibid.
41 For more on the Pacific Islander indentured labour trade, see Tracey Banivanua-Mar, *Violence and Colonial Dialogue: The Australian-Pacific indentured labor trade*, University of Hawai'i Press, Honolulu, 2007; Raymond Evans, Kay Saunders & Kathryn Cronin, *Race Relations in Colonial Queensland: A history of exclusion, exploitation and extermination*, 3rd edn, University of Queensland Press, Brisbane, 1993, pp. 147–234.
42 Mabel Quakawoot, interview with Noah Riseman, Mackay, Qld, 5 June 2011.
43 ibid.
44 ibid.
45 ibid. Other ex-servicewomen similarly argue that different treatment did not necessarily equate to discrimination. See Bronwyn Lowe, 'Reflections on Gender and Memory: Personal experiences of women of the WAAAF during the Second World War', *Melbourne Historical Journal*, vol. 39, 2011, pp. 167–8.
46 Mabel Quakawoot, interview.
47 See Desmond Martin (ed.), *Backing up the Boys: The Australian Women's Army Service and Albury Army area*, Thomsons Printing Pty Ltd, Albury, NSW, 1988, pp. 31, 33, 37, 39; Ollif, *Women in Khaki*, pp. 46–7, 51, 57–8; Howard, *Where Do We Go from Here?*, p. 87; Buckley, Irwin & Kinsella, *We Also Served*, pp. 16, 27, 36, 40.
48 Mabel Quakawoot, interview.

49 ibid.
50 ibid.
51 Marj Tripp, in *For Love of Country*, directed by Malcolm McKinnon, produced by Reconciliation South Australia, DVD, 19 mins, 2011. See also Mattingley & Hampton (eds), *Survival in Our Own Land*, pp. 106, 288.
52 Patricia Lees, interview with Colleen Hattersley, Brisbane, 13 June 2001, *Bringing Them Home Oral History Project*, TRC 5000/300, NLA, Canberra.
53 Jacqueline Shaw, interview.
54 ibid.
55 *Dawn*, August 1967, p. 12.
56 Jacqueline Shaw, interview.
57 Kathryn Spurling, 'From Exclusion to Submarines', p. 37. See also Agostino, 'Femininities and Masculinities in the Royal Australian Navy', p. 75; Smith & McAllister, 'The Changing Military Profession', p. 372.
58 Jacqueline Shaw, interview.
59 See Smith & McAllister, 'The Changing Military Profession', pp. 369–91; Australian Human Rights Commission, *Report on the Review into the Treatment of Women at the Australian Defence Force Academy: Phase 1 of the review into the treatment of women in the Australian Defence Force*, vol. 1, Australian Human Rights Commission, Canberra, 2011; Australian Human Rights Commission, *Review into the Treatment of Women in the Australian Defence Force: Phase 2 report*, vol. 2, Australian Human Rights Commission, Canberra, 2012.
60 Jacqueline Shaw, interview.
61 ibid.
62 Agostino, 'Femininities and Masculinities in the Royal Australian Navy', p. 75; Smith & McAllister, 'The Changing Military Profession', p. 372.
63 Jacqueline Shaw, interview.
64 ibid.
65 ibid.
66 For published Second World War examples, see Alice Lovett, in Jackomos & Fowell, *Forgotten Heroes*, pp. 38–42; 'Oodgeroo Noonuccal', in Hall, *Fighters from the Fringe*, pp. 111–33.

5 RACISM, INDIGENOUS PEOPLE, AND THE AUSTRALIAN ARMED FORCES

1 Gerard Warber, interview with John Bannister, Perth, 26 March 2000, *Bringing Them Home Oral History Project*, TRC 5000/101, NLA, Canberra.
2 Hugh Smith, 'Minorities and the Australian Army: Overlooked and

Notes

underrepresented?', in Peter Dennis & Jeffrey Grey (eds), *A Century of Service*, pp. 129–49.

3   Traditional historiography has deemed Captain Reg Saunders to be the first Aboriginal commissioned officer during the Second World War, but Andrea Gerrard of the University of Tasmania has recently identified Tasmanian Aboriginal man Second Lieutenant Alfred Hearps from the First World War. See Michelle Paine, 'Tales of Illegal Heroes', *The Mercury* (Hobart), 9 November 2012, p. 23. The first known Aboriginal graduate from the Royal Military College, Duntroon, was Wesley Aird, during the 1980s.

4   Christopher Bates Doob, *Racism: An American cauldron*, HarperCollins College Publishers, New York, 1993, p. 5.

5   Doob, *Racism*, p. 6. See also David Hollinsworth, *Race and Racism in Australia*, 3rd edn, Cengage Learning, Melbourne, 2006, pp. 42–51.

6   Hollinsworth, *Race and Racism in Australia*, p. 48; Doob, *Racism*, p. 6.

7   Noel Tovey, *Little Black Bastard*, Hachette Australia, Sydney, 2005, p. 144.

8   Ken Colbung, in 'Ken Colbung', *Message Stick*, produced and directed by Kelrick Martin, produced by the ABC, 2004, abc.net.au/tv/messagestick/stories/s1070887.htm, accessed 27 January 2015.

9   Bob Blair, interview.

10 Ron Wenitong, interview.

11 Mial Bingarape, interview with Noah Riseman, Cairns, 7 November 2011.

12 Mabel Quakawoot, interview.

13 Sue Gordon, interview with Noah Riseman.

14 ibid.

15 Yin Paradies, 'A Systematic Review of Empirical Research on Self-reported Racism and Health', *International Journal of Epidemiology*, vol. 35, no. 4, 2006, p. 891.

16 Sue Gordon, interview with Noah Riseman; David Cook, interview with Noah Riseman; Noah Riseman, 'The Stolen Veteran', pp. 57–77; Phil Prosser, in *The Forgotten*, directed by Glen Stasiuk; Geoff Shaw, in *I Hope the War Will Be Over Soon*, directed by John Ruane.

17 Anthony Bergin, Robert Hall, Roger Jones & Ian McAllister, 'The Ethnic Composition of the Australian Defence Force: Management, attitudes & strategies', Australian Defence Studies, working paper no. 11, University College, University of New South Wales, Australian Defence Force Academy, Canberra, May 1993, p. 10.

18 George Akee, interview with Noah Riseman, Thursday Island, 11 November 2011.

19 Ezra Anu, interview with Noah Riseman, Canberra, 27 September 2010.

20   Ed Bailey, interview with Noah Riseman, Canberra, 11 April 2012.
21   Neil Macdonald, interview with Noah Riseman, Canberra, 3 December 2009; Hollinsworth, *Race and Racism in Australia*, p. 48.
22   Linda McBride-Yuke, interview with Noah Riseman, Zillmere, Qld, 20 June 2010.
23   Frank Mallard, interview.
24   Warren L Young, *Minorities and the Military: A cross-national study in world perspective*, Greenwood Press, Westport, CT, 1982, pp. 26–9. See also Charles C Moskos, Jr, 'Racial Integration in the Armed Forces', *The American Journal of Sociology*, vol. 72, no. 2, September 1966, pp. 132–48.
25   James E Westheider, *Fighting on Two Fronts*, p. 113.
26   Major General Michael Jeffery, interview with Richard Trembath, Canberra, 22 February 2012.
27   Hall, *The Black Diggers*, p. 69.
28   Dick Bligh, interview.
29   Steve Maloney, interview with Noah Riseman, Brisbane, 24 September 2012.
30   George Bostock, interview with Noah Riseman. See also John Schnaars, interview with Noah Riseman.
31   Dick Bligh, interview.
32   Laughton, *Not Quite Men, No Longer Boys*, p. 44.
33   Ezra Anu, interview. See also George Akee, interview.
34   Australia, Department of Defence, 'Department of Defence Census 2011 Public Report', Roy Morgan Research, Canberra, May 2012, p. 44.
35   Jason Sears, '1919–1929: An imperial service', in David Stevens (ed), *The Royal Australian Navy: The Australian centenary history of defence*, vol. III, Cambridge University Press, Melbourne, 2001, p. 71.
36   Bergin, Hall, Jones & McAllister, 'The Ethnic Composition of the Australian Defence Force', p. xviii.
37   Linda McBride-Yuke, interview; Private Cedric 'Ned' Egglestone & Don McLeod, Royal Australian Infantry Corps, interview with Bill Bunbury, RSL, Reservoir, 3 September 1998, AWM S01907, AWM, Canberra; Lieutenant DG Bowen, RAN, to HJ Green, Aborigines Welfare Board, 6 September 1962, in David Cook Welfare File, provided to authors courtesy of David Cook.
38   David Cook, interview.
39   Marsat Ketchell, interview with Noah Riseman, Thursday Island, 11 November 2011.
40   Linda McBride-Yuke, interview; Marsat Ketchell, interview; Ezra Anu, interview; David Williams, interview with Noah Riseman, Merrylands, NSW, 4 November 2011.

Notes

41 Bergin, Hall, Jones & McAllister, 'The Ethnic Composition of the Australian Defence Force', p. 10.
42 Neil Macdonald, interview.
43 Linda McBride-Yuke, interview.
44 Brian White, in George Bray, Kenny Laughton & Pat Forster (eds), *Aboriginal Ex-servicemen of Central Australia*, IAD Press, Alice Springs, 1995, p. 17.
45 *As a Matter of Fact: Answering the myths and misconceptions about Indigenous Australians*, Office of Public Affairs, ATSIC, Canberra, 1998, p. 60; John Gardiner-Garden, 'Defining Aboriginality in Australia', Current Issues Brief no. 10, 2002–03, aph.gov.au/About_Parliament/Parliamentary_Departments/Parliamentary_Library/Publications_Archive/CIB/cib0203/03Cib10#definitions, accessed 29 June 2012. See also Scott Bennett, *White Politics and Black Australians*, Allen & Unwin, Sydney, 1999, p. 31; Geoffrey Partington, *Hasluck versus Coombs: White politics and Australia's Aborigines*, Quakers Hill Press, Sydney, 1996, p. 57.
46 Andrew Bolt, 'It's So Hip to be Black', *The Herald-Sun* (Melbourne), 15 April 2009; Federal Court of Australia, *Eatock v. Bolt* [2011] FCA 1103, 28 September 2011, austlii.edu.au/au/cases/cth/FCA/2011/1103.html, accessed 29 June 2012.
47 Ezra Anu, interview.
48 Mick Pittman, interview with Noah Riseman, Gosford, NSW, 21 January 2010.
49 See, for instance, Riseman, 'The Stolen Veteran', p. 65.
50 Frank Mallard, interview.
51 Major Jo West, interview with Richard Trembath, Brisbane, 5 July 2013.
52 Stan Phoenix, interview with Noah Riseman, Singleton, NSW, 18 January 2010.
53 Young, *Minorities and the Military*, p. 249.
54 ibid., pp. 248–51.
55 McGregor, *Indifferent Inclusion*, p. xi.
56 On civil rights and activism in the 1960s–70s, see Jennifer Clark, *Aborigines & Activism: Race, Aborigines and the coming of the sixties to Australia*, University of Western Australia Press, Perth, 2008; Sue Taffe, *Black and White Together: FCAATSI: The Federal Council for the Advancement of Aborigines and Torres Strait Islanders 1958–1973*, University of Queensland Press, Brisbane, 2005; *Vote Yes for Aborigines*; Chesterman, *Civil Rights*.
57 Murray Goot & Tim Rowse, *Divided Nation? Indigenous affairs and the imagined public*, Melbourne University Press, Melbourne, 2007, p. 38;

Scott Bennett, *White Politics and Black Australians*, pp. 22–4; Scott Bennett, *Aborigines and Political Power*, Allen & Unwin, Sydney, 1989, pp. 53–4. See also McGregor, *Indifferent Inclusion*, pp. 157–8.

58 Goot & Rowse, *Divided Nation?*, p. 59. See also Bennett, *Aborigines and Political Power*, p. 59.

59 Jennifer Clark, *Aborigines & Activism*, pp. 158–9; Mickler, *The Myth of Privilege*, pp. 93–129. See also Haebich, *Spinning the Dream*, p. 192.

60 Sarah Maddison, *Beyond White Guilt: The real challenge for Black–white relations in Australia*, Allen & Unwin, Sydney, 2011, p. 107.

61 Goot & Rowse, *Divided Nation?*, p. 93. On the 1980s public backlash, see also Mickler, *The Myth of Privilege*, pp. 198–247; Hawke & Gallagher, *Noonkanbah*, pp. 318–19; Bennett, *White Politics and Black Australians*, p. 33; Bennett, *Aborigines and Political Power*, p. 157.

62 Lee Sigelman & Susan Welch, 'The Contact Hypothesis Revisited: Black–white interaction and positive racial attitudes', *Social Forces*, vol. 71, no. 3, March 1993, p. 783.

63 Goot & Rowse, *Divided Nation?*, p. 173. See also Bennett, *White Politics and Black Australians*, pp. 24–37.

64 Irene Moss, 'Are Australians Racist?', *The Age*, 27 January 1994, p. 12.

65 Brigadier Nagy Sorial, interview with Richard Trembath, Melbourne, 18 July 2013.

6 A CHANGING DEFENCE FORCE AND RECONCILIATION

1 Japarta Maurie Ryan, interview with Glenys Dimond, Berry Springs, NT, 10 April 2000, *Bringing Them Home Oral History Project*, TRC 5000/233, NLA, Canberra.

2 Bergin, Hall, Jones & McAllister, 'The Ethnic Composition of the Australian Defence Force', p. 23.

3 Paul Keating, 'The Redfern Park Address', 10 December 1992, in Michelle Grattan (ed.), *Reconciliation: Essays on Australian Reconciliation*, Black Inc., Melbourne, 2000, p. 63.

4 See Grattan (ed.), *Reconciliation*; Andrew Gunstone, *Unfinished Business: The Australian formal Reconciliation process*, Australian Scholarly Publishing, Melbourne, 2007.

5 Paul A Rosenzweig, *Ever Vigilant: The regimental history of the North West Mobile Force (NORFORCE) 1981–2001*, North West Mobile Force, Darwin, 2001, p. vii.

6 Grey, *A Military History of Australia*, pp. 262–4.

7 Rosenzweig, *Ever Vigilant*, p. vii.

Notes

8   Grey, *A Military History of Australia,* pp. 264–5.
9   Lieutenant General David Morrison, chief of army, at Senate Estimates, Foreign Affairs, Defence and Trade Legislation Committee, Senate Committee Hansard, 2 June 2014, p. 140.
10 Grey, *A Military History of Australia*, p. 265.
11 Rosenzweig, *Ever Vigilant*, p. 13.
12 ibid., p. 67.
13 Colonel Ashley Gunder, CO of 51 FNQR, January 2000 – December 2001, interview with Richard Trembath, Brisbane, 5 July 2013.
14 Lieutenant General David Morrison, chief of army, at Senate Estimates, Foreign Affairs, Defence and Trade Legislation Committee, Senate Committee Hansard, 3 June 2013, pp. 143–4; 'Force Charged with Guarding WA's Vast Frontier', *The West Australian*, 27 August 2011.
15 Lieutenant Colonel Cameron Hooke, CO of the Pilbara Regiment, 1994–95, email to Richard Trembath, 22 November 2012.
16 Brigadier Nagy Sorial, interview.
17 See *No Bugles, No Drums*; Berndt & Berndt, *End of an Era*; Noah Riseman, *Defending Whose Country?*, chapters 1 and 2.
18 David Hancock, 'Putting on the Green Skin', *Australian Geographic*, January–March 2009, pp. 70–7.
19 'Australia's Last "Tracker" Barry Port Retires', *Brisbane Times*, 4 July 2014, brisbanetimes.com.au/queensland/australias-last-tracker-barry-port-retires-20140704-zsvrm.html, accessed 12 September 2014.
20 John Connor, 'The Frontier War That Never Was', in Craig Stockings (ed.), *Zombie Myths of Australian Military History*, NewSouth Publishing, Sydney, 2010, pp. 10–28.
21 Bergin, Hall, Jones & McAllister, 'The Ethnic Composition of the Australian Defence Force', pp. 147, 166–7.
22 Brigadier Nagy Sorial, interview.
23 Colonel Clay Sutton, CO of Norforce, May 2003 – December 2004, interview with Richard Trembath, 3 December 2012. See also Colonel Tim Simkin, interview with Richard Trembath, Brisbane, 8 July 2013.
24 Brigadier Mal Rerden, CO of 51 FNQR, January 1996 – December 1997, interview with Richard Trembath, 3 December 2012.
25 Colonel Tim Simkin, interview.
26 Major General Michael Jeffery, interview.
27 Colonel Clay Sutton, interview.
28 Kathy Marks, 'Brothers in Arms', *Good Weekend*, 10 December 2011, pp. 22–6.

29 'Norforce', *Message Stick*, produced and directed by Penny Smallacombe, ABC, 2004.
30 Colonel Ashley Gunder, interview.
31 WO1 Reg Davies, 'Diary of the First Aboriginal Recruit Course, 02–18 October 1981', Appendix Four, in Rosenzweig, *Ever Vigilant*, pp. 343–58. Emphasis in original.
32 'Green Warriors', *Message Stick*, directed by Douglas Watkin, produced by the ABC, 2008.
33 *Living Black*, 22 April 2012; also aired on 'Soldier – Artist', *SBS World News Australia*, 1 April 2012.
34 'Green Warriors', *Message Stick*.
35 'The Work of Norforce', *SBS World News Australia*, 31 March 2012.
36 'Green Warriors', *Message Stick*.
37 'The Work of Norforce', *SBS World News Australia*.
38 'Green Warriors', *Message Stick*.
39 'Norforce', *Message Stick*.
40 John C Blaxland, *The Australian Army from Whitlam to Howard*, Cambridge University Press, Melbourne, 2014, p. 289.
41 Blaxland, *The Australian Army from Whitlam to Howard*, pp. 321–2.
42 Jane Ashby-Cliffe, 'Reaching the End', *Army – The Soldiers Newspaper*, no. 1202, 13 November 2008, p. 4.
43 Warren Snowden, minister for defence science and personnel, cited in Ashby-Cliffe, 'Reaching the End', p. 4.
44 'Norforce Boost', *ABC News NT*, 15 May 2009.
45 'Black Force', *Living Black*, 28 September 2009.
46 ibid.
47 For the history of Australia's involvement in the Persian Gulf War, see David Horner, *The Gulf Commitment: The Australian Defence Force's first war*, Melbourne University Press, Melbourne, 1992; David Horner, *Australia and the 'New World Order': From peacekeeping to peace enforcement: 1988–1991*, *The official history of Australian peacekeeping, humanitarian and post–Cold War operations*, vol. 2, Cambridge University Press, Cambridge, 2011, pp. 269–498.
48 Neil Macdonald, interview.
49 ibid.
50 Bergin, Hall, Jones & McAllister, 'The Ethnic Composition of the Australian Defence Force', Annex 1–9.
51 For a history of the Somalia campaign, see Bob Breen, *A Little Bit of Hope: Australian Force – Somalia*, Allen & Unwin, Sydney, 1998; Peter Londey,

Notes

Other People's Wars: A history of Australian peacekeeping, Allen & Unwin, Sydney, 2004, pp. 179–93.
52 Chris Townson, interview with Noah Riseman, Townsville, 26 September 2012.
53 ibid.
54 For a history of INTERFET and Australia's role, see Bob Breen, *Mission Accomplished – East Timor: Australian Defence Force participation in International Force East Timor*, Allen & Unwin, Sydney, 2001; Londey, *Other People's Wars*, pp. 231–61.
55 Steve Maloney, interview.
56 ibid.
57 ibid.
58 ibid.
59 See Hugh Smith, 'The Dynamics of Cultural Change and the Australian Defence Force', *Armed Forces & Society*, vol. 21, no. 4, 1995, pp. 531–51.
60 Bergin, Hall, Jones & McAllister, 'The Ethnic Composition of the Australian Defence Force', pp. 4–7.
61 Major Jo West, interview.
62 Bergin, Hall, Jones & McAllister, 'The Ethnic Composition of the Australian Defence Force', pp. 224–7.
63 Senator John Faulkner, 5 May 1993, *Hansard*, p. 134.
64 James Swanwick, 'Aborigines Get Call to Arms', *The Courier-Mail*, 23 February 1998.
65 Australia, Department of Defence, 'Defence Reconciliation Action Plan 2010–2014: Reconciliation through our people', December 2009, reconciliation.org.au/raphub/wp-content/uploads/raps/federal/defencereconciliationactionplan2010-14.pdf, accessed 27 January 2016.
66 Australia, Department of Defence, 'Australian Defence Force Indigenous Employment Strategy 2007–17', 10, defence.gov.au/fr/publications/ADF%20IES%20-%20External%20Version_04Dec08.pdf, accessed 3 July 2012.
67 'About IPRC', Indigenous Pre Recruitment Course, iprc.aboriginallearningcircle.com/about-iprc, accessed 12 January 2015; 'Indigenous Pre-Recruitment Course', The Centre of Diversity Expertise: Indigenous Affairs, defence.gov.au/code/indigenous/career/adf/iprc.asp, accessed 12 January 2015.
68 In Peter Foley, 'Military Life Meets Indigenous Culture', *The Queensland Times*, 6 June 2014, qt.com.au/news/trio-ready-to-serve-after-special-defence-course/2281368/, accessed 12 January 2015.

69 'Defence Indigenous Development Program', The Centre of Diversity Expertise: Indigenous Affairs, defence.gov.au/code/indigenous/career/adf/didp.asp, accessed 12 January 2015.

70 'More Indigenous Recruiting Officers Join Army Ranks', *The Australian Army*, army.gov.au/Our-people/Army-Indigenous-community/More-Indigenous-Recruiting-Officers-join-Army-ranks, accessed 12 September 2015; 'Indigenous Students Get a Taste for Air Force Life', Department of Defence Media Release, 17 April 2013, news.defence.gov.au/2013/04/17/indigenous-students-get-a-taste-for-air-force-life/, accessed 12 January 2015; 'Army's First Indigenous Elder', *The Australian Army*, army.gov.au/Our-people/Army-Indigenous-community/Armys-first-Indigenous-Elder, accessed 22 September 2015; Des Paroz, 'Twenty Three Indigenous Australians Graduate from the First Navy-run Defence Indigenous Development Program', *Navy Daily*, 25 July 2014, news.navy.gov.au/en/Jul2014/Events/1253/Twenty-three-indigenous-Australians-graduate-from-the-first-Navy-run-Defence-Indigenous-Development-Program.htm#.VLPkj005CUk, accessed 12 January 2015.

71 *Survival School*, directed by Luigi Acquisto and David Bradbury, produced by Luigi Acquisto and Stella Zammatro, produced by the ABC, 55 mins, 2007; 'Local Aboriginal Women Teach Bush Skills to Troops', *ABC News*, 22 May 2011.

72 'Short Stay', *Living Black*, 14 October 2012.

73 'Soldiers Take Historic Steps', *Army News*, 24 November 2011, army.gov.au/Our-people/Army-Indigenous-community/Stories-of-interest/Soldiers-take-historic-steps, accessed 12 September 2015; 'Army Indigenous Initiatives', *The Australian Army*, army.gov.au/Our-people/Army-Indigenous-community/Army-Indigenous-initiatives, accessed 12 September 2015.

EPILOGUE: COMMEMORATING INDIGENOUS SERVICE

1 Inglis, *Sacred Places*, p. 356.

2 Darryl 'Rocky' Wallace, interview with George Bostock, 11 April 1991, BOSTOCK_G01-016549-50, AIATSIS, Canberra; Jane Munday, 'Lest We Forget the Aborigines Who Fought', *The Age*, 26 April 1985, p. 5; 'Aboriginal Anzac March', *The Canberra Times*, 20 March 1985, p. 9; 'Ruxton Plans to Stop Aboriginal Group March', *The Canberra Times*, 5 March 1985, p. 3.

3 Liz Reed, *Bigger than Gallipoli: War, history and memory in Australia*, University of Western Australia Press, Perth, 2004, p. 174; Cecil Fisher, 'Anzac Day Marching on the Gold Coast in 1993', *Koori Mail*, 2 May 2001, p. 9.

4 Eloise Dortch & Minh Lam, 'Marchers Break New Ground', *The West Australian*, 26 April 2001, p. 5; *The Forgotten*, directed by Glen Stasiuk; Jodi

Notes

    Hoffman, 'Aboriginal Pride to the Fore in Anzac Day March', *Koori Mail*, 2 May 2001, p. 11.

5   Yuko Narushima, '300 Attend Coloured Diggers March', *The Sydney Morning Herald*, 26 April 2007, smh.com.au/news/national/300-attend-coloured-diggers-march/2007/04/25/1177459766290.html, accessed 13 January 2015; 'The Coloured Diggers Project', Babana Aboriginal Men's Group Redfern, babana.org.au/#!coloured-digger-project/c1xg3, accessed 13 January 2015.

6   'Fed: Thousands Gather in Canberra for Dawn Service', Australian Associated Press, 25 April 2004; Aboriginal & Torres Strait Islander Veterans & Services Association, atsivsa.com, accessed 13 January 2015.

7   'Indigenous Cultural Events and Commemorative Events', Department of Veterans' Affairs, dva.gov.au/i-am/aboriginal-andor-torres-strait-islander/indigenous-cultural-events-and-commemorative-events, accessed 12 September 2015; David Mclennan, 'Black Soldiers: They were "fighting for their land"', *The Canberra Times*, 7 July 1999, p. 3; 'Theme and Host City', NAIDOC, naidoc.org.au/about/theme-and-host-city, accessed 13 January 2015.

8   John Schnaars, in 'The Last Post', *Message Stick*.

9   See Inglis, *Sacred Places*, especially pp. 355–6; 'AUSTRALIAN GOVERNMENT: Aboriginal War Memorial unveiled at Point Pearce', M2 PRESSWIRE, 15 November 1999; 'Qld – Torres Strait War Memorial Planned', Australian Associated Press, 30 September 2000; Georgia Warner, 'Black Flag in Right Place', *The Mercury*, 26 April 2000, p. 7; 'Aboriginal War Memorial Rededicated', *Illawarra Mercury*, 21 April 2000, p. 4.

10   Anne Brennan, 'Lest We Forget: Military myths, memory, and Canberra's Aboriginal and Torres Strait Islander memorial', *Memory Connection*, vol. 1, no. 1, 2011, pp. 35–44.

11   Frank Lampard, speech, copy provided to authors.

12   *YININMADYEMI Thou didst let fall*, City Art Sydney, cityartsydney.com.au/artwork/yininmadyemi-thou-didst-let-fall, accessed 13 January 2015; Melanie Kembrey, 'Tony Albert's "Confronting" Tribute to Indigenous Diggers Unveiled in Sydney's Hyde Park', *The Sydney Morning Herald*, 31 March 2015, smh.com.au/entertainment/art-and-design/tony-alberts-confronting-tribute-to-indigenous-diggers-unveiled-in-sydneys-hyde-park-20150331-1mbuzo.html, accessed 27 April 2015.

13   'The Work of Norforce: The first marines to train in the Northern Territory may arrive as early as next month', *SBS World News Australia*, 31 March 2012.

BIBLIOGRAPHY

PRIMARY SOURCES

Interviews

Akee, George, interview with Noah Riseman, Thursday Island, 11 November 2011.
Anu, Ezra, interview with Noah Riseman, Canberra, 27 September 2010.
Atkinson, Graham, interview with George Bostock, April 1991, BOSTOCK_G01-016549, AIATSIS, Canberra.
Bailey, Ed, interview with Noah Riseman, Canberra, 11 April 2012.
Bingarape, Mial, interview with Noah Riseman, Cairns, 7 November 2011.
Blair, Bob, interview with Noah Riseman, Rockhampton, 22 June 2010.
Bligh, Dick, interview with Noah Riseman, Perth, 25 November 2010, ORAL TRC 6260/4, NLA, Canberra.
Bostock, George, interview with Noah Riseman, Brisbane, 18 June 2010.
Colbung, Ken, interview with Lily Kauler, Canberra, 22 October 2001, *Bringing Them Home Oral History Project*, TRC 5000/336, NLA, Canberra.
Cook, David, interview with Noah Riseman, Raymond Terrace, NSW, 20 January 2010.
Egglestone, Private Cedric 'Ned' & Don McLeod, Royal Australian Infantry Corps, interview with Bill Bunbury, RSL, Reservoir, 3 September 1998, AWMY S01907, AWM, Canberra.
Gage, Dianne, interview with Noah Riseman, Brisbane, 1 June 2011.
Gardner, Max, interview with George Bostock, 28 April 1991, BOSTOCK_G01-016546, AIATSIS, Canberra.
Gordon, Sue, interview with John Bannister, Perth, 12 October 1999, *Bringing Them Home Oral History Project*, TRC 5000/52, NLA, Canberra.

Bibliography

—— interview with Noah Riseman, Perth, 25 November 2010, ORAL TRC 6260/5, NLA, Canberra.
Gunder, Colonel Ashley, interview with Richard Trembath, Brisbane, 5 July 2013.
Hooke, Lieutenant Colonel Cameron, interview with Richard Trembath, Canberra, 4 December 2012.
James, Glenn, interview with Ina Bertrand, Templestowe, Vic, 23 January 2001, *Victorians at War – Oral history project*, victoriansatwar.net/archives/james.html, accessed 18 February 2013.
Jeffery, Major General Michael, interview with Richard Trembath, Canberra, 22 February 2012.
Ketchell, Marsat, interview with Noah Riseman, Thursday Island, 11 November 2011.
Lampard, Frank, interview with Noah Riseman, Adelaide, 28 November 2013.
Lees, Patricia, interview with Colleen Hattersley, Brisbane, 13 June 2001, *Bringing Them Home Oral History Project*, TRC 5000/300, NLA, Canberra.
'Louise', interview with Noah Riseman, Canberra, 12 April 2012.
McBride-Yuke, Linda, interview with Noah Riseman, Zillmere, Qld, 20 June 2010.
McCormack, Jeff, interview with Noah Riseman, Monarto, SA, 9 July 2012.
Macdonald, Neil, interview with Noah Riseman, Canberra, 3 December 2009.
Mallard, Frank, interview with Noah Riseman, Perth, 24 November 2010, ORAL TRC 6260/2, NLA, Canberra.
Maloney, Steve, interview with Noah Riseman, Brisbane, 24 September 2012.
Mummery, Michael, interview with Richard Trembath, Adelaide, 17 September 2012.
Ogilvie, Leonard, interview with John Bannister, 25 May 2001, *Bringing Them Home Oral History Project*, TRC 5000/274, NLA, Canberra.
—— interview with John Bannister, 10 February 2004, item 26869, IWM, London.
Phoenix, Stan, interview with Noah Riseman, Singleton, NSW, 18 January 2010.
Pittman, Mick, interview with Noah Riseman, Gosford, NSW, 21 January 2010.
Prosser, Phillip, interview with John Bannister, Perth, 22 January 2000, *Bringing Them Home Oral History Project*, TRC 5000/183, NLA, Canberra.
Quakawoot, Mabel, interview with Noah Riseman, Mackay, 5 June 2011.
Rerden, Brigadier Mal, interview with Richard Trembath, Canberra, 3 December 2012.
Ryan, Japarta Maurie, interview with Glenys Dimond, Berry Springs, NT, 10 April 2000, *Bringing Them Home Oral History Project*, TRC 5000/233, NLA, Canberra.
Schnaars, John, interview with Noah Riseman, Perth, 23 November 2010, ORAL TRC 6260/1, NLA, Canberra.

Shaw, Jacqueline, interview with Noah Riseman, Cairns, 27 September 2012.
Simkin, Colonel Tim, interview with Richard Trembath, Brisbane, 8 July 2013.
Sorial, Brigadier Nagy, interview with Richard Trembath, Melbourne, 18 July 2013.
Sutton, Colonel Clay, interview with Richard Trembath, Canberra, 3 December 2012.
Townson, Chris, interview with Noah Riseman, Townsville, 26 September 2012.
Wallace, Darryl 'Rocky', interview with George Bostock, 11 April 1991, BOSTOCK_G01-016549-50, AIATSIS, Canberra.
Warber, Gerard, interview with John Bannister, Perth, 26 March 2000, *Bringing Them Home Oral History Project*, TRC 5000/101, NLA, Canberra.
Wenitong, Ron, interview with Noah Riseman, Cairns, 23 June 2010.
West, Major Jo, interview with Richard Trembath, Brisbane, 5 July 2013.
Whyman, Hewitt, interview with George Bostock, 26 April 1991, BOSTOCK_G01-016548, AIATSIS, Canberra.
Williams, David, interview with Noah Riseman, Merrylands, NSW, 4 November 2011.

Newspapers and media

The 7.30 Report
ABC News
ABC News NT
The Advertiser (Adelaide)
The Advocate (Burnie)
The Age (Melbourne)
The Argus (Melbourne)
Army (Australian Army)
The Australian
Australian Associated Press
Australian Geographic
Australian Playboy
The Barrier Miner (Broken Hill)
Brisbane Times
The Bulletin
The Cairns Post
The Canberra Times
Centralian Advocate (Alice Springs)
The Courier-Mail (Brisbane)
The Daily Bulletin (Townsville)
The Daily News (Perth)
Dawn
Good Weekend
The Herald (Melbourne)
The Herald-Sun (Melbourne)
Illawarra Mercury
Koori Mail
Living Black
M2 PRESSWIRE
The Mail (Adelaide)
The Mercury (Hobart)
The Mirror (Sydney)
The Morning Bulletin (Rockhampton)
Morwell Advertiser
Mufti (Victorian RSL magazine)
Navy Daily (Royal Australian Navy)
The Northern Standard (Darwin)
The Portland Guardian
The Queensland Times
SBS World News Australia

Bibliography

The Standard (Warrnambool)
Stateline WA
The Sun (Melbourne)
The Sunday Herald (Sydney)
Sunday Observer (Melbourne)
The Sunday Times (Perth)
The Sydney Morning Herald
Townsville Daily Bulletin
The West Australian (Perth)

Archives
AIATSIS
MS 3012, George Bostock, 'Black veterans of Vietnam', unpublished manuscript

Australian War Memorial
AWM, series AWM263, item D/2/6
AWM, series AWM263, item D/2/7
AWM, FO1992
AWM, FO7535
AWM, P01795.001
AWM, PR 91/163
AWM, S01906
AWM, S01907

Central Army Records Office (CARO)
Various Korean War and Vietnam War service records

David Cook Welfare File
Provided to authors courtesy of David Cook

National Film and Sound Archives
Title no. 452926

National Archives of Australia
NAA Canberra, series A452, item NT1964/7194
NAA Canberra, series A452, item NT1967/2081
NAA Canberra, series A463, item 1962/3685, part 1
NAA Canberra, series A463, item 1968/3222
NAA Canberra, series A816, item 72/301/23
NAA Canberra, series A1734, item NT1972/23
NAA Canberra, series A2354, item 1968/1
NAA Canberra, series A2487, item 1919/3202
NAA Canberra, series A2671, item 45/1940
NAA Canberra, series B2458, item 337678
NAA Melbourne, series B337, item 664
NAA Melbourne, series MP742/1, item 275/1/696
NAA Perth, series K38, item 1971/3551

National Library of Australia
NLA, item 1862902
NLA, MSS 6609 (RSL papers)
NLA, MSS 9904 (Bruce Ruxton papers)

State Records Office, WA
RSO, series 2030, item 1965/0317

Legislation and court cases
Australia, *Defence Act*
—— *Defence Legislation Amendment Act 1992*, No. 91, 1992
—— *Eatock v. Bolt* [2011] FCA 1103, 28 September 2011
—— *National Service Act 1951*
—— *National Service Act 1964*
—— *National Service Regulations 1964*

Unpublished theses
Agostino, Katerina, 'Femininities and Masculinities in the Royal Australian Navy: Workplace discourses', PhD thesis, Department of Psychology and Sociology, James Cook University, 1997.
Johansen, Grace, 'The AWAS: A social history of the Australian Women's Army Service during the Second World War', BA (Honours) Thesis, History Department, Central Queensland University, 1996.
Pratt, Rod, '"By Cripes! I'll Fight for White Australia!": Queensland Aborigines in the First AIF', Thesis for Master of Literary Studies, University of Queensland, 1990.
Spurling, Kathryn Leslie, 'The Women's Royal Australian Naval Service: A study in discrimination 1939–1960', MA thesis, History Department, The University of New South Wales at the Australian Defence Force Academy, 1988.

Other unpublished sources
Aboriginal & Torres Strait Islander Veterans & Services Association, atsivsa.com, accessed 13 January 2015.
'About IPRC', *Indigenous Pre-Recruitment Course*, iprc.aboriginallearningcircle.com/about-iprc, accessed 12 January 2015.
'Army Indigenous Initiatives', *The Australian Army*, army.gov.au/Our-people/Army-Indigenous-community/Army-Indigenous-initiatives, accessed 12 September 2015.
'Army's First Indigenous Elder', *The Australian Army*, army.gov.au/Our-people/

Bibliography

Army-Indigenous-community/Armys-first-Indigenous-Elder, accessed 22 September 2015.

'The Coloured Diggers Project', Babana Aboriginal Men's Group Redfern, babana.org.au/#!coloured-digger-project/c1xg3, accessed 13 January 2015.

'The Coronation Contingent of 1953', *Australian War Memorial*, awm.gov.au/blog/2009/03/11/the-coronation-contingent-of-1953/, accessed 17 December 2013.

'Defence Indigenous Development Program', Centre of Diversity Expertise: Indigenous Affairs, defence.gov.au/code/indigenous/career/adf/didp.asp, accessed 12 January 2015.

'Indigenous Cultural Events and Commemorative Events', Department of Veterans' Affairs, dva.gov.au/i-am/aboriginal-andor-torres-strait-islander/indigenous-cultural-events-and-commemorative-events, accessed 12 September 2015.

'Indigenous Pre-Recruitment Course', Centre of Diversity Expertise: Indigenous Affairs, defence.gov.au/code/indigenous/career/adf/iprc.asp, accessed 12 January 2015.

'Indigenous Students Get a Taste for Air Force Life', Department of Defence Media Release, 17 April 2013, news.defence.gov.au/2013/04/17/indigenous-students-get-a-taste-for-air-force-life/, accessed 12 January 2015.

Ken Colbung, interview with Kerrie Jean Ross, *Awaye!*, ABC Radio National, 27 August 2007, nma.gov.au/exhibitions/first_australians/resistance/yagan/awaye_audio_program_transcript, accessed 27 January 2015.

Lampard, Frank, speech, dedication of Adelaide memorial to Aboriginal and Torres Strait Islander military service, 10 November 2013.

Lieutenant Colonel Cameron Hooke, CO of the Pilbara Regiment, 1994–95, email to Richard Trembath, 22 November 2012.

'Maryborough (Queensland) Military and Colonial Museum', maryboroughmuseum.org/malayan.html, accessed 27 January 2013.

'More Indigenous Recruiting Officers Join Army Ranks', *The Australian Army*, army.gov.au/Our-people/Army-Indigenous-community/More-Indigenous-Recruiting-Officers-join-Army-ranks, accessed 12 September 2015.

One People, prepared by the Commonwealth Department of Territories, for use by the National Aborigines' Day Observance Committee on the celebration of National Aborigines' Day, 14 July 1961.

'Sgt Cecil Anderson – Indigenous soldier in three wars', *Remember Them*, garriehutchinson.com/2013/11/13/sgt-cecil-anderson-indigenous-soldier-in-three-wars/, accessed 8 February 2015.

'Steve Abala', Monument Australia, monumentaustralia.org.au/display/80218-steve-abala, accessed 6 April 2015.

'Theme and Host City', NAIDOC, naidoc.org.au/about/theme-and-host-city, accessed 13 January 2015.

'Yininmadyemi – Thou didst let fall', City Art Sydney, cityartsydney.com.au/artwork/yininmadyemi-thou-didst-let-fall/, accessed 13 January 2015.

SECONDARY SOURCES

Adam-Smith, Patsy, *Australian Women at War*, 2nd edn, Penguin, Melbourne, 1996.

Agostino, Katerina, 'Women in Uniform: Challenging feminisms', in Kathryn Spurling & Elizabeth Greenhalgh (eds), *Women in Uniform: Perceptions and pathways*, School of History, University College, UNSW, Australian Defence Force Academy, Canberra, 2000, pp. 64–82.

Anderson, Fay & Richard Trembath, *Witnesses to War: The history of Australian conflict reporting*, Melbourne University Press, Melbourne, 2011.

As a Matter of Fact: Answering the myths and misconceptions about Indigenous Australians, Office of Public Affairs, ATSIC, Canberra, 1998.

Australia, Department of Defence, 'Australian Defence Force Indigenous Employment Strategy 2007–17', defence.gov.au/fr/publications/ADF%20IES%20-%20External%20Version_04Dec08.pdf, accessed 3 July 2012.

—— 'Defence Reconciliation Action Plan 2010–2014: Reconciliation through our people', December 2009, reconciliation.org.au/raphub/wp-content/uploads/raps/federal/defencereconciliationactionplan2010-14.pdf, accessed 27 January 2016.

—— 'Department of Defence Census 2011 Public Report', Roy Morgan Research, Canberra, May 2012.

Australia, Department of Veterans' Affairs, *Study of Returned Servicewomen of the Second World War*, Australian Government Publishing Service, Canberra, 1985.

—— *Morbidity of Vietnam Veterans: A study of the health of Australia's Vietnam veteran community: Volume 1 – male Vietnam veterans*, Canberra, 1998–99.

Australia, National Inquiry into the Separation of Aboriginal and Torres Strait Islander Children from their Families, *Bringing Them Home: National inquiry into the separation of Aboriginal and Torres Strait Islander children from their families*, Human Rights and Equal Opportunity Commission, Sydney, 1997.

Australia, Senate, Community Affairs Reference Committee, *Forgotten Australians: A report on Australians who experienced institutional or out-of-home care as children*, 2004.

—— Estimates, Foreign Affairs, Defence and Trade Legislation Committee, Senate Committee Hansard, 3 June 2013.

—— Estimates, Foreign Affairs, Defence and Trade Legislation Committee, Senate Committee Hansard, 2 June 2014.

Australian Human Rights Commission, *Report on the Review into the Treatment of*

Bibliography

Women at the Australian Defence Force Academy: Phase 1 of the review into the treatment of women in the Australian Defence Force, vol. 1, Australian Human Rights Commission, Canberra, 2011.

—— *Review into the Treatment of Women in the Australian Defence Force: Phase 2 report*, vol. 2, Australian Human Rights Commission, Canberra, 2012.

Banivanua-Mar, Tracey, *Violence and Colonial Dialogue: The Australian-Pacific indentured labor trade*, University of Hawai'i Press, Honolulu, 2007.

Bassett, Jan, *Guns and Brooches: Australian Army nursing from the Boer War to the Gulf War*, Oxford University Press, Melbourne, 1992.

Bennett, Scott, *Aborigines and Political Power*, Allen & Unwin, Sydney, 1989.

—— *White Politics and Black Australians*, Allen & Unwin, Sydney, 1999.

Beresford, Quentin, *Rob Riley: An Aboriginal leader's quest for justice*, Aboriginal Studies Press, Canberra, 2006.

Bergin, Anthony, Robert Hall, Roger Jones & Ian McAllister, 'The Ethnic Composition of the Australian Defence Force: Management, attitudes & strategies', prepared for Director General Recruiting, Headquarters Australian Defence Force, 2 vols, Unisearch, February 1993.

—— 'The Ethnic Composition of the Australian Defence Force: Management, attitudes & strategies', Australian Defence Studies, working paper no. 11, University College, University of New South Wales, Australian Defence Force Academy, Canberra, May 1993.

Berndt, Ronald M & Catherine H, *End of an Era: Aboriginal labour in the Northern Territory*, Australian Institute of Aboriginal Studies, Canberra, 1987.

Beveridge, Jean, *AWAS: Women making history*, Booralong Publications, Chevron Island, Qld, 1988.

Blair, Anne, *Ruxton: A biography*, Allen & Unwin, Sydney, 2004.

Blaxland, John C, *The Australian Army from Whitlam to Howard*, Cambridge University Press, Melbourne, 2014.

Bomford, Janette, *Soldiers of the Queen: Women in the Australian Army*, Oxford University Press, Melbourne, 2001.

Bray, George, Kenny Laughton & Pat Forster (eds), *Aboriginal Ex-Servicemen of Central Australia*, IAD Press, Alice Springs, 1995.

Breen, Bob, *A Little Bit of Hope: Australian Force – Somalia*, Allen & Unwin, Sydney, 1998.

—— *Mission Accomplished – East Timor: Australian Defence Force participation in International Force East Timor*, Allen & Unwin, Sydney, 2001.

Brennan, Anne, 'Lest We Forget: Military myths, memory, and Canberra's Aboriginal and Torres Strait Islander Memorial', *Memory Connection*, vol. 1, no. 1, 2011, pp. 35–44.

Briscoe, Gordon, *Racial Folly: A twentieth century Aboriginal family*, ANU E Press and Aboriginal History Incorporated, Canberra, 2010.

Broome, Richard, *Aboriginal Australians: A history since 1788*, Allen & Unwin, Sydney, 2010.

Buckley, M, L Irwin & H Kinsella, *We Also Served*, MJ Buckley, Goonellabah, NSW, 1995.

Carroll, Colonel OM (Max) (RL), '"They Were Foremost Australian Soldiers": An oral account of Aboriginal and Thursday Island soldiers who served in Malaya and Vietnam: 1957 to 1967', *Aboriginal History*, vol. 16, no. 1, 1992, pp. 99–105.

Chesterman, John, *Civil Rights: How Indigenous Australians won formal equality*, University of Queensland Press, Brisbane, 2005.

Clark, Jennifer, *Aborigines & Activism: Race, Aborigines and the coming of the sixties to Australia*, University of Western Australia Press, Perth, 2008.

Connor, John, *The Australian Frontier Wars: 1788–1838*, UNSW Press, Sydney, 2002.

—— 'The Frontier War that Never Was', in Craig Stockings (ed.), *Zombie Myths of Australian Military History*, NewSouth Publishing, Sydney, 2010, pp. 10–28.

Cook, Kevin & Heather Goodall, *Making Change Happen: Black and white activists talk to Kevin Cook about Aboriginal, union and liberation politics*, ANU E Press, Canberra, 2013.

Costello, Judy, '"Why Would a Woman Want a Job Like That?" A personal reflection', in Peter Dennis & Jeffrey Grey (eds), *A Century of Service: 100 years of the Australian Army. The 2001 chief of army's military history conference*, Army History Unit, Department of Defence, Canberra, 2001, pp. 121–8.

Curtis-Otter, Margaret, *WRANS*, 2nd edn, The Naval Historical Society of Australia, Sydney, 1996.

Davison, Graeme, John Hirst & Stuart Macintyre (eds), *The Oxford Companion to Australian History*, Oxford University Press, Melbourne, 1998.

de Matos, Christine, 'A Very Gendered Occupation: Australian women as "conquerors" and "liberators"', *US–Japan Women's Journal*, vol. 33, 2007, pp. 87–107, available from University of Wollongong Research Online, ro.uow.edu.au/cgi/viewcontent.cgi?article=1186&context=artspapers, accessed 12 September 2015.

Dennis, Peter & Jeffrey Grey, *Emergency and Confrontation: Australian military operations, Malaya and Borneo, 1950–1966*, Allen & Unwin in association with the Australian War Memorial, Sydney, 1996.

Donaldson, Carina & Marilyn Lake, 'Whatever Happened to the Anti-war Movement?' in Marilyn Lake & Henry Reynolds (eds), *What's Wrong With Anzac? The militarisation of Australian history*, NewSouth Publishing, Sydney, 2010, pp. 71–93.

Bibliography

Doob, Christopher Bates, *Racism: An American cauldron*, HarperCollins College Publishers, New York, 1993.
Duguid, Charles, *No Dying Race*, Rigby, Adelaide, 1963.
Edwards, Peter, *Australia and the Vietnam War*, NewSouth Publishing, Sydney, 2014.
Evans, Raymond, Kay Saunders & Kathryn Cronin, *Race Relations in Colonial Queensland: A history of exclusion, exploitation and extermination*, 3rd edn, University of Queensland Press, Brisbane, 1993.
Flagg, Simon & Sebastian Gurciullo (eds), *Footprints: The journey of Lucy and Percy Pepper*, National Archives of Australia and Public Record Office of Victoria, Canberra, 2008.
For Love of Country, directed by Malcolm McKinnon, produced by Reconciliation South Australia, 19 mins, DVD, 2011.
Forbes, Cameron, *The Korean War: Australia in the giants' playground*, Macmillan, Sydney, 2010.
The Forgotten, directed by Glen Stasiuk, originally aired as an episode of *Message Stick* on the Australian Broadcasting Corporation (ABC), 27 April 2003, videocassette.
Forsyth, Sue, 'Telling Stories: Nurses, politics and Aboriginal Australians, circa 1900–1980s', *Contemporary Nurse*, vol. 24, no. 1, February 2007, pp. 33–44.
Freney, Denis, *A Map of Days: Life on the left*, William Heinemann Australia, Melbourne, 1991.
Gaffney, Ellie, *Somebody Now: The autobiography of Ellie Gaffney, a woman of Torres Strait*, Aboriginal Studies Press, Canberra, 1989.
Gallaway, Jack, *The Last Call of the Bugle: The long road to Kapyong*, University of Queensland Press, Brisbane, 1994.
Gardiner-Garden, John, 'Defining Aboriginality in Australia', Current Issues brief no. 10, 2002–03, aph.gov.au/About_Parliament/Parliamentary_Departments/Parliamentary_Library/Publications_Archive/CIB/cib0203/03Cib10#definitions, accessed 29 June 2012.
Gerster, Robin, *Big-noting: The heroic theme in Australian war writing*, Melbourne University Press, Melbourne, 1987.
—— *Travels in the Atomic Sunshine: Australia and the occupation of Japan*, Scribe, Melbourne, 2008.
Goodall, Heather, 'Too Early Yet or Not Soon Enough? Reflections on sharing histories as process', *Australian Historical Studies*, vol. 33, no. 118, 2002, pp. 7–24.
Goodman, Rupert, *Queensland Nurses: Boer War to Vietnam*, Boolarong Publications, Brisbane, 1985.
—— *Our War Nurses: The history of the Royal Australian Army Nursing Corps*

1902–1988, Boolarong Publications, Brisbane, 1988.

Goold, Sally S & Kerrynne Liddle (eds), *In Our Own Right: Black Australian nurses' stories*, eContent Management, Maleny, Qld, 2005.

Goot, Murray & Tim Rowse, *Divided Nation? Indigenous affairs and the imagined public*, Melbourne University Press, Melbourne, 2007.

Gordon, Harry, *The Embarrassing Australian: The story of an Aboriginal warrior*, Lansdowne Press, Melbourne, 1965.

Grattan, Michelle (ed.), *Reconciliation: Essays on Australian Reconciliation*, Black Inc., Melbourne, 2000.

'Green warriors', *Message Stick*, directed by Douglas Watkin, produced by the ABC, 2008.

Grey, Jeffrey, *A Military History of Australia*, 3rd edn, Cambridge University Press, Melbourne, 2008.

Gunstone, Andrew, *Unfinished Business: The Australian formal Reconciliation process*, Australian Scholarly Publishing, Melbourne, 2007.

Haebich, Anna, *Broken Circles: Fragmenting Indigenous families*, Fremantle Arts Centre Press, Fremantle, 2000.

—— *Spinning the Dream: Assimilation in Australia, 1950–1970*, Fremantle Press, Fremantle, 2008.

Hall, Robert, *Fighters from the Fringe: Aborigines and Torres Strait Islanders recall the Second World War*, Aboriginal Studies Press, Canberra, 1995.

—— *The Black Diggers: Aborigines and Torres Strait Islanders in the Second World War*, 2nd edn, Aboriginal Studies Press, Canberra, 1997.

Ham, Paul, *Vietnam: The Australian war*, HarperCollins, Sydney, 2007.

Hamel-Green, Michael E, 'The Resisters: A history of the anti-conscription movement 1964–1972', in Peter King (ed.), *Australia's Vietnam: Australia in the Second Indo-China War*, Allen & Unwin, Sydney, 1983, pp. 100–28.

Hammond, JE, *Winjan's People: The story of the South-West Australian Aborigines*, edited by Paul Hasluck, Imperial Printing Co., Perth, 1933.

Hardisty, Sue (ed.), *Thanks Girls and Goodbye!: The story of the Australian Women's Land Army 1942–45*, Viking O'Neil, Melbourne, 1990.

Haskins, Victoria, *One Bright Spot*, Palgrave Macmillan, Basingstoke, 2005.

Hasluck, Paul, *Black Australians: A survey of native policy in Western Australia, 1829–1897*, Melbourne University Press in association with Oxford University Press, Melbourne, 1942.

—— *Native Welfare in Australia: Speeches and addresses*, Paterson Brokensha, Perth, 1953.

—— *Shades of Darkness, Aboriginal Affairs 1925–1965*, Melbourne University Press, Melbourne, 1988.

Bibliography

Hawke, Steve & Michael Gallagher, *Noonkanbah, Whose Land, Whose Law*, Fremantle Arts Centre Press, Fremantle, 1989.

Hegarty, Ruth, *Is That You, Ruthie?*, University of Queensland Press, Brisbane, 1999.

Hollinsworth, David, *Race and Racism in Australia*, 3rd edn, Cengage Learning, Melbourne, 2006.

Horner, David, *The Gulf Commitment: The Australian Defence Force's first war*, Melbourne University Press, Melbourne, 1992.

—— *Australia and the 'New World Order': From peacekeeping to peace enforcement: 1988–1991, the official history of Australian peacekeeping, humanitarian and post–Cold War operations*, vol. 2, Cambridge University Press, Cambridge, 2011.

Howard, Ann, *You'll Be Sorry!*, TARKA Publishing, Sydney and Melbourne, 1990.

—— *Where Do We Go from Here?*, TARKA Publishing, Sydney, 1994.

Huggins, Jackie, 'Indigenous Women and Leadership: A personal reflection', *Indigenous Law Bulletin*, vol. 6, no. 1, March/April 2004, pp. 5–7.

Huggonson, David, 'Aborigines and the Aftermath of the Great War', *Australian Aboriginal Studies*, vol. 11, no. 1, 1993, pp. 2–9.

—— 'The White Australia Ideal and Australia's Defence Policy', *Journal of the Royal Historical Society of Queensland*, vol. 17, no. 8, November 2000, pp. 373–9.

Huie, Shirley Fenton, *Ships Belles: The story of the Women's Royal Australian Naval Service in war and peace 1941–1985*, The Watermark Press, Sydney, 2000.

Hunter, Tamara, 'The Myth of Equality: The denial of citizenship rights for Aboriginal people in Western Australia', *Studies in Western Australian History*, vol. 22, 2001, pp. 69–82.

I Hope the War Will Be Over Soon, directed by John Ruane, produced by Juniper Films, 1988, DVD.

Inglis, Ken S, *Sacred Places: War memorials in the Australian landscape*, 3rd edn, Melbourne University Press, Melbourne, 2008.

Jackomos, Alick & Derek Fowell, *Forgotten Heroes: Aborigines at war from the Somme to Vietnam*, Victoria Press, Melbourne, 1993.

James, Jan 'Kabarli', *Forever Warriors*, Scott Print, Perth, 2010.

Janowitz, Morris, 'Military Institutions and Citizenship in Western Societies', *Armed Forces and Society*, vol. 2, no. 2, 1976, pp. 185–204.

Jordens, Ann-Mari, 'An Administrative Nightmare: Aboriginal conscription 1965–72', *Aboriginal History*, vol. 13, no. 2, 1989, pp. 124–34.

Kartinyeri, Doreen, *Ngarrindjeri Anzacs*, Aboriginal Family History Project, South Australian Museum and Raukkan Council, Adelaide, 1996.

—— & Sue Anderson, *My Ngarrindjeri Calling*, Aboriginal Studies Press, Canberra, 2008.

'Ken Colbung', *Message Stick*, produced and directed by Kelrick Martin, produced by the ABC, 2004, abc.net.au/tv/messagestick/stories/s1070887.htm, accessed 27 January 2015.

Kerin, Rani, *Doctor Do-Good: Charles Duguid and Aboriginal advancement 1930s–1970s*, Australian Scholarly Publishing, Melbourne, 2011.

Kolig, Erich, *The Noonkanbah Story*, University of Otago Press, Dunedin, 1987.

Kristianson, GL, *The Politics of Patriotism: The pressure group activities of the Returned Servicemen's League*, ANU Press, Canberra, 1966.

Langton, Marcia, 'They Made a Solitude and Called it Peace', in Rachel Perkins & Marcia Langton (eds), *First Australians: An illustrated history*, The Miegunyah Press, Melbourne, 2008, pp. 25–37.

'The Last Post', *Message Stick*, directed by Adrian Wells, produced by the ABC, 2006, DVD.

Laughton, Kenny, *Not Quite Men, No Longer Boys*, Jukurrpa Books, Alice Springs, 1999.

Lee, David, 'McBride, Sir Philip Albert (1892–1982)', *Australian Dictionary of Biography*, National Centre of Biography, Australian National University, adb.anu.edu.au/biography/mcbride-sir-philip-albert-15051/text26249, accessed 31 December 2013.

Lennox, Gina, *Forged by War: Australians in combat and back home*, Melbourne University Press, Melbourne, 2006.

Levett, Robin, *The Girls*, 2nd edn, Hudson Publishing, Newstead, Vic, 2005.

Londey, Peter, *Other People's Wars: A history of Australian peacekeeping*, Allen & Unwin, Sydney, 2004.

Loos, Noel & Koiki Mabo, *Eddie Koiki Mabo: His life and struggle for land rights*, University of Queensland Press, Brisbane, 1996.

Lowe, Bronwyn, 'Reflections on Gender and Memory: Personal experiences of women of the WAAAF during the Second World War', *Melbourne Historical Journal*, vol. 39, 2011, pp. 159–73.

MacGregor, Sandy, as told to Jimmy Thomson, *No Need for Heroes*, CALM Pty Limited, Sydney, 1993.

Macintyre, Stuart, *Australia's Boldest Experiment: War and reconstruction in the 1940s*, NewSouth Publishing, Sydney, 2015.

Maclean, Pam, 'An Almost Universal Scheme of National Service in Australia in the 1950s', *Australian Journal of Politics and History*, vol. 52, no. 3, 2006, pp. 378–97.

McGregor, Russell, *Indifferent Inclusion: Aboriginal people and the Australian nation*, Aboriginal Studies Press, Canberra, 2011.

Maddison, Sarah, *Beyond White Guilt: The real challenge for Black–white relations in Australia*, Allen & Unwin, Sydney, 2011.

Bibliography

Martin, Desmond (ed.), *Backing up the Boys: The Australian Women's Army Service and Albury Army area*, ed. for the Army Women's Service Club, Bandiana, Thomsons Printing Pty Ltd, Albury, NSW, 1988.

Martin, Kingsley, *The Magic of the British Monarchy*, Little, Brown and Company, Boston and Toronto, 1962.

Mattingley, Christobel & Ken Hampton (eds), *Survival in Our Own Land: 'Aboriginal' experiences in 'South Australia' since 1836*, Hodder & Stoughton, Sydney, 1992.

Maynard, John, '"Let Us Go" … It's a "Blackfellows' War" – Aborigines and the Boer War', *Aboriginal History*, vol. 39, 2015, pp. 143–62.

Mickler, Steve, *The Myth of Privilege: Aboriginal status, media visions, public ideas*, Fremantle Arts Centre Press, Perth, 1998.

Mill, Lorna, *Been There – Done That*, L Mill, Melbourne, 1984.

Moremon, John, 'After "the Girls" Came Home: Ex-servicewomen of Australia's Wartime Women's Auxiliaries', in Martin Crotty and Craig Barrett (eds), *When the Soldiers Return: November 2007 conference proceedings*, RMIT Publishing in association with the School of History, Philosophy, Religion and Classics, University of Queensland, Melbourne, 2009, pp. 203–11.

Moskos Charles C, Jr, 'Racial Integration in the Armed Forces', *The American Journal of Sociology*, vol. 72, no. 2, September 1966, pp. 132–48.

Murphy, John, *Harvest of Fear: A history of Australia's Vietnam War*, Allen & Unwin, Sydney, NSW, 1993.

Murray, Suellen, John Murphy, Elizabeth Branigan & Jenny Malone, *After the Orphanage: Life beyond the children's home*, Sydney, UNSW Press, 2008.

Nicoll, Fiona, 'War by Other Means? Sovereignty and the Aboriginal Tent Embassy', in Gary Foley, Andrew Schaap & Edwina Howell (eds), *The Aboriginal Tent Embassy: Sovereignty, Black power, land rights and the state*, Routledge, Abingdon, 2014, pp. 267–83.

No Bugles, No Drums, produced by Debra Beattie-Burnett, directed by John Burnett, Seven Emus Productions in association with Australian Television Network, 49 mins, videocassette, 1990.

'Norforce', *Message Stick*, produced and directed by Penny Smallacombe, ABC, 2004.

Ollif, Lorna, *Women in Khaki*, Ollif Publishing Company, Sydney, 1981.

—— *Colonel Best and Her Soldiers: The story of 33 years of the Women's Royal Australian Army Corps*, Ollif Publishing Company, Sydney, 1985.

O'Neill, Robert, *Australia in the Korean War 1950–1953, Volume 1, Strategy and Diplomacy*, Australian War Memorial and the Australian Government Publishing Service, Canberra, 1981.

—— *Australia in the Korean War 1950–1953, Volume 2, Combat Operations*, Australian War Memorial and the Australian Government Publishing Service, Canberra, 1985.

Osborne, Elizabeth, *Torres Strait Islander Women and the Pacific War*, Aboriginal Studies Press, Canberra, 1997.

Paradies, Yin, 'A Systematic Review of Empirical Research on Self-Reported Racism and Health', *International Journal of Epidemiology*, vol. 35, no. 4, 2006, pp. 888–901.

Partington, Geoffrey, *Hasluck versus Coombs: White politics and Australia's Aborigines*, Quakers Hill Press, Sydney, 1996.

Pederson, Howard & Banjo Woorunmarra, *Jandamarra & the Bunuba Resistance*, 3rd edn, Magabala Books, Broome, 2011.

Pilkington, Doris (Nugi Garimara), *Under the Wintamarra Tree*, University of Queensland Press, Brisbane, 2002.

Pottinger, Paul, 'The Unknown Soldier', *The Australian Magazine*, 4 November 2000, pp. 30–36.

Pratt, Rod, 'Queensland's Aborigines in the First Australian Imperial Force', in P Whitney Lackenbauer, R Scott Sheffield & Craig Leslie Mantle (eds), *Aboriginal Peoples and Military Participation: Canadian & international perspectives*, Canadian Defence Academy Press, Kingston, ON, 2007, pp. 215–36.

Reed, Liz, *Bigger than Gallipoli: War, history and memory in Australia*, University of Western Australia Press, Crawley, WA, 2004.

Reynolds, Henry, *Fate of a Free People: The classic account of Tasmanian Wars*, 2nd edn, Penguin, Melbourne, 2000.

—— *The Other Side of the Frontier: Aboriginal resistance to the European invasion of Australia*, 3rd edn, UNSW Press, Sydney, 2006.

—— *Forgotten War*, NewSouth Publishing, Sydney, 2013.

Richter, Bill & Margie, *Radio Operator: Vietnam War; School of Signals; healing journey*, Bill & Margie Richter, Maleny, Qld, 2013.

Riseman, Noah, 'The Stolen Veteran: Institutionalisation, military service and the Stolen Generations', *Aboriginal History*, vol. 35, 2011, pp. 57–77.

—— *Defending Whose Country? Indigenous soldiers in the Pacific War*, University of Nebraska Press, Lincoln, 2012.

—— 'Equality in the Ranks: The lives of Aboriginal Vietnam veterans', *Journal of Australian Studies*, vol. 36, no. 4, December 2012, pp. 411–26.

—— 'The Curious Case of Mervyn Eades: National service, discrimination and Aboriginal People', *Australian Journal of Politics and History*, vol. 59, no. 1, 2013, pp. 64–80.

—— 'Racism, Indigenous People and the Australian Armed Forces in the

Bibliography

Post–Second World War Era', *History Australia*, vol. 10, no. 2, 2013, pp. 159–79.

—— 'Enduring Silences, Enduring Prejudices: Australian Aboriginal participation in the First World War', in David Monger, Katie Pickles & Sarah Murray (eds), *Endurance and the First World War: Experience and legacies in New Zealand and Australia*, Cambridge Scholars Publishing, Newcastle upon Tyne, 2014, pp. 178–95.

—— 'Aboriginal Military Service and Assimilation', *Aboriginal History*, vol. 38, 2014, pp. 155–78.

—— 'Escaping assimilation's grasp: Aboriginal women in the Australian women's military services', *Women's History Review*, vol. 24, no. 5, 2015, pp. 757–75.

Rosenzweig, Paul A, *Ever Vigilant: The regimental history of the North West Mobile Force (NORFORCE) 1981–2001*, North West Mobile Force, Darwin, 2001.

Rowse, Tim (ed.), *Contesting Assimilation*, API Network, Perth, 2005.

'The Sapphires: Where are they now?', *Australian Geographic*, 5 September 2012, australiangeographic.com.au/topics/history-culture/2012/09/the-sapphires-where-are-they-now, accessed 8 September 2014.

Scarlett, Philippa, *Aboriginal and Torres Strait Islander Volunteers for the AIF: The Indigenous response to World War One*, Indigenous Histories, Canberra, 2011.

Scott, Kim & Hazel Brown, *Kayang & Me*, Fremantle Arts Centre Press, Fremantle, 2005.

Sears, Jason, '1919–1929: An imperial service', in David Stevens (ed.), *The Royal Australian Navy: The Australian centenary history of defence volume III*, Cambridge University Press, Melbourne, 2001, pp. 81–102.

Sekuless, Peter & Jacqueline Rees, *Lest We Forget: The history of the Returned Services League 1916–1986*, Rigby, Sydney, 1986.

Sigelman, Lee & Susan Welch, 'The Contact Hypothesis Revisited: Black–white interaction and positive racial attitudes', *Social Forces*, vol. 71, no. 3, March 1993, pp. 781–95.

Smith, Hugh, 'The Dynamics of Cultural Change and the Australian Defence Force', *Armed Forces & Society*, vol. 21, no 4, 1995, pp. 531–51.

—— 'Minorities and the Australian Army: Overlooked and under-represented?', in Peter Dennis and Jeffrey Grey (eds), *A Century of Service: 100 years of the Australian Army. The 2001 chief of army's military history conference*, Army History Unit, Department of Defence, Canberra, 2001, pp. 129–49.

—— & Ian McAllister, 'The Changing Military Profession: Integrating women in the Australian Defence Force', *Australian and New Zealand Journal of Sociology*, vol. 27, no. 3, November 1991, pp. 369–91.

Spurling, Kathryn, 'From Exclusion to Submarines – The integration of Australian women naval volunteers', *Australian Defence Force Journal*, vol. 139, November/December 1999, pp. 35–40.

Stevenson, Clare & Honor Darling (eds), *The WAAAF Book*, Hale & Iremonger, Sydney, 1984.

'Strong Indigenous Women Speak on Leadership', *Indigenous Law Bulletin*, vol. 7, no. 1, November 2007, p. 2.

Survival School, directed by Luigi Acquisto & David Bradbury, produced by Luigi Acquisto & Stella Zammatro, produced by the ABC, 55 mins, 2007.

Sykes, Roberta B, *Black Majority*, Hudson Publishing, Melbourne, 1989.

Sykes, Roberta (ed.), *Murawina: Australian women of high achievement*, Doubleday, Sydney and New York, 1993.

Taffe, Sue, *Black and White Together: FCAATSI: the Federal Council for the Advancement of Aborigines and Torres Strait Islanders 1958–1973*, University of Queensland Press, Brisbane, 2005.

Thomson, Alistair, 'Anzac Stories: Using personal testimony in war history', *War & Society*, vol. 25, no. 2, October 2006, pp. 1–21.

—— *ANZAC Memories: Living with the legend*, rev. ed., Monash University Publishing, Melbourne, 2013.

Thomson, Donald, *Donald Thomson in Arnhem Land*, revised edn, compiled and introduced by Nicolas Peterson, The Miegunyah Press, Melbourne, 2005.

Thomson, Joyce, *The WAAAF in Wartime Australia*, Melbourne University Press, Melbourne, 1991.

Tovey, Noel, *Little Black Bastard*, Hachette Australia, Sydney, 2005.

Trembath, Richard, *A Different Sort of War: Australians in Korea 1950–53*, Australian Scholarly Publishing, Melbourne, 2005.

Tucker, Margaret, *If Everybody Cared: Autobiography of Margaret Tucker MBE*, Ure Smith, Sydney, 1977.

Vote Yes for Aborigines, written and directed by Frances Peters-Little, produced by Ronin Films, 2007, DVD.

Wells, Julie & Michael Christie, 'Namatjira and the Burden of Citizenship', *Australian Historical Studies*, vol. 31, no. 114, 2000, pp. 110–30.

Westheider, James E, *Fighting on Two Fronts: African Americans and the Vietnam War*, New York University Press, New York and London, 1997.

—— *The African American Experience in Vietnam: Brothers in arms*, Rowman and Littlefield, Lanham, MD, 2008.

Winegard, Timothy, *Indigenous Peoples of the British Dominions and the First World War*, Cambridge University Press, Cambridge, 2012.

Young, Warren L, *Minorities and the Military: A cross-national study in world perspective*, Greenwood Press, Westport, CT, 1982.

INDEX

Note: The term 'Indigenous' here refers to Aboriginal people and Torres Strait Islanders.

Abala, Steve 184 n. 10
  serves in BCOF 18
Abbott government 155
Afghanistan
  Indigenous service in 3, 164
Akee, George
  serves in army 125, 126
Allie, Harry
  appointed Air Force Indigenous Elder 168
Anderson, Alan
  navy recruit 169
Anderson, Sgt Cecil
  serves in three conflicts 22
Anu, Ezra
  serves in army 125–6, 129, 133
Anzac Day 9, 25, 33, 55, 108
  and Indigenous marches 2, 4, 171, 172; Coloured Diggers March 172
  services 173, 173
Atkinson, Graham
  Vietnam veteran 65, 79–80, 81, 87, 88–9
Australia: Indigenous affairs to WWII
  attacking Aboriginal culture: child removal 94; limiting employment opportunities 94; urban relocation 94
Australia: Indigenous affairs postwar
  assimilation policy 13, 16–17, 26, 29, 59, 66, 85; and citizenship 17, 30, 31; information pamphlets 30–1; and military service 16, 30, 31, 66, 82–6; and 'model' Aboriginal people 28, 29, 48
  child removal 1, 8, 59
  conditions and civil rights of Indigenous people 37, 40–1, 63, 137, 138; and 'development' 40
  inquiries: *Bringing Them Home* 88; Royal Commission into Aboriginal Deaths in Custody 88, 142
  international criticism over treatment of Aboriginal people 25, 46
  larger federal role in Indigenous affairs 138
  1960s–1970s: interest in and support for Indigenous civil rights 63, 64–5, 85, 137; referendum of 1967 66, 83–4, 137
  1990s: Reconciliation movement 51, 139, 142, 143, 170, (Council for Aboriginal Reconciliation), 142–3; National Reconciliation Week 121, 173, 174; opposition to 139; and politics 139
  non-Indigenous understandings of Aboriginal identity, culture 133, 134–5, 136, 138–9, 149; little personal contact 138
  politics of racism 47–8, 53, 133; under *National Service Act* 65, 67–9, 82–6
  see also Indigenous Australians

Australia: to 1945
  conscription plebiscites 6
  European settlement: and violence on the frontier 3–5
  soldier settlement schemes: and Aboriginal veterans 8, 42
  White Australia Policy 6
Australia: postwar
  immigration 48; Asian 53
  1960s–1970s: anti–Vietnam War movement 57, 84–5, 86–7; concern over events in Southeast Asia 63; opposition to conscription 84, 86, 87; *Racial Discrimination Act 1975* 131; social activism 57
  1990s: changing social attitudes 164–5; race and Indigenous Australians 165
  and racism in civil society 136–8, 140
  and White Australia Policy 137
Australian defence policy postwar
  caution about over-commitment 22
  Department of Defence: and considering Indigenous cultural norms 165; Defence Indigenous Development Program 168; promoting Reconciliation 143, 167
  policy initiatives of 1980s–90s: Dibb Report 144; *Defence of Australia* white paper 144, 164; altering recruitment practices 166–7
  women: expanded opportunities 117; and marriage 102, 110
Australian Imperial Force (1st AIF)
  Infantry: 21st Battalion 8
  Light Horse: 6th Regiment 8
Australian military postwar
  Army: Air Service: 2nd Squadron 76; 1st Field Squadron: 3 Field Troop 57, 71, 73, 78; Royal Australian Armoured Corps, Detachment 74; Royal Australian Corps of Signals 70; Royal Australian Engineers: 17th Construction Squadron 72; Royal Australian Infantry: 1st Royal Australian Regiment 25, 57, 160–1; 2RAR 22, 25, 33, 72, 73; 3RAR 24, 33, 76; 4RAR 75; 7RAR 78; 8RAR 72; 9RAR 73; Royal Corps of Australian Electrical and Mechanical Engineers 70: 1st Armoured Regiment 80; Royal Regiment of Australian Artillery, 1st Field Regiment 72
  as Australian Defence Force (ADF) 91; and border protection 155; changing dynamics, operations 143–4, 157–8, 164, (range of commitments) 155–6, 164; policy of recruitment diversity 166, 167–8
  K Force (Korea) 22, 23, 24
  RAN 74; and racism 130–1
  Regional Force Surveillance Units (Army 2nd Division): 51 FNQR 144, 145, 147, 152; NORFORCE 144, 145, 146–7, 148, 150, 151, 152, 154–5, 156; Pilbara Regiment 140, 144, 145, 147, 155, 156
  RFSUs: areas of operation 145, 147–8, 154–5; Indigenous component 144, 145, 146–7, 148–51, 156–7; interracial relations 140, 150, 152, 153–4; links with earlier units 154; recruitment 150, (adjustments), 149; as reserve units 54, 144–5; roles 145, 146, 149, (modified), 155–6; working with local Indigenous communities 143, 144, 145, 146, 148, 150–1, 155, 156, 165, (and history of discrimination and exclusion), 147–8, (mentoring role of recruits), 157
  Special Air Service (SAS) 61, 145
  state of readiness 22, 23
  women in ADF 58; acquiring skills 93–4; difficult paths 116; and discrimination 98; and glass ceiling 93; and opportunities 117; study at Duntroon 98
  women's services: 190 n. 5; acquiring skills 97; disbanded 98; forced to leave on marriage 102, 110, (rule change), 204 n. 22; opportunities for women 97, (limited), 115; pay 97; RAANC 58, 97, 101; something new 10; WRAAC 97; WRAAF 97; WRANS 97, 115
  see also Indigenous servicewomen; racism, Indigenous people and the armed forces
Australian military postwar: Indigenous enlistment and Reconciliation
  ADF 91; pre-entry courses 167–8, (and

Index

Indigenous culture), 168; promoting Reconciliation and Indigenous service 121, 140, 143, 144, 152, 157, 170, (partnerships with Indigenous communities) 169, 170; RFSUs 144, 145, 146–7, 148–9, 150, (bridging courses), 156–7, 167, 168, (challenges), 152; success of programs 170; training courses, (to combat ignorance), 140, (for Indigenous youth), 168, 169–70

Army: appoints Indigenous Elder 168; Army Aboriginal Community Assistance Program 170; Indigenous recruitment officers, mentors 168; lifts restrictions 20; discrimination remains 20–1

evolving policies on 16; greater recognition 27; tolerating enlistees 21, 22

exclusions for BCOF in Japan 18–19, (protests), 19–20

RAAF: exclusions 21, 49; appoints Air Force Indigenous Elder 168; Indigenous Youth Program 168–9

RAN: Defence Indigenous Development Program 169; exclusions 21, 49; recruitment drives 113–14; strengthening ties with Indigenous communities 169

Reconciliation services 2, 121

Australian War Memorial 55
commemorating Indigenous service 172–3; and memorial 174
and Indigenous resistance to colonialism 4

Bailey, Ed
serves in RAAF 126
Baker, Anthony 157
Baker, Frazer 157
Basset, Jan 101
BCOF. *See* Japan
Bennett, Scott 137
Bingarape, Mial
veteran of Indonesian Confrontation 124
Black Diggers (Wright) ix, x, 90, 171
Blair, Bob 69–70
Vietnam veteran 61, 72, 90, 91, 124
Blair, Harold 29, 48

Bland, HA 63–4, 66
Bligh, Dick
military service 90; Vietnam veteran 60, 61, 72–3, 75, 76, 90, 128–9
Boer War
Aboriginal soldiers and trackers 3; left in South Africa? 5–6
Bolt, Andrew 133
Bostock, George
military service 89; Vietnam veteran 61, 75, 77, 80–1, 88, 128
as playwright: *It Seems Like Yesterday* x, 90
Briscoe, Gordon x
Britain
and enlistment of 'coloureds' 5
and influence in East Asia 18
and Malayan Emergency 21–2
Broome, Richard 40
Brown, Hazel 31–2

Carroll, Col. OM 57
cases:
Bolt vilification case 133
Commonwealth v. Tasmania (1983) 133
Chifley, Ben 37, 39
Chifley government 39, 40
churches in Australia
and Indigenous rights 34, 47, 48
Clark, Jennifer 138
Coe, Paul 86
Colbung, Kenneth
military service 27; veteran of BCOF and Korean War 19, 23, 26, 124
Connor, John 4
Cook, L/Cpl David
early life 1, 88
military service 70; navy 130; Vietnam veteran 1, 78, 79, (police harassment), 88
Cook, Kevin 86
Cook, PH 84–5
Coolburra, Billy
Vietnam veteran 71–2, 78, 80
Cooper, JE 83
Cosgrove, Peter 143–4, 145
leads INTERFET 162
Costello, Judy 93
Council for Aboriginal Affairs 66, 85
Crafter, Anthony 169

235

Davies, WO1 Reg 152
de Matos, Christine 18
Dexter, BG 68
Dodd, Stephen
  Korea veteran 25
Donovan, Cecil 16
Doob, Christopher Bates 122
Duroux, Jeffrey
  Vietnam veteran 62
Duroux, Lionel
  Vietnam veteran 89

Eades, Mervyn 82–3, 85, 86, 87
East Timor: INTERFET 155, 162
  Australian contingent 162; some troops remain 162
  Indigenous service in x, 2, 13, 128, 162, 163
Egglestone, Cedric
  military service 27; veteran of WWII and Korea 23, 26
Elizabeth II
  coronation 44–5; Australian contingent 45, (controversy), 45–8
  royal tour of 1954 47
Enoch, Wesley ix
Evatt, Clive 43

Faulkner, John 167
Federal Council for the Advancement of Aborigines and Torres Strait Islanders 64
First World War
  the AIF and Aboriginal enlistment 6–7
  casualties 6
  commemoration of x
  Indigenous enlistment and service ix, 2, 3, 6–7; and equal treatment 121
Fisher, Cecil
  Korea veteran 25; return to civilian life 32–3
Fitzgerald, Joe 64
Forbes, Cameron 24
Forde, Frank 18, 20
Francis, Josiah 45
Fraser government 118
Freney, Denis 86

Gaffney, Ellie 100
Gage, Dianne 62
Gardner, Max 89

Garland, Alf 53
Goodall, Heather x–xi
Goot, Murray 137, 139
Gordon, Harry 24
Gordon, Sue
  early years 104–5; education 105; removed from family 104, 105
  in the army (WRAAC) 105–6, 108, 124
  as ex-servicewoman: career in Indigenous affairs 106–7; contacts with the WRAAC 108; reconnects with family 107; senior and leadership positions, roles 107–8, 119; skilled work 106; training course 106; university study 107
Grassby, Al 52
Grey, Jeffrey 4, 54, 144, 145
Gulf War 158
  Australian commitment 158; RAN vessels and roles, 158–9
  Indigenous military service in x, 13, 131, 158, 159
Gumballa, Leon 157
Gunder, Lt Col. Ash 152

Haebich, Anna 16, 28
Hall, Robert 128
Hanson, Pauline 139
Hasluck, Paul
  influence on Indigenous matters 40
Hearps, 2nd Lt Alfred
  serves in WWI 207 n. 3
Henry, Stephen 68–9
Holt, Harold 72
Houston, L/Cpl Stanley 25
Howard government
  and border protection 155
Huggins, Jackie 95
Hughes, Timothy
  WWII veteran 31
Hull, Rev. Crookes 48
Human Rights and Equal Opportunity Commission
  and complaint of racism in navy 132
Hussein, Saddam 158

In Our Town (play) x
Indigenous Australians to 1950s
  activism 13, 17, 20; for citizenship rights 43

Index

and assimilation 13, 28, 29, 30, 94, 101, 125; interpretations 16–17, 32; linked with armed forces and citizenship 17, 30, 31–2

fighting to defend country: frontier wars 3–5, (as military service), 4

history of persecution and discrimination/racism 2, 7, 12, 28–9, 101, 121, 125; in training and employment 12, 100–1

Indigenous women: limited opportunities 94, 100, 105; discrimination in training and employment 100–1; and domestic work x, 94, 98, 100, 105

and legislation: *Commonwealth Electoral Act* 12, 50; *Commonwealth Electoral (War-time) Act* 39; *Commonwealth Electoral Act 1949* 39, 43; *Defence Act 1903* 6, 21; drinking laws 33, 38, 43; national service x, 21, 63; voting rights 43

marginalisation of 5

as 'native police', trackers 4, 5, 149

non-Indigenous supporters of rights 34, 47, 48

popular and media opinion of: Aboriginal people 25–6, 30, 31; Torres Strait Islanders 25, 26, 29–30

and state protection regimes 8, 9, 10, 23, 29, 59, 94, 99; promoting enlistment 15–16, 30

stereotyping of 30, 31–2

Stolen Generations 23, 59–60, 88, 104, 106, 125

Indigenous Australians from 1960

activism and politics 51, 86; Aboriginal Tent Embassy 51; Black Power 86, 87; civil rights 57, 64, 85, 87; land rights 51, 52, 87, 107

child abuse 108

discrimination, racism 53–4, 87–8, 121, 124, 148; official 64, 66, 84–6, 87

impact of collaboration with RFSUs 143, 144, 145, 146, 148, 150–1, 156; training courses 156

Indigenous business community 90, 91

Indigenous culture: and military service 165, 168; Dreamtime Cultural Centre 90–1; theatre ix, x, 90

and Indigenous identity 51, 53, 84, 133

Indigenous women: discrimination, sexism 104; and education 95; and leadership 95, 107, 119–20; and opportunity 104

and legislation: *National Service Act* and *Regulations* 62–4, 66, 86, (inconsistencies), 65, 67–9, 84, (prosecutions), 69, 82–3, 85, 86, 87

NAIDOC Week 55, 172, 173

and state governments, welfare regimes 67–8, 82, 113

stereotyping of 149

support in communities for ADF 165

Indigenous Australian servicemen

backgrounds: abuse 59; experience of racism 60, 125; institutionalisation (Stolen Generations) 23, 59–60, 92, 125; low education levels 70; out-of-home care 60; unskilled work 60, 70

experiences as veterans ix, 1; as advocates for Indigenous empowerment 13; conditional/partial rights 13, 39–40, 43; continuing discrimination in civilian life 3, 8, 28–9, 32–4, 125, (right to purchase alcohol) 33, 43–4; denied access to pay and entitlements 8, 10; education 164; forgotten 26; friendships with army mates 26; post-traumatic stress disorder: (Korea) 26, (Somalia), 161; pride in service x, 9, 26, 141, 163; and rehabilitation 20, (traditional healing), 161, 162; welcome home 25

experiences as Vietnam veterans 14; ambivalence of communities 87; as community leaders, Elders 59, 90; confronting legacy of unpopular war 87, 91, 92; and employment 88–9, 90, (in army), 90; involvement in Aboriginal affairs 58, 88–9; opposition to Australian involvement 81; post-traumatic stress disorder 1, 14, 59, 87, 92; racial discrimination 87–8, 125; readjustment difficulties/ social dislocation 14, 58, 59, 87, 92, (alcoholism, marriage breakdown), 87; study 88

impact on family and community 2, 8, 9, 11, 33, 61–2

237

military service and citizenship 17, 30, 35
motivations to enlist 7, 23, 58, 151; as alternative social paradigm 2, 13; continue family tradition 12, 61, 154; defending country 12, 62, 175; as employment and advancement opportunity 2, 7, 12, 13, 23, 32, 61, 151, 159; financial 24, 60; loyalty 7, 12; offers stability 60, 151; as protest 65; as route to empowerment and rights 2, 11; seeking adventure 7, 12, 61
number of; in Gulf War 159; in Korean War 22–3; in Vietnam War 14, 58, 91; in WWI 7; in WWII 10, 11
and recognition ix, x, 9, 12–13, 18, 20, 22, 47, 54–5; and non-Indigenous veterans 9, 19, 38–9
see also the various conflicts; RSL and Indigenous Australians
Indigenous Australian servicemen: experiences in the armed forces
awards and honours 7, 22, 25
combat and hardship 24, 58, 74, 75, 92, 127, 128, 138; ambush 73; casualties 7, 22, 23, 58, 73
fitting in 23, 60; comfortable with discipline 70
gaining self-confidence 59
interpersonal relationships with other Australian personnel 71, 73, 78, 128, 160; friendships 70, 71–2, 92
learning skills, gaining education 32, 59, 92, 153, 166; training 69, 169, (at Duntroon), 135
on lower pay 10, 12; not paid 11
in minority 69
naval escort, patrols 74; protecting assets 159; waiting 159
at Nui Dat base, Vietnam 74–5, 77; entertainment 75, (female Aboriginal singers), 194 n. 6
patrols 72–3, 74; checking Viet Cong tunnels 74; not knowing who is an enemy 72
peacekeeping 160–1; patrols 161
playing sport: boxing 70–1; football codes 70
racism and stereotyping 19, 70–1, 128, 130

in Regional Force Surveillance Units (RFSUs) 143, 144, 151
relations with American servicemen 76, 77, 79–81, (with black soldiers), 80, 81; opinion of 77, 80, 81, (racism) 77–9, 81, 92
rest and recreation at Vung Tau, Vietnam 80; poor behaviour 75–7, 80–1
retaining culture 32, 153
training for Vietnam 69, 128
treated as equals 3, 7, 11, 19, 23, 32, 57, 58, 81, 87, 92, 121, 123–4, 128, 138
venereal disease 76
witnessing aftermath of conflict, war 23, 71, 163–4
Indigenous Australian servicemen and women (ADF)
changed role of 170
commemorating Indigenous service ix–x, 2, 4, 25, 55, 171, 172, (on centenary of WWI), 171, (Honouring Indigenous War Graves organisation), 90, 108, 173; involvement of Indigenous communities 173; in NAIDOC Week 172, 173; with non-Indigenous Australians 172, 175; Veterans' Affairs Department 121, 173
and memorials dedicated to Indigenous service 173–5; Aboriginal and Torres Strait Islander War Memorial Committee 174; Coloured Diggers Project 174
numbers: in Gulf War 159
as officers 19, 24, 28, 165–6, 207 n. 3; and women's services 98
as percentage of ADF members 129, 165; among officer ranks 165
and pre-recruitment course 167–8
RFSUs 144, 145, 146–7, 148–50, 156–7; experiences 152–3, 157
see also racism, Indigenous people and the armed forces
Indigenous Australian servicewomen
background: institutionalisation (Stolen Generations) 104, 106, 113, 125; limited education, employment options 94, 98, 100, 105, 109–10, 166; under assimilation regime 95, 98

Index

experiences as ex-servicewomen: fighting for Indigenous rights 94, 107, 108, 119–20; further education, training 106, 107, 112, 117–18, 119; involvement in non-profit projects 111; as leaders, in senior roles 94, 95, 107, 119–20; links with other ex-servicewomen 108, 112; in skilled employment 106; working with Indigenous communities 103, 106–7, 111, 112, 113, 117–18

motivations to enlist: adventure 101; to challenge gender and racial discrimination 94; escape from domestic service, assimilation 95, 109–10, 119; inspired by example 114; offers opportunities, security 94, 104, 105, 110, 112, 114; something different 101

numbers 94; increasing 116

Indigenous Australian servicewomen: experiences in the armed forces (women's services)

acquiring new skills 94, 97–8, 106, 110, 112, 118, 153

adapting to army life, discipline 106, 108, 119

in ADF 119; navy 160

conformity and expressing Aboriginality 118–19

discrimination in pay and work 98, 110, 115; racial 116

equal treatment based on race 98, 104, 106, 110, 116, 119

forced to leave on marriage 102, 110

forming contacts, friendships 106, 115

in navy (WRANS) 113, 115; gender relations 116; and racism 116; on recruitment drives 113–14; restrictions on roles 115, 116–17

in Second World War 13, 36, 94, 113

significant responsibilities 106

training 101, 106, 110, 115, 119

Indigenous histories (Australian)

focus on colonialism and assimilation 91

of Indigenous participation in armed forces in two world wars 91

Indigenous peoples and clans

Bidjigal 5

Bunuba 5

Djungutti 1

Gumbaynggirr 1, 159

Ierganadu 107

Jirrbal 114

Khungarakung 184 n. 10

Kombumerri 172

Noongar 31

Noonuccal 162

Quandamooka 162

Yamatji 104

Yorta Yorta 65

Indigenous veterans' groups 171

Aboriginal and Torres Strait Islander Veterans and Services Association of Australia 173

Honouring Indigenous War Graves 90, 108, 173

National Aboriginal and Islander Ex-Services Association 171–2

WA Aboriginal and Torres Strait Islander Veterans and Services Association 172

Inglis, Ken 173

Iraq War

Indigenous service in 2, 164

James, Glenn

military service 70; Vietnam veteran 68, 72, (as VFL umpire), 90

James, Jan 'Kabarli'

Forever Warriors 94

Jandamarra (Aboriginal warrior) 5

Japan

British Commonwealth Occupation Force 17–18; Australian personnel in 18, 19, (women), 102

Indigenous Australians serving in BCOF 18

US occupation force 17, 19

and WWII 11, 12, 17

Jeffery, Michael

and RFSUs 127–8, 145–6, 150–1

Joseph, Samantha 95

Joye, Col 75

Keating, Paul

Redfern address on Indigenous disadvantage 142

Kennedy, George

veteran of WWI 8

239

Kerin, Rani 16, 29, 32
Ketchell, Marsat
　serves in navy 130–1
Keys, Sir William, 53
Korean Veterans Association of Australia
　Indigenous members 26
Korean War 18, 22, 25
　Australian commitment 22, 23, 102
　as forgotten war 26
　Indigenous service in 2, 13, 22–3, 26, 27, 124, 130

Lampard, Frank 174
Laughton, Kenny
　Not Quite Men, No Longer Boys 129
　Vietnam veteran 129
Lees, Patricia
　serves in WRANS 113; on recruitment drives 113–14
Lightning, Pte Desmond
　serves in NORFORCE 151
Little Pattie 75
'Louise' (Torres Strait Islander)
　early years 99–100; trains as nurse 100, 101
　in the army (RAANC) 101; forced to leave on marriage 102; meets her husband 102; training and work 102
　as ex-servicewoman: and further training 103, 119; involvement with WA and ACT Aboriginal health services 103; raises a family 103, 19; works as nursing aide in aged care 102–3

MacArthur, Gen. Douglas 17
McBride, Bill
　serves in RAN 126, 132
McBride, Philip 46, 49
McBride, Stan
　serves in WWII 130
McBride-Yuke, Linda 126, 130, 132
McCormack, Jeff 3
Macdonald, Neil
　naval veteran of Gulf War x, 126, 131–2, 136; experience, 159–60
McGirr government 43
McGregor, Russell 16, 137
Maclean, Pam 66
Mabo, Eddie Koiki 63
Maddison, Sarah 138

Malayan Emergency 21–2
　Australian forces 22; Indigenous service in 2, 13
Mallard, Frank
　military service 90; Army Reserve 134; Vietnam veteran 61–2, 92, (in Vietnam), 73–4, 75–6, 77, 78, 80, 127
　peacekeeping in Balkans 90
Maloney, Steve 164
　military service 162–3; East Timor 128, 162, 163–4
Maza, Rachael 155
media in Australia
　ABC television: *Message Stick* 155
　coverage of Korean War 24–5; Indigenous contribution 24–5, 27
　and Indigenous Australians (Reg Saunders), 24–5, 27, 28, 46, 47;
　coverage of Indigenous issues 138, (negative from 1980s), 138–9; and RFSUs 148–9, 151, 155; status of 83, 85–6, 138
　Indigenous media 148, 155
　see also newspapers and magazines
Mene, Charles 25
Menzies government 40, 67
　introduces national service 62, 63
Mickler, Steve 137, 138
Moss, Irene 140
Mummery, Michael 194 n. 65
Muntz, Robert 86
Murray, Pte JS 19

Namatjira, Albert 29, 48
Newie, L/Cpl Eccles
　serves in 51 FNQR 154
newspapers and magazines
　Advertiser (Adelaide) 46, 47
　Age 140
　Argus 39, 40–1, 49
　Australasian Post 61
　Australian 54, 83, 85–6
　Australian Geographic 148–9
　Australian Playboy 53
　Bulletin 44
　Cairns Post 29
　Dawn and *New Dawn* 15–16, 30, 115
　Herald (Melbourne) 28
　Herald-Sun 133

Index

Medical Journal of Australia 27
Morning Bulletin 25
Mufti (RSL magazine) 27, 49
Reveille (RSL magazine) 9
Sunday Herald (Sydney) 45
Sunday Times (Perth) 19, 46
Sydney Morning Herald 43–4
West Australian 25, 46
New South Wales
  easing drinking restrictions for Aboriginal people 43–4; opposition 44
New South Wales Aborigines Welfare Board/Native Welfare Department
  promoting enlistment 15–16, 115
Noonuccal, Oodgeroo 172
Northern Territory
  and child abuse 108
  Northern Territory Emergency Response Taskforce (the Intervention) 108; and army 155–6, (RFSUs), 156; controversial 156

Ogilvie, Leonard
  military service 27; Korea 23–4, 26
Onus, William (Bill) 20

Parfitt, L/Cpl Des
  Korea veteran 33–4
Pemulwuy (Aboriginal man) 5
Pepper, Percy
  veteran of WWI 8
Perkins, Charles 51–2, 53
Peters, Aunty Dot 173
Phoenix, Stan
  serves in army 135–6
Pitt, Tylisha 168
Pittman, Mick
  serves in RAAF 134
Prosser, Phillip 31
  Vietnam veteran 60, 61, 88, 172
Purantatameri, Patrick
  serves in NORFORCE 153

Quakawoot, Mabel
  background and early life 109; education 109; racism, discrimination 109
  early employment: domestic service 109, (encouraged), 109
  as ex-servicewoman: household duties, raising family 110, 119; involved in non-profit projects 111–12, 113; odd jobs 110; as special education teacher 110–11, 113, 119; study 112; works for Indigenous education 112, 119
  family members in military 112–13
  in WRAAF 109–10, 112, 124; discharged on marriage 110
Queensland
  and Indigenous policy 67; legislation regulating people's lives 99, 109; Stolen Wages 8, 10
  racism 109
Queensland Theatre Company ix

racism, Indigenous people and the armed forces
  ADF and racism 119, 140–1; anti-racism and Reconciliation Action Plans 143; efforts to stop racial discrimination 122; failure to tackle racial vilification 131–2; policies against racial vilification 140
  armed forces and presence of racism 122, 140
  expectations of racism 125
  factors in experience of racism 122; branch of service 140, (army), 135–6, (navy), 129–32; combat vs peacetime 127–8, 138, 140; skin colour 132–5, 136, 140; in training (instructors) 128–9
  incidents of racial discrimination 122, 123; covert 123, 126, 136; overt 123, 130–1, 134, (responses to), 130–1
  Indigenous ex-servicemen's perceptions of racism 122; absence of 121, 122, 123–4, 134; as existing 19, 70–1, 126, 128; low level 124–5, 138; taunts, name-calling 125, 126, 133; as pervasive 125–6
  Indigenous ex-servicewomen's perceptions: absence of racism 124; minor 124–5; taunts, name-calling 125, 133
  increase in perceptions of racism over time 122, 123; in 1980s–90s 125, 126, 130–1, 139
  racism defined 122
  underlying denigrating attitudes 126
Rerden, Brig. Mal 150

Rowse, Tim 137, 139
RSL (Returned and Services League)
  immigration 53; and support for White Australia Policy x, 42, 49–50
  as pressure group 36
  reactionary outbursts 36, 51–2
  as single-sex organisation 36, 189 n. 5
RSL and Indigenous Australians
  alienates veterans 54, 171
  discrimination, belittling 9, 50–1, 53–4
  Indigenous Australians generally 36, 53; and activism 53; loss of interest 49, 50; and rights 42, 44
  supporting Indigenous enlistment 27, 36–7, 48–9
  support for Indigenous veterans x, 9, 50, 54; citizenship rights 41; and the Coronation Contingent 45–7; on drinking laws 35, 38, 43, 44; and recognition 37, 46, 55, 174, 194 n. 65, (Victorian branch), 173, (WA branch), 172; voting rights 37–40, 41
  and Torres Strait Islanders 36
  and Vietnam War 87
Returned Servicewomen's League (Mackay) 112
Reynolds, Henry 4
Ruxton, Bruce 51–2, 53, 54, 171, 172
Ryan, HJ 82

Sambono, Barak
  serves in NORFORCE 151
Saunders, Chris Jr 29
Saunders, Chris Sr
  veteran of WWI 46
Saunders, Dorothy 28, 29
Saunders, Glenda (later Hume) 28
Saunders, Capt. Reg 19, 25, 53, 54, 207 n. 3
  and assimilation 29, 31
  challenges in civilian life 25; discrimination 28–9
  and the Coronation Contingent 44, 45–6, 47, 48
  featured in media 24–5, 27, 28, 46, 47
  military service: training national servicemen 25; veteran of WWII and Korea 24–5, 27
Schnaars, John
  Vietnam veteran 65, 74, 89, 90, 128, 173

science
  and racial hierarchies 27
Scott, Lt Col. WJR 11
Sears, Jason 130
Second World War
  the AIF (2nd) and Indigenous enlistment 10, 11, 130
  Australian Women's Land Army 95
  Indigenous military service 2, 3, 64; and equal treatment 121; Indigenous units in north 10–11; women 13, 36, 93, 94, 113
  Pacific War 10, 11; involvement of Indigenous Australians 10–12, 37, 95, 148; North Australian Observer Unit 145, 154–5; and remote Australia 11–12, (bombings), 12
Shaw, Geoff
  Vietnam veteran 61, 73, 88, 89
Shaw, Jacqueline
  early years 114; education 114; nursing training 114
  as ex-servicewoman: raises a family 117; study 117–18; works for federal Department of Aboriginal Affairs 117; works for Indigenous bodies, on a board 117
  in navy (WRANS): fails her as black woman 118; friendships 115; gender relations 116; leaves 117; racism 116; restricted role 115–17; sees position as tokenistic 118; training 115, 118
Sigelman, Lee 139
Simkin, Lt Col. 150
Simms, Eric 69
Somalia international peacekeeping mission 160
  Australian commitment 160; 1RAR 160
  Indigenous personnel in 160–2
Sorial, Brig. Nagy 140, 148, 150
South Sea Islanders 109, 111
  commemorating military service of 112
Spender, Dale 93–4
Spurling, Kathryn 115
Sunshine Club, The (play) x
Sutton, Col. Clay 150, 151

Tasmania
  Black War in 4
Thomson, Alistair 26, 59

Index

Thomson, Donald 11
Torenbeek, Ptl Com. Chris 153
Tovey, Noel
  serves in RAAF 123
Townson, Chris
  veteran of Somalia 160–2
Tripp, Marj
  serves in WRANS 113
Tyson, Pte Nathaniel
  serves in 51 FNQR 153, 154

United Nations 25
United States
  race relations in 139
  rise of Black Power and Black Panther79, 86
  and Vietnam War 57, 58, 77; anti-war protests 86; racial tensions, segregation 77–9, 80–1, 127

Veterans' Affairs, Department of
  commemorations honouring Indigenous service 121, 173
  and promoting Reconciliation 143
Vietnam War
  Australia commitment and role in 57–8; Battle of Long Tan 58; casualties 58; gradual withdrawal 58
  Indigenous military service in x, 13, 57, 58, 71–80, (and racism), 127, 128; as (volunteer) national servicemen 62, 64, 65
  non-Indigenous veterans 53, 71–2; experiences 58–9, 75, 78, 80; experiences after war 87, 92; and Indigenous servicemen 57, 71–2
  the war in popular memory 91 and forgotten histories of Indigenous servicemen 91, 92

Wallace, Darryl
  Vietnam veteran 76–7, 80, 88
Wannan, William 38–9
Ward, Stanley 85, 86, 87
Ware, Cpl Mary
  serves in 51 FNQR 153
Welch, Susan 139
Wenitong, Ron
  Vietnam veteran 61, 78–9, 89, 124
Wentworth, William 84
West, Maj. Jo 134–5, 166
Western Australia
  legislation: *Aborigines Act* 13; *Native Welfare Act 1963* 82
Westheider, James 79, 127
White, Brian
  Vietnam naval veteran 132
Whitlam government 118
  repeals *National Service Act* 87
Whyman, Hewitt
  Vietnam veteran 54, 72, 81, 88
Williams, David
  serves in navy 65, 131
Wilson, ND 47, 49
Wilson, Snow 71–2
Winegard, Timothy 7
Wood, James
  serves in NORFORCE 153, 154, 175
Wright, Tom ix

Young, Warren 127, 136

www.ingramcontent.com/pod-product-compliance
Ingram Content Group UK Ltd.
Pitfield, Milton Keynes, MK11 3LW, UK
UKHW021327180426
11947UKWH00017B/1490